D1525276

Advance Praise for

trust and the public good

"The first person I sent this book to was my son who is just entering academic life. Everybody involved in academic life, faculty and staff and alumni, would profit enormously as well. It is the most original and important book on the culture and future of higher education that I've read."

Warren Bennis, University Professor & Distinguished Professor of Business, University of Southern California

"*Trust and the Public Good* is another major contribution by William G. Tierney, the country's most creative scholar on higher education. Tierney links theories of social capital and trust with the risk taking that must occur for institutions of higher education to respond to the major changes he identifies. The four case studies provide invaluable practical laboratories to demonstrate how Tierney's theory applies to reality."

Neil Hamilton, Professor of Law, Director of the Center for Ethical Leadership in the Professions, University of St. Thomas School of Law

"William G. Tierney has thought deeply about the role of and need for trust in academic institutions. As social capital trust cannot be overvalued; as a condition for promoting the public good trust should never be underestimated. His book is a cautionary account of why faculty involvement in governance is crucial to building trust; and explains how tenure-track and tenured faculty sustain the bonds of trust that make shared governance work well in an academic community. He also reminds all of us in the academy why we must think creatively about earning and keeping the public's trust."

Roger W. Bowen, General Secretary, American Association of University Professors, Former President of State University of New York at New Paltz (1996–2001)

"In *Trust and the Public Good,* William G. Tierney ponders the big questions about the role of universities in contemporary society in relation to the lived lives of faculty and administrators. Using organizational culture as a lens for viewing trust in relation to community within academe, he raises questions about collective and individual responsibilities of members of universities as stewards of the public good. Not only is Tierney's book a good read, but it gives food for thought to anyone who cares about the qualify of academic life and the future of academe."

Edward P. St. John, Algo D. Henderson Collegiate Professor of Education, University of Michigan

trust

and the public good

Studies in the
Postmodern Theory of Education

Joe L. Kincheloe and Shirley R. Steinberg
General Editors

Vol. 308

PETER LANG
New York • Washington, D.C./Baltimore • Bern
Frankfurt am Main • Berlin • Brussels • Vienna • Oxford

William G. Tierney

trust

and the public good

Examining the Cultural
Conditions of Academic Work

PETER LANG
New York • Washington, D.C./Baltimore • Bern
Frankfurt am Main • Berlin • Brussels • Vienna • Oxford

Library of Congress Cataloging-in-Publication Data

Tierney, William G.
Trust and the public good: examining the cultural conditions
of academic work / William G. Tierney.
p. cm. — (Counterpoints: studies in the postmodern theory of education; v. 308)
Includes bibliographical references and index.
1. Universities and colleges—United States—Administration.
2. Universities and colleges—United States—Faculty.
3. Educational change—United States. 4. College teachers—
Professional relationships—United States. 5. College teaching—
Social aspects. 6. Trust. 7. Social capital (Sociology). I. Title.
LB2341.T594   378.1'2—dc22   2006022717
ISBN 0-8204-8650-7
ISSN 1058-1634

Bibliographic information published by **Die Deutsche Bibliothek**.
Die Deutsche Bibliothek lists this publication in the "Deutsche
Nationalbibliografie"; detailed bibliographic data is available
on the Internet at http://dnb.ddb.de/.

Cover design by Lisa Barfield

© 2006 Peter Lang Publishing, Inc., New York
29 Broadway, New York, NY 10006
www.peterlang.com

Printed in the United States of America

FOR BARRY, WHO HAS TAUGHT ME ABOUT TRUST
FOR 23 YEARS, AND HOPEFULLY MANY, MANY MORE.

Acknowledgments

As with any intellectual undertaking, this project has benefited from many people in many ways. In the Center for Higher Education Policy Analysis at the University of Southern California, Monica Raad and Diane Flores provided the logistical support in getting me to where I was supposed to go, and in keeping track of the multiple versions of chapters that came to them from multiple locales at various times over the course of three years. Karri Holley was more than a research assistant with me; her writing skills are excellent and she not only was able to track down the odd missing reference, but also helped in paring down prose in dire need of pruning. She will be a superb faculty member. I undertook the case studies that account for part two with James T. Minor; conversations with him led to the genesis of the idea for this book, and he remains a trusted critic and good friend. Ted Hullar, was the program director of the Higher Education Program at Atlantic Philanthropies that funded the research for this book. Ted was the perfect program director—thoughtful, demanding, creative, and encouraging; his comments usually forced me to rethink one or another idea I had concocted, and always made me think about new strategies to accomplish what I wanted to do.

Phil Altbach, Ed St. John and Steve Van Luchene gave very helpful feedback on parts of this book. Jay Dee and Brian Pusser went beyond the call of duty in providing very specific comments that forced me to rewrite the text when I wanted it to be done. Other writers should be so lucky to have such careful readers.

Over the past three years I had the opportunity to test and refine my ideas in a series of workshops, conferences and lectures. The trial of one's ideas in front of colleagues is an essential part of academic life and I was fortunate to be able to work out drafts of this work with colleagues at seminars and lectures over the last several years at the Consortium of Higher Education Researchers in Finland, the Neil Rappaport Lecture for the American Association of University Professors, the American Educational Research Association in Canada, and the Association for the Study of Higher Education in Kansas City.

Los Angeles
Santa Fe
Kabul

Table of Contents

PART ONE

Theorizing Trust

Commencement

The Challenges Awaiting Us

The morning haze has almost dissipated as the faculty comes together to walk in Commencement. "Another year, another graduation," my colleague murmurs, "but I still have this sense of anticipation, of celebration, even after all these years." The campus is jammed with parents, friends, and graduates and is replete with balloons and ceremonial banners. As we enter the main plaza, a voice announces that the faculty members have entered. Applause arises from the crowd as we walk down the path dressed in our multicolored academic robes. The band plays the processional; amidst the academic flags of the schools, we proceed to our seats.

I ask a friend on my left how he will spend the summer, and he talks briefly about multiple consulting opportunities. Someone behind us breaks in and laughingly says, "Jim's going to get rich this summer. We won't see him until after Labor Day." I nod, responding, "The real rich guy is actually Bob. We'll be lucky if we see him before October." Bob, immediately behind me, says, "Hey, wait a minute. How much I make is overrated." Jim interrupts, shakes his head, and says, "Higher education is the only industry where you can be criticized for making money. We're supposed to feel bad for making a buck." "Badly," my colleague corrects. "We're supposed to feel badly, Jim."

Later that day, I attend a baseball game to unwind, watching my childhood favorites, the Los Angeles Dodgers. A batter comes up in the early innings. The stadium board provides not only the hitter's batting average, but also lets the fans know that he "attended Cal State Fullerton for three seasons before going to the

Dodgers' farm system." After a quiet evening of watching the Dodgers rally in the late innings, I return home and prepare for bed. I hit the return button on my keyboard before I turn in to see if any email messages have arrived.

My niece, Meg, has sent a message from Katmandu. Meg graduated two years ago from Bowdoin. She spent her junior year in Nepal studying religion and the role of women in rural villages. After graduation, she backpacked around South America with her friends and tried to figure out what to do with her life. She applied for, and received, a Fulbright to continue her studies in Nepal. Meg's parents worry about her being halfway across the world, and while they are excited for her, they wonder what she will do when she returns to the States. I have quietly been encouraging my niece to think about getting a doctorate and pursuing a faculty career. She has just as quietly resisted any firm plan for her future. "Hi, Uncle Bill," she writes. "I've been thinking about what you wrote, about graduate school. I actually might consider it! But tell me, what's it like being a professor anyway? Really."

How might I best respond? If I were to rephrase my niece's question, what she is really interested in is not an exegesis on academe's gloried past, or troubled present, but about what is on the horizon. What does the future portend for academe in general and the faculty in particular? Although I am not a prophet of doom, I am sanguine about the multiple challenges that lie ahead. And these challenges call for academic organizations populated with individuals who are able to change, innovate, and take risks.

In some respects, I could replay for Meg all of the vignettes I have just offered and say to her that they are academe in a 21st-century composite. Indeed, when she was born, we did not have the capability to send and receive instantaneous messages with colleagues around the world. If she so decides, she will apply to graduate school online and be able to take a virtual tour of potential campuses. Many of our most recent technologies are disruptive; rather than merely improving the way we use current technologies, they force us to think and act in new ways. Technological innovations of the late 20th century have been disruptive to academe in ways that other technologies (audiovisual and television, for example) have not. New technologies will fundamentally reshape the nature of academic life.

Some changes are merely continuations from the past. Just as the leisurely pace of a baseball season stretches languidly over the course of a summer and into the fall, colleges and universities continually make minor changes to one or another aspect of their organization. A professor who retired 25 years ago might have a difficult time growing accustomed to the Internet and World Wide Web, but the pace of the academic year, the requirements for gaining entry and promotion in the professorate, and the ceremonies and tempo of academe remain basically the same— or at least are in the same ballpark—as a generation ago.

The fiscal environment has changed. Encroachments on how academe defines itself come from all sides. A college student who plays baseball during spring semester has morphed instead into a college baseball player, like the Dodger who attended Fullerton for three "seasons," not semesters. Students are consumers. And as I will further elaborate in this text, the state no longer sees higher education as a public good that should be publicly subsidized; education is training and the state is a provider that pays for goods and services. Although faculty consulting may provoke teasing, a sense of entrepreneurialism is pervasive in institutions perceived as on the move. In that sense, how faculty members spend their time and what they work on are undergoing reanalysis and change.

But ultimately, colleges and universities are still punctuated with the same ceremonies and symbols that have endured for centuries. The academic community still gathers to celebrate the graduation of a student at Commencement. Graduation asserts that the individual has acquired the vocational and intellectual skills imparted by the faculty of the institution and supported by the administration so that the student may commence an adult life. In this text, I work from the assumption that the academic worlds of the future will be significantly different from what currently exists, but that the core values of academe must remain intact. Indeed, I argue that the central mission of academe had better remain or it will be, in the words of José Ortega y Gasset, "love's labor's lost."

The sense of many in higher education is that the academy's future is troubled and the focus is unclear. Should higher education embrace technology or ignore its ramifications for teaching and learning and continue doing what has proven successful in the past? Are for-profit institutions a competitor that will overtake traditional colleges and universities, or merely a new sector undergoing rapid growth by expanding the consumer pool? Should accreditation be strengthened or eliminated? The answers to these and other such complicated questions that confront higher education are neither a simple yes nor no. Such conundrums call for sophisticated and thoughtful responses that not only think about future markets but also consider fundamental questions of purpose. What I sense, however, is a palpable tension and inability to even deal with the questions on the part of many who work in academe—administrators and faculty alike. Individuals are so overwhelmed either by their own daily tasks or by the magnitude of the changes that loom in front of them that the easiest path to take is to continue as if tomorrow will be like yesterday.

My argument is that for individuals to confront forthrightly the challenges ahead, the conditions for trust need to exist on two fronts. First, individuals within the institution need to find the organization and one another trustworthy. Second, colleges and universities need to be seen as worthy of the public's trust. Colleges and universities are historically decentralized and relatively nonhierarchical organizations. Faculty are organized by rank, and a clear pecking order exists between the metaphorical have's and have-not's. Yet when compared with business and industry, the military, or government agencies, postsecondary organizations provide their employees with a remarkable degree of latitude about how to design their workday, objectives, and goals. On a systemic level, over the last century public funding for postsecondary institutions has been characterized by a willingness to let institutions spend public monies in ways that each institution's leaders have seen fit. Obviously, the hands-off attitude has changed dramatically. While fiscal support for public higher education has declined, accountability measures have increased. I suggest that the idea of education as a public good has lost support while the public's trust in public education has declined. To be sure, a metaphorical "chicken and egg" question may be raised, but my purpose here is to focus on trust and to consider ways that trust might be enhanced within and outside of postsecondary institutions.

Decentralized organizations have distinct advantages over hierarchical institutions, but when changes need to be made, no such equivalent of a CEO or a general exists in a college or university. Collaboration and cooperation are necessary ingredients for any successful decentralized organization. Cooperation needs to occur within the organization. Collaboration with external constituencies is a necessity. I propose that trust is a foundational requirement for collaboration and cooperation to succeed within the institution, as well as for postsecondary institutions to be perceived as a public good worthy of public support.

When trust is absent, individuals will be less willing to change, particularly if the changes contemplated involve risk. Adherence to the status quo may seem to be a doomed strategy, but when the path ahead is unclear and trust is absent, individuals cling to whatever is familiar. Trust permeates institutional relationships. Accordingly, in Part 1, I discuss how to build trust in colleges and universities so that those who work in postsecondary organizations as well as those external to the institution are able to support change. I begin by delineating the theoretical parameters of trust, then focus on what has been meant by trust in organizations and what I intend in writing about trust in postsecondary organizations.

In Part 2, I turn to four facets of academic life. In a case study on *social networks,* I analyze the cultural ties that bind individuals in the organization together and create the conditions for trust to develop. A subsequent case study deals with the *dissolution of academic community* and considers how betrayal and distrust have become pervasive at one institution. I suggest that the organization's actors are caught in an endless cycle where distrust breeds more distrust. Any chance at increasing academic quality erodes, as different parties are unable to trust one another. Chapter 7 pertains to how *organizational communication* plays a vital role in enabling trust to occur. I make the case that communication needs to be evident if an organization expects individuals to have the social capital to participate actively in an academic community. The subsequent chapter on *the limits of trust* acknowledges that trust is a not a cure-all for every problem that ails an institution. Individuals are on a fool's errand if they think of trust as an end unto itself rather than a process that enables quality to occur.

In Part 3, I examine trust as defined by how the public views postsecondary organizations. My purpose in this chapter is neither to indict colleges and universities for perceived failures nor to offer a polemic against increasing privatization such that the public good of education becomes a vestige of the past. Instead, I suggest that trust and definitions of the public good go hand in hand regardless of societal contexts. The challenge in the 21st century is to simultaneously reinvigorate a dialogue about how postsecondary institutions serve the public good and to create the conditions for trust to exist between postsecondary organizations and their publics.

Colleges and universities need to change dramatically, but at the same time, the core ideals of postsecondary education need to be maintained. Before initiating a discussion of social capital and trust, I present a brief overview of five meta-changes that confront academe, the implications of these changes for colleges and universities, and what the core values of the academy have been.

Academic transformations in the 21st century

Changes to the structure of the system of higher education

For at least a century, but especially for the last 50 years, the structure of higher education has been relatively stable. The Carnegie classification system defines the universe of postsecondary institutions. Although criticism and revisions have ensued, there is general agreement about the population and existent hierarchy. By and large, the postsecondary system may be characterized as a mature industry that is closed to competition. Funding mechanisms, credentialing requirements, organizational arrangements, and inter-organizational relationships have not been in a massive state of flux. Change has been gradual and evolutionary. Community colleges, for example, came of age in the 20th century. Their relationship in the structure has been relatively unchanged.

Similarly, although organizational transformations have occurred so that a teachers college can change to a state college and then to a state university, such change has been at a moderate pace. Nothing like the "dot.com" boom of the 1980s and 1990s has occurred in academe. Even revolutionary new kinds of organizations or different structural arrangements have not really taken hold. Indeed, the most experimental time in higher education over the last half-century was in the 1960s. A great many new colleges and universities originated with distinct claims about how they would differ from mainstream organizations. With the benefit of hindsight, two points stand out about these experimental institutions. First, virtually all of the experiments have regressed to the norm. They are more alike than different from the very institutions from which they sought distinction. Second, the experiments were actually not very experimental. Individuals created new institutions that were very much like what one expected of colleges and universities. An administrative structure existed with a president; faculty taught students in courses over a set time period, and eventually the students received a degree based on credits; faculty had tenure, and so on.

Research, also, has had a relatively static quality. European universities created research institutes that were distinct from their postsecondary institutions. During and after World War II in the United States, however, the federal government developed a research infrastructure that was heavily geared toward investment in higher education. Even stand-alone research units such as the Lawrence Livermore or Jet Propulsion Laboratories had academic oversight. If one looked for research, the university was a likely place to find it.

My sense, however, is that in the future the closed market in which higher education operates will change. Different providers will be numerous, and competition for students and research will be much more common. For-profit institutions, corporate universities, and companies that excel in distance learning will enter the market and create new ways of thinking about higher education. A significant change in the way individuals see the role of the federal and state government will also lead to different configurations. State appropriations to institutions will continue to diminish, which will necessitate new ways for institutions to interface with one another and their publics. Relationships among business, industry, and higher education will become more common.

The structure of the system of higher education as it has been realized in the last generation is due for dramatic reconfiguration. Many institutions will, of course, exist in some permutation similar to what they are today. They will still educate traditionally aged students with a faculty that has tenure in organizations with familiar structures. Postsecondary organizations will be two- or four-year institutions that recruit in an established manner. The revenue streams will not be remarkably changed.

However, a great number of institutions will be quite different from what existed at the turn of the 21st century. Some institutions will be closed, owned, or merged in ways that would have been unthinkable a generation ago. When someone says that he or she wants a degree, the obvious question will no longer be, "Which college are you going to attend?" Multiple providers will offer multiple opportunities. Indeed, the common comment will not be that someone wants a "degree." Those, too, will be only one of several options available in the postsecondary universe in ways that are uncommon today. Changes of this sort can occur

by organizational drift, where external demands move an organization in a particular direction. Alternatively, when an organization's members are able to act in a
determined manner they have the potential to choose a particular path. I suggest
in Parts 2 and 3 that the ability to act in a collaborative way is in part determined
by the conditions of trust that exist within the organization and between the organization and the larger society.

Changes to the internal structure of colleges and universities

Another factor that will necessitate changes to colleges and universities pertains to
the nature of knowledge and the internal organizational locus for where and how
knowledge is produced. Throughout the 20th century, academics increasingly
viewed themselves as professionals who worked within the disciplines. The profession and the discipline defined their raison d'être according to internally regulated
rules about what counts for knowledge.

The profession of the professorate was one key factor in how individuals
thought about knowledge. The credential of the Ph.D., for example, became the sine
qua non of academic standing. By and large, without a terminal degree, individuals were viewed as professionally suspect. The belief was that without a terminal
degree, individuals were not able to make informed judgments about the various
issues that arose pertaining to knowledge production. How might one be able to
judge a candidate's suitability for tenure if the evaluator did not have a terminal
degree in the field being considered?

Further, the assumptions of individuals in disciplines helped outline not only
the parameters of how they defined knowledge but also how they studied issues,
what counted for an educated person, how they constructed curricula, what they
looked for in hiring and retaining faculty, and how they structured departments.
Whether one viewed the external world as "socially constructed" or a "real" entity
depended in large part on the interpretation of knowledge that the discipline held.
Of consequence, the department became the building block of postsecondary
institutions.

Faculty taught graduate students a specific area of knowledge. As the 20th century drew to a close, individuals had an increasingly narrow intellectual purview.
Departmental structures, of course, are not simply lines on an organizational chart.
Individuals populate these units; although intellectual thought initially generates a
departmental configuration, human interaction also produces political machinations.
A department chair, for example, seeks to expand the department not because of an
intellectual necessity, but because of a political one—the desire for more resources
and personnel. The result is that departmental configurations became stronger
over the course of the 20th century.

I suggest that the configuration of the 21st century will be quite different. The discipline and, hence, departments have outlived their usefulness. In an age that many see as postmodern and/or globalized, theoretical and practical thought is increasingly oriented toward interdisciplinarity and what Donald Stokes has called "use-informed" research (1997). Such an assertion is less an argument than a statement of fact and belief by an increasing number of faculty in numerous disciplines. Departments and schools will be a 21st-century artifact; postsecondary organizations will develop a much more flexible structure where individuals come together around an idea or problem with the expectation that faculty with multiple perspectives will work together.

A common concern with restructuring is the fear that faculty will lose their power. The assumption is that faculty have their greatest input at the departmental level. If the structure of the department is eliminated in favor of more temporary units, then a faculty voice can be muted. Such a concern relates precisely to the point of this book. One can understand the concern that what little power one may have amassed will be lost if the structure is eliminated, but surely alternative possibilities exist. Departments ought not to be seen as fiefdoms isolated from current changes and needs. Indeed, the impetus for moving away from a departmental structure has more to do with intellectual advances and overlapping interests of the professorate over the last generation than with any needs relating to institutional efficiency or effectiveness. But changing from the familiar to the new and different is a risk, a risk that inherently involves trust.

Changes to the temporal nature of the organization

Time has been a fixed commodity in U.S. higher education. Courses are divided into units that occur over a defined period. Students are expected to take a specific number of years to attain a degree. After the student has amassed the necessary credits, the institution provides the candidate with a degree. Traditional colleges and universities usually have a set tempo. Fall and spring is when students are in residence, and summers are generally much slower. The country has offered an agrarian model of education since the 19th century, when students needed to return to their families and work to earn money.

In the past, the temporal structure offered benefits in a system where flexibility was difficult. Students attended classes with other students, so there was a definite limit to the number of courses that could be offered based on the availability of classrooms. Classes that began and ended at the same time provided greater coordination insofar as course schedules coincided. If one individual spent a similar amount of time as another student in a class, in a major, and in a degree program, the assumption was that the learning experiences of those students would be equivalent.

One would be hard pressed, however, to assume that such rigidity produces the kind of teaching and learning necessary for the 21st century. Rather than seat time, future classes will be geared toward a student's mastery of the material. Some students will learn the material faster than others and proceed at a quicker pace than their peers. Indeed, learning will involve much more than simply what a professor has to impart and what can be found in the library for the final term paper. Instead, learning will occur in various locales that necessitate greater temporal flexibility.

In many respects, one could argue that American higher education has determined its learning experiences in part through the temporal structure of its system. Learning stops at the end of the semester and begins anew in the fall. The professor who wants to extend his or her class beyond the confines of a semester is sure to run into problems with the registrar. Individuals who decide that the best way for students to learn is through short courses that occur intensively over the course of a matter of weeks are likely to be told not about whether the suggestion is intellectually useful, but about its impracticality.

The future, however, will be much more flexible and synthetic. Although ceremonies such as graduation will likely always populate the culture of academe, the sharp differentiation between temporal units called "semesters" or "quarters" is likely to give way sooner rather than later. The freedom to schedule classes without the concern of overlapping courses or inadequate seat capacity will enable instructors to teach units that differ from a traditional academic term. Time to degree will also vary significantly; learning will be defined not by what takes place in a course taught by an instructor in a lecture hall. Instead, learning will be defined by what the individual actually has learned.

Such changes, of course, have significant ramifications for those who do the teaching—the faculty. Higher education is an industry where those who have mastered the technology have done quite well by repeatedly using the same technology. Although faculty frequently update their course syllabi, the changes are minor. The manner in which they have taught throughout their careers has been more similar than different. Indeed, an argument could be made that the component of academe that has changed the least since World War II is the pedagogic unit. The model remains a professor standing in front of the classroom. Given the advances in technology and the increased competition from alternative providers, one could equally make the case that the most significant changes are likely to be in the nature of coursework. In consequence, those who teach will experience significant upheavals and needs.

Changes to faculty work and appointments

Each change is interrelated. A temporal change is in part dependent on changes in the internal and external environments and vice versa. Similarly, if changes occur with regard to the external environment, the manner in which interdisciplinary work is defined, and the temporal nature of the institution, then how faculty work is constituted and the nature of faculty appointments will also change. The current standard is relatively uniform, although variations do exist. Individuals enter academic life as assistant professors and over time gain tenure. They are promoted to associate, then full professor. The quality of faculty work is generally judged by what they produce as researchers and how they teach in the classroom.

Faculty will still exist in colleges and universities, but who they are, what they do, how they are remunerated, and their relationship to their institutions will undergo a significant transformation. In some respects, changes to faculty work and appointments have been taking place for a generation. As an overall percentage, there are fewer tenure-track faculty today than a generation ago. Part-time faculty are greater today than a generation ago, and the traditional professorate is no longer expanding at the rate it has done in the recent past. Full-time non-tenure-track faculty are also increasing. Although research still remains the academic coin of the realm, non-research universities have little reason to reward research when classes need to be taught. Many individuals are hired simply to teach, and their contract says nothing about research or service.

Tenure will still exist in the future, but in all but the most prestigious institutions, its ranks will be vastly reduced. The change will not occur through vigorous debate, swiftly, or because of an asserted effort by conservative administrators or legislators. Indeed, when the elimination of tenure becomes the goal of a group, they are likely to meet with stiff resistance. The change will instead occur gradually so that no one will notice the reduction in tenure year by year. Only after a series of years will the reduction be seen. The causes of tenure's demise will be multiple, but the clearest culprit will be the continuing fiscal shortfalls of postsecondary institutions.

How tenure gets defined will also change. Currently, in the vast majority of institutions, tenure is equivalent to 100% of an individual's salary. Although individuals may earn more income through consulting, teaching summer classes, or securing a grant, the norm is that a tenure-track faculty member earns the bulk of his or her salary via the institution. In the future, faculty are likely to be more entrepreneurial since their university salary will only cover a portion of their tenure-line salary. That is, although a tenured professor might earn $100,000 a year, the institution may guarantee only a certain part of it—such as 60%, or $60,000. The individual will be expected to bring in the remaining portion of his or her income through additional teaching, grants, and other such activities. Although this practice has been rare in traditional colleges and universities, it has seen greater use in medical schools where faculty generate a great deal of income through private practices and service contracts. The future will determine if this kind of arrangement will be possible in traditional fields where resource streams are not so plentiful. The strength of such a system is that some individuals are likely to generate a higher salary. The weakness is that it undermines, if not destroys, the basic idea of tenure.

Further, the assumption that a professor's class notes are owned by the individual and that whatever he or she chooses to teach in a class is acceptable will change. Although classes will have greater interdisciplinarity and breadth of scope, it is possible that the curricula will be more tightly coupled. A teacher's idiosyncratic ways of teaching a class will be less likely and the standardization of curricula will increase. Standardized curricula offer a portrait of faculty as interchangeable parts where courses and faculty are decoupled. If anyone with a particular set of credentials can teach the established syllabus, then one crucial instrumental aspect of the need for faculty has been eliminated.

Research will continue, but it will be greatly circumscribed. Rather than an aspiration of most faculty, it will be in the hands of a relative few who work in elite research universities. Medical schools, always a sign that a university is replete with external research dollars, are likely to be fewer in number and have a different relationship with academic institutions. Thus, the research function of academe will diminish within the entire system, although premier research universities will still attract funding.

The result is that the work of the faculty will be significantly changed. I do not believe that a system that currently holds over 4,000 institutions will be entirely reconfigured so that the central constituency who does the work for the industry—the faculty—will be eliminated. Higher education in the 21st century is not the steel industry of the 1960s, and the faculty are not steelworkers. However, one ought to expect a continued decline in tenure. The profile for every institution will no longer be full-time, tenure-track faculty.

The ramifications of such a portrait are highly contingent on the kind of institutions in which faculty work. Elite research universities will probably have a faculty profile similar to that of today. One wonders—if these assumptions are correct—how it will affect those who think about entering, and those who remain in, the academy. The profession will be impacted considerably if the realization is that, in an already limited job market, jobs will become even more elusive.

Changes to the funding mechanisms of higher education

50 years ago, funding was relatively straightforward. Colleges and universities had dedicated funding streams: the federal government, the state government, parents of students (and some students themselves), and alumni. Today some of those streams are drying up while others have many new tributaries. The federal government still provides research income for major universities, but their grant program for student aid is gradually becoming a loan program. Resources that were earmarked for buildings have been dramatically cut back.

Business and industry have begun to fund higher education initiatives—if the initiatives conform to their needs. Unique arrangements between universities, or departments within universities, and companies will only increase. The fiscal arrangements will have broad ramifications for how faculty conduct research, whether a professor's findings can be published in the public domain, and ultimately where an individual's allegiances reside. If the only way to get funded, for example, is to sign a contract that stipulates all of the research is confidential, then the manner in which faculty have typically gone about their work will undergo significant redefinition.

Although tuition still accounts for a significant percentage of an institution's total revenue stream, capital campaigns and entrepreneurial activities have taken hold in a manner that no one would have been able to consider 50 years ago. Naming rights to football stadiums and the like more closely approximate what occurs in the for-profit sector than in not-for-profit institutions. The exclusive merchandizing of a product on a campus and a host of other market-oriented decisions have refashioned how institutions are able to save and generate income.

Although many fiscal changes have occurred, none is more significant than the inability and/or unwillingness of state governments to fund their public systems of higher education. Indeed, in some institutions, state appropriations are no greater than 10% of the entire budget of an institution. Even in the 1990s, when state appropriations increased in actual dollars given to postsecondary institutions, the actual percentage of fiscal resources provided to institutions was reduced. In consequence, what one means by a public institution of higher education is under analysis. This analysis, I suggest, has a great deal to do with issues surrounding trust and the public good. What a citizenry expects of its public institutions in some way gets determined by the manner in which the organization is perceived and trusted. The mission of a public institution is not merely a marketing tool; an organization's mission in part announces to the public how the trust that the organization has been given is going to be enacted.

As I shall discuss in Chapter 9, the movement to a market economy has ramifications beyond the basketball team wearing Nike or different fiscal arrangements being made regarding intellectual property rights. When an institution needs to be sensitive to market demands, it presumably hires individuals in senior-level executive positions who are experienced in that domain. The concern is that those who are versed in one academic area will not be as conversant in other areas. Although a concern for management principles ought not to be seen as inconsistent with academic organizations, one can also see how different skills will undoubtedly influence individuals.

These changes should not be understood in a deterministic fashion insofar as they will undoubtedly be utilized and implemented in different ways depending upon institutional type, history, and location, to name but a few such factors. Yet they are representative of larger trends. The successful postsecondary institution will neither run helter-skelter into the future nor act ostrich-like with its head buried in the sands of time. Change is upon us. I believe that the internal determinants of trust by actors within the organization, and the external relationships that the organization develops with the larger society, are critical. Trust is not an answer but a way to approach critical issues. How best to respond to these dilemmas? An initial response is to define the core values of the organization and then to consider these values in light of the trends.

Values to the core

The enduring importance of academic freedom

Some characteristics of colleges and universities, although perceived to be fundamental, are more a means to an end, rather than ends in and of themselves. Two of the clearest examples pertain to tenure and shared governance. Throughout the 20th century, both concepts became enshrined as hallmarks of American higher education. In reality, however, both ideas were means to an end—the ability of academics to search for truth no matter where it took them, otherwise known as academic freedom.

At times, the interpretation of academic freedom has been confused. Academic freedom has little, if anything, to do with a professor stating that he or she wants to teach at a certain time of day or day of the week merely to accommodate a busy schedule. Simply because a math professor holds a belief for or against homosexuality does not mean that those views may be promulgated in a calculus class. An individual's academic freedom is not infringed if he or she is arrested for participating in an online chat room with underage youth that leads to sexual liaisons between the academic and the minor.

Academic freedom is a value and ideal of the community. The college or university asserts that the search for truth is intrinsic to teaching, learning, and research activities. Whether one subscribes to an objective and empirical notion of reality or to a view that is more interpretive, the point of the rigid adherence to academic freedom is that one may work in the classroom or laboratory without external interference. In consequence, faculty have substantial autonomy in the conduct of their work and the unfettered freedom of inquiry into different domains of thought, however unpopular such domains may be.

Tenure is the structure that safeguards academic freedom. The assumptions are twofold. First, when an individual has tenure, he or she has job security that encourages research without fear of the loss of employment. Second, those who have tenure are presumed to be guardians of academic freedom on their campus. If an injustice is done to someone on campus, then it is the obligation of the tenured faculty to protect that individual. Without tenure, the campus presumably has no one to protect academic freedom.

Shared governance upholds academic freedom in the decision-making processes of the institution. The assumption is that when faculty who hold tenure are involved in the governance of the institution, they will create policies that protect academic freedom. Most importantly, procedures will be put in place by tenured faculty that ensure individuals are able to air their disagreements and grievances when they feel their academic freedom has been infringed. The hiring of faculty, promotion and tenure review, and grievance policies are examples of procedures that have been built through shared governance that presumably protect academic freedom.

If other structures or processes are able to provide the same protections, then they should be considered. The core value, however, should be maintained. The obligation of the scholarly community is to set itself on a path that seeks to advance knowledge by way of the search for truth. Such a value is unique to higher education. To lose this value is to lose part of the essential core of academe.

The centrality of access

Throughout much of U.S. history, but especially since the late 19th century, higher education has been perceived as the great equalizer. Education was a way out and a way up. The Morrill Acts (which led to the establishment of land-grant institutions), the GI Bill, and the relatively low cost of tuition at public institutions are all examples of the citizenry's recognition of the importance of a college education. Affirmative action is another such policy designed to advance a core value—access to higher education. As with tenure and shared governance, however, affirmative action is the vehicle to enable a desired end. There is nothing sacred about affirmative action as a policy in and of itself. If another policy can be found that fosters a similar result, then it should be considered.

However, a concern for access has been embedded in the heart of postsecondary education as a core value. The citizenry of the United States has held as an ideal that whether an individual is born poor or rich, he or she should be able to prosper and participate in the democratic sphere. Education is the means to enable success and participation. Both K-12 education and postsecondary education were viewed as a public good—individuals not only had a claim on the public good, but by using a public good, the public benefited as well. A college degree was not a private good that benefited only the individual; a well-educated workforce made the country stronger. Education created less unemployment and more participation in the public sphere.

Throughout the 20th century, a spirited debate took place about the benefits to the individual and society when someone attained a degree. When an individual received a college education, how much did his or her earnings increase over the course of a lifetime? Although the increase to the individual was clear, what were the benefits to society? If the answer was that society did not benefit at all, then a reasonable argument could be made that the state should reduce its investment in higher education. By the late 20th century, however, a curious dualism developed where it was clear that America needed a highly skilled workforce if it were to retain its preeminence in a global economy, but the assumption was that the individual should pay for the cost of education as long as the government facilitated a loan program. The assumption had less to do with education than with a shift in public thinking about the nature of government and what counted as a public good.

Often overlooked in such discussions were the benefits that accrued to society by the increased ability of the individual to participate in the democratic public sphere. The tradition has held, for example, that a college education increases participation in a democracy by virtue of almost all traditional indicators (such as voting patterns or volunteerism). Presumably if one wants to encourage active participation in a democracy, then attendance in some form of postsecondary education is useful. The irony here is that participation in the civic life of the community clearly is a public good. But as I later discuss, recently the assumption has held that it is no longer the role of the federal or state government to facilitate that participation. Thus, going to college has enabled individuals to be more competitive in the economy and more civically engaged, but the obligation to pay for that education seems to increasingly fall on the individual.

If postsecondary education no longer has such a purpose, then one may rightfully raise three questions. First, who will foster an increase by the citizenry into the global economy? The country needs highly skilled workers. The country is at a stage where, to remain competitive, we must focus on educating the workforce. Second, if civic engagement is the scaffolding upon which democracy rises or falls, what structure will replace education's role? And finally, if higher education eschews its core value of access, then what is its mission? An institution must represent something.

The necessity of excellence and inquiry

Academic traditions and structures have been built over time to ensure that the best possible decisions are made rather than political or capricious ones. Blind reviews of academic work, for example, presumably enable the reader to focus on the quality of the ideas in the article rather than the name of the author. Whether the review is for a journal article, a book, or a proposal to the National Science Foundation, the assumption is that committees and editors reach decisions by concentrating on the merits of the idea. The multiple rings of reviews that a tenure candidate endures are an attempt to lessen the political nature of the decision and increase the probability that the ultimate decision is based on the excellence of his or her scholarship. When a candidate goes for a job interview, the "job talk" allows the candidate to demonstrate mastery of the material.

The idea of merit has been of importance to the academy as a means to help individuals judge work—not because of someone's background, race, or gender, but instead on the quality of ideas. Although the meritocracy has a much-debated history with regard to its efficacy, its central ideal remains in place in academe. Although one may fault the SAT for racial bias or for some methodological or scoring flaw, the motivation for standardized testing was to remove academic decisions from individuals who might make judgments that had little, if anything, to do with the quality of the applicant's work. In the early 20th century, for example, the commitment to a meritocracy benefited Jewish students who gained entrance to academe based on academic criteria whereas they had previously had been denied for no other reason than their religion.

A commitment to excellence also implies that the search for truth will be constant. Rather than a static notion of the enterprise that teaches eternal truths and little more, excellence and inquiry suggest that the organization is a dynamic entity that searches out new ways of thinking in any number of arenas. Although some might argue that colleges and universities are slow to adapt and are change-averse, if one examines the transformations in knowledge production that have occurred in higher education over the last century, a different conclusion can be drawn.

Colleges and universities, and the faculties within them, have continually sought out new ways of thinking and acting. Over 4,000 patents are annually issued to academic researchers for scientific innovations (Agres, 2003). Philosophical and scientific breakthroughs have occurred in the lab, classroom, and faculty offices.

One needs merely to read histories of the men and women who populated academe at the turn of the 20th century to see the ferment that existed. John Dewey, Franz Boas, William James, Margaret Mead, and legions of other academics were literally stripping away previous ideas and inventing new ways of seeing and acting in the world. Their successors were no less ambitious. American higher education became the envy of the world after World War II—not simply because of abundant resources, but also intellectual commitment. Academics sought new ways of interpreting phenomena as well as resolving some of the pressing problems that society faced. A static, reticent academic environment is one that would betray a central notion of American higher education throughout the last century. Ironically, then, the culture of the academy with regard to knowledge production has been one of intellectual inquiry and change, while the structure and function of the academy have simultaneously remained relatively stable.

Turning to Trust

While one may celebrate or bemoan the permutations that I have outlined, few will disagree that academic organizations are now undergoing changes as significant as any they have encountered in a century. The point is no longer simply a reduction in resources for a year or two that forces minor adjustments in the budget. Academe's purpose seems up for grabs, and the changes that colleges and universities face are alterations to basic processes and structures. I devote the remainder of this book to a relatively unstudied aspect of academic organizations—the idea of what constitutes trust and trustworthiness. What might be done to increase the ability of individuals within the organization to engage with the problems that are on academe's doorstep—both with one another and with those external to the institution?

Academic life has been one marked by unclear tasks and technologies. Professors teach students in a classroom and develop research projects that are relatively unencumbered from oversight and monitoring. The assumption has been that, as professionals in a unique organization, faculty are best suited to develop curricula and undertake research. Their colleagues—other faculty—determine the quality and worth of their work. However, the challenges noted call into question these basic suppositions. One way to respond to external and internal demands is to clarify tasks and technologies and to tighten what has historically been a loosely coupled system. Legalistic contracts and behavioral objectives change the role of faculty to that of "managed professionals," as Gary Rhoades (1998) has suggested. However, an increasing body of literature argues that trust is a preferred alternative to secure compliance over mandates and regulations. Although compliance may occur in any number of ways (threat, coercion, incentives, and contractual arrangements, to name a few), organizations that operate in dynamic environments where participation is not mandatory are more likely better off to call upon trusting relationships.

The changes I have outlined make one point certain: the status quo is untenable. Whether institutions change their values, or deal with the external environment by developing online courseware, or consider mergers and cooperative agreements with different organizations, or any number of other possible responses to the problems that exist, the future holds a high degree of uncertainty. The organization's participants will be called on to take risks. Innovation and experimentation demand that what is known may be changed or dropped in favor of what is unknown. When individuals take risks in an organization, they need to trust the organization and one another.

Accordingly, in the next chapter I outline the scaffolding for trust—the idea of social capital. As I explain, social capital has many theoretical frames. All of them see trust and trustworthiness as constituted by (and constituting) social capital. Organizations rich in social capital are likely to generate the conditions for trust. These organizations are better suited to meet the challenges that lie ahead and determine how best to deal with the assault on the core values of academe.

CHAPTER ONE

Framing Social Capital

Trust is inevitably social and relational. Of course, someone might say, "I don't trust myself when it comes to junk food, so I avoid having it around the house." Such a statement, however, has little to do with trust in a social organization and more to do with an individual's internal fortitude and resolve. To trust involves trusting others. A generalized meaning of trust is embedded in networks of social relations. From multiple perspectives, trust pertains to one party trusting another party.

Trust is neither something fully developed that simply exists regardless of who the individuals are, nor a trait of one person or group irrespective of the social organization in which the actors function. As I discuss in the following chapter, contexts matter. Trust cannot be understood as an abstraction; it cannot be merely treated as trust between individuals when the discussion centers on an organization. The social relations of individuals within specific contexts create meaning. Although pre-existing meaning exists, such meaning is influenced by the behavior of organizational actors.

Social capital is the scaffolding that makes trust possible. Social capital is the inherited meanings that exist in organizations awaiting interpretation by the actors. As I elaborate, the sturdier the scaffolding, the more likely it is that conditions of trust will prevail. Without scaffolding, trust becomes difficult, if not impossible, to achieve. Thus, prior to a discussion about how to define trust, I examine the concept of social capital. I first consider the roots of social capital and the competing conceptions employed by its two most prominent proponents, James Coleman and

Pierre Bourdieu. I then offer my definition by delineating the elements of social capital, its uses, and how social capital constitutes (and is constituted by) trust.

Defining social capital

Social capital is a framework that enables or disables individuals and groups to accomplish particular goals. The term is derived from sociology, albeit with distinct economic overtones. In some respects, the ideas behind social capital have been a mainstay of the discipline since the work of Emile Durkheim (1867/1966). Simply stated, involvement and affiliation with a group have positive benefits. Anomie and suicide were more likely to occur, posited Durkheim, in individuals who had less systematic involvement with social institutions such as the church, the neighborhood, or local community organizations. Accordingly, social capital pertains to interpersonal networks that provide people with resources that they can then exploit in other areas of social life. A wealth of social capital enables individuals to gain leverage in the pursuit of economic and cultural capital and encourages engagement in the democratic public sphere. A lack of social capital makes it harder for people to develop economic and cultural capital, precluding civic engagement.

Table 1.1: Elements of social capital

ELEMENT	DESCRIPTION
Form	The structural aspects of social ties and relations
Norms of obligation	A sense of investment with an expectation for return and reciprocity
Resources	Both within the network as well as potential external resources

Social capital is the actual (or potential) resources developed within a network of more or less institutionalized relationships of mutual acquaintances. Families and communities are primary examples of units where social capital occurs. Families where the parents have gone to college, for example, are more likely to have children who have access to college; such students attend and participate in an array of college-preparation activities. Vermont villages where town hall meetings still occur are examples of communities that are rich in social capital. When individuals accumulate social capital, they have greater access to economic and cultural privileges, and the communities have a more engaged citizenry.

The term 'social capital' implies an economic value. In common parlance, *cap-*

ital refers to the economic resources an individual or group accumulates over time. Capital can be acquired, spent, exchanged, increased, depleted, lost, or recaptured due to its communal and relational nature. It is rarely static. Capital occurs within groups and societies; one cannot acquire or exchange capital with one's self.

Individuals also have a constant potential of gaining access to capital. When an individual is judged to have significant capital, the judgment is partially in relation to the capital of others. "I just won a hundred dollars!" may seem like a trivial statement in the 21st century to those in the middle- or upper-class. If the statement had been made a century ago, or in a third-world village today, the speaker would have won a significant amount.

Individuals also decide whether they have an adequate amount of capital based on its potential use. Some individuals grow up in communities, for example, where they want to ensure that everyone has access to healthcare and sustenance. Economic wealth is not a goal. Other individuals see the accumulation of wealth as a primary goal in life. Again, such judgments are contextual, relational, and idiosyncratic. The individual who grows up in a wealthy family also learns a different meaning of a perceived adequate amount of capital than the individual's counterpart in a poor family. While in the rampantly market-driven modern American economy of the 21st century there is no ceiling for how much capital an individual may have, there have been modest attempts to ensure that no one falls below a particular level. The result is that there are enormous differences in wealth. Such is also the case with social capital.

Capital provides access to a variety of goods, services, and related physical and symbolic commodities. The use of the term 'social' capital implies that capital is not only economic. Different forms of capital exist that nevertheless function in a manner akin to economic capital. *Human capital,* for example, is the stock of skills, training, and productive knowledge possessed by individuals and groups. During the Industrial Revolution, craftspeople claimed that their skills constituted a form of capital. Software engineers and webmasters are modern-day counterparts of craftspeople who possess such specified skills. *Cultural capital* pertains to the linguistic and cultural tools useful in obtaining economic and social goods. Cultural capital has less to do with specific skills and more with dispositions that individuals acquire through interactions within social institutions such as schools, churches, museums, and theaters.

One of the more confusing aspects of the sociological use of 'capital' as a metaphor is the manner in which the terms overlap and constitute one another. The question of "Which came first?" frequently develops. Millionaires are able to send their children to private schools and colleges, thereby creating cultural capital. The sons and daughters of the wealthy take a summer course in Italy and learn the Italian language. As they grow up, they continue to develop these summer relationships.

Thus, economic wealth enables, in part, social, human, and cultural capital to occur. Did the social capital of the summer abroad create cultural capital, or did the cultural capital earned enable social capital to develop? The answer is not clear-cut insofar as multiple actions take place concurrently where one form of capital frequently constitutes and is constituted by another. Nevertheless, it is useful to recognize that different forms of capital exist, providing avenues for opportunity to those who are able to access them. The challenge is to understand how these multiple forms of capital function in real and symbolic manners as distinct entities, while simultaneously recognizing their constitutive nature.

Obviously, then, these terms are related to one another and often, although not always, overlap. Presumably, a professor's family may be rich in cultural capital but not necessarily economic capital. A software engineer may have a great deal of human and economic capital but not always a great deal of social or cultural capital. A poet who is fluent in Russian may have a great deal of human and cultural capital but a minimal amount of economic and social capital. The intangible character of social capital adds to the confusion. Alejandro Portes observed, "Whereas economic capital is in people's bank accounts and human capital is inside their heads, social capital inheres in the structure of their relationships. To possess social capital, a person must be related to others, and it's those others, not himself, who are the actual source of his or her advantage" (1998, p. 7). The result is that one cannot speak of social capital as an abstraction. To understand social capital demands an investigation of local contexts.

The inheritors of Durkheim's concept, who popularized the notion of capital, are James Coleman and Pierre Bourdieu. Coleman, an American, and Bourdieu, a Frenchman, are sociologists who have garnered a great deal of respect for their work. Both acknowledge their Durkheimian roots, although Coleman's is more overt by way of structural functionalism. Bourdieu's work is linked more closely to theories of social reproduction. They are frequently seen as having competing conceptions of social capital; Bourdieu is more of a neo-Marxist, whereas Coleman employs rational choice. For the purposes of advancing an understanding of trust, however, I see their work more as complementary rather than contradictory. A brief review is in order.

Coleman's version of social capital

Coleman focuses on the relationship between social and human capital. His assumption is that relationships which actors develop within a web of social networks are likely to produce positive outcomes. Coleman writes, "These social relationships which come into existence when individuals attempt to make best use of their individual resources need not only be seen as components of social structure, however.

They may also be seen as resources for the individuals" (1990, p. 300). These resources inhere within the networks of social relations that get built within school and community and have positive consequences.

Coleman's assumption is that, as with economic capital, social capital is capable of producing positive outcomes. Without social capital, certain ends will not be achieved. From this perspective, social capital is not something inherent to an individual. Instead, it is built by the web of social relationships in which individuals reside. My use of the passive voice here—"social capital is built"—is purposive. Although individuals may be able to create, build, and maintain social capital as individuals, the norm is that individuals enter into preexisting networks and make of them what they will.

As I discuss below and in subsequent chapters, such an observation has crucial implications for the maintenance of equality and the creation of trust. Some individuals, for example, will enter organizations where trust is absent. Such a context dramatically differs from one where trust exists through the networks in which people involve themselves. Nevertheless, social capital's function is to increase opportunities for individuals to accomplish acts that otherwise may not be able to take place.

Although there are distinct drawbacks to such an interpretation, one should also note the strengths of the direction toward which Coleman is pointing social theorists. Insofar as the underpinnings of social capital assume the importance of networks and social interaction, Coleman's work moves social theorists away from an overly individualistic notion of how society changes. As he noted, "Individuals do not act independently, goals are not independently arrived at, and interests are not wholly selfish" (1990, p. 301). Rather than a 'great man' theory of change where leaders imbued with preordained traits direct society or the assumption that society is one vast meritocracy where individuals rise or fall strictly based on their competence, Coleman suggests that change happens in large part because of the interactions that take place within social networks and structures.

The analysis of networks and structures is particularly useful in understanding the acquisition of educational credentials. In Coleman's worldview, generalized reciprocity enables societies to function. Reciprocity is only able to occur when individuals share common bonds with one another. One individual helps another not as an altruistic gesture but because of the underlying acceptance of reciprocity. The individual who helps another knows that—at some point—he or she will also need help. Common bonds unite a community because there is goodwill available to individuals within the group (Adler & Kwon, 2002, p. 23). Communal interactions, as Durkheim first pointed out, enable individuals and the community to benefit. Without social capital, the community will be cast into divisiveness and self-aggrandizement to the long-term detriment of the society. Indeed, Xavier de Souza

Briggs goes so far as to assert, "Businesses have never thrived, nor have economies flourished, without social capital. . . . [Social capital] greases the gears of commerce, along with other areas of life" (1997, p. 111).

Coleman's assumption is that social capital acts as a regulator where norms exist; the community works to maintain them. When social capital functions in this manner, trust is built and maintained, which Coleman believes is necessary for societies to function effectively. The portrait that Coleman develops is of communities where order and discipline exist because of social capital. As Dika and Singh observe, Coleman's world is one framed by "traditional values, rigorous discipline, and hierarchical order and control" (2002, p. 34). Without social capital, children are denied opportunities and the community becomes dysfunctional.

The concern with Coleman's approach is that, in some respects, he raises the stark individualism that he sought to reject to the social structural level. He never addresses how societal inequality functions. In Coleman's view, social capital occurs in large part through familial connections. When children do not gain access to social capital, they most likely will not accrue the benefits of economic and cultural capital. The source of the lack of social capital is the family. Norms exist—if the family is truly motivated, then they will be able to gain social capital.

Such an assumption, of course, neither questions the values of these norms nor contextualizes why some have access to social capital and others do not. If social capital is an economic concept, then it stands to reason that key areas for investigation are analyses that come to terms with unequal power relations within society. Social capital cannot be a network analysis that assumes only good and productive outcomes. Some individuals will be excluded. Others will have to assimilate to norms that may be at odds with their backgrounds and value systems. "The potential for the development of supportive ties is always set in the context of interlocking class, race, and gender hierarchies" (Stanton-Salazar, 1997, p. 9). At a minimum, investigations of social capital must consider how inequality is created and what kinds of structures exist within networks that privilege some and silence others.

As problematically, the manner in which Coleman has presented social capital formation is tautological. Access to social capital begets social capital. Successful communities have social capital while unsuccessful communities do not. Individuals are successful because they reside in communities with social capital; unsuccessful individuals do not. In many respects such an analysis places individuals in a deterministic situation, where social capital is simultaneously a cause and effect. What is not taken into account by such an analysis is how communities break the cycle so that they are able to acquire social capital, or how successful communities became unsuccessful. "Defining social capital as equivalent with the resources thus obtained," according to Portes, "is tantamount to saying that the successful succeed" (1998, p. 5). The circularity of Coleman's framework ensures that those who are successful today will be successful tomorrow. What gets lost in such an analysis is an understanding of the ability of humans to interact and change the structures in which they reside as well as how those structures are power-laden. I do not wish to dismiss Coleman's analyses. They have useful implications for how trust functions in colleges and universities. Of necessity, however, one should modify Coleman's framework and take into account how change takes place, how power functions to qualify some and disqualify others, and what abilities individuals bring to social interactions that affect the structures in which they reside.

Pierre Bourdieu's concept of social capital

The thoughtful work of Pierre Bourdieu is frequently obscured by the obliqueness of his language. His work also suffers from a lack of contextualization—even though he acknowledges the need for context. He notes: "Social capital is the aggregate of the actual or potential resources which are linked to possession of a durable network of more or less institutionalized relationships of mutual acquaintance and recognition—or in other words, to membership in a group—which provides each of its members with the backing of the collectively-owned capital, a 'credential' which entitles them to credit, in the various senses of the word" (1986, p. 249). Indeed. To translate: social capital is not a single act, but a series of acts, or networks, that are lasting and institutionalized. The interactions occur among individuals who know one another because they are members in the same network or group. Membership in the group has social obligations that enable benefits to the individual such as a credential.

A useful analogy might be membership in a country club. One joins, or rather, is admitted, to a country club. Membership brings with it any number of possible interactions with other members—dinner, tennis, a round of golf, and the like. A member must meet certain obligations—annual dues, a dress code, or appointments for tee time. In turn, the member not only gains the benefits of membership but also increases his or her social capital. Members create networks with one another that will enable the member and his or her family to benefit in ways that are made more difficult without membership. How often, for example, has the observation been made that business deals are closed on the golf course or over drinks at the bar after a tennis match?

Such networks frequently overlap with one another. The members of the golf club also are members of the same congregation or business organization. Members may have gone to school together or graduated from the same university. The overlapping networks strengthen and extend the social capital of the individual. In turn, economic and cultural capital increases in ways that would be difficult, if not impossible, if an individual were not a member. The criticism of Coleman is that he rightly observes the venues where social capital occurs and increases, but he overlooks the structure of inequality. Enter Pierre Bourdieu.

Bourdieu focuses on the function and reproduction of inequality and power. Accordingly, when he studies social capital, he emphasizes the properties that reproduce inequality. Dika and Singh summarize Bourdieu's definition of social capital as "the investment of the dominant class to maintain and reproduce group solidarity and preserve the group's dominant position" (2002, p. 33). The manner in which reproduction occurs is a dynamic process that has unstated and seemingly arbitrary rules. Thus, at one point in time membership in a golf club is essential for the wealthy and powerful, but gradually membership in one network can become less prestigious. Individuals who were previously denied admittance may become members. In the meantime, power has moved on to another network. Bourdieu's fascination is with the dynamics of change and how power maintains privilege. Unlike Coleman's more focused look at social capital at a particular point in time, Bourdieu is interested in how networks change so that the powerless are unable to increase their social capital.

Bourdieu assumes that structural relationships exist such that individuals are able to accumulate capital. Certain individuals are able to accrue benefits while others are not. The accumulation of social capital enables individuals to access economic and cultural resources. Like Coleman, he emphasizes the intangible nature of social capital, which necessitates, of consequence, the microanalysis of how inequality functions.

However, Bourdieu has significant differences from Coleman's version of social capital. Bourdieu does not assume that social networks are preexistent and value-neutral. Individuals constantly create and recreate networks as investments in reproducing the status quo so that group relations become institutionalized. Social capital is not simply a "good." By allowing access to some individuals, the structure of social capital denies it to others. Whereas Coleman sees social capital as a positive form of social regulation that enables society to function, Bourdieu argues that it serves as a form of social regulation that empowers some and disempowers others.

Coleman and his successors (Putnam, 1995a, 1995b) argue that social capital does not only occur in golf clubs and retreats to fancy resorts by the wealthy and powerful. Social capital, they claim, is a neutral term that occurs in any number of associational networks—church picnics, neighborhood potlucks, family get-togethers, and PTA meetings. Thus, one ought not to equate social capital with privilege and power but instead try to chronicle where social capital takes place and in what forms and shapes. The goal is to come to terms with the outcomes of these associational formations. Coleman and Putnam believe that the eventual endpoint is an increase in civic engagement. The more social capital that exists only provides greater opportunity for the expansion of democracy.

Bourdieu fundamentally disagrees. His focus is not on the expansion of democracy but on how inequality flourishes. His concept of social capital is inextricably tied to notions of power. Although Bourdieu never takes up Coleman's assumptions, Alejandro Portes (1998) offers a trenchant analysis of social capital that closely follows Bourdieu's approach. He criticizes Coleman and his supporters for their overemphasis on social capital's positive consequences and lack of analysis of its negative aspects. He points out, as does Bourdieu, that membership in groups such as golf clubs are exclusionary; they bar certain people from joining. Group membership also restricts individual freedom. Norms are established to which individuals must adhere. These norms inevitably reinforce the status quo. In effect, Portes raises another key sociological precept by pointing out that social capital may well enforce community solidarity and at the same time restrict individual freedom.

Portes has commented sparingly about social capital in low-income groups, but his work complements Bourdieu's analysis of social reproduction. Portes states:

> There are situations in which group solidarity is cemented by a common experience of adversity and opposition to mainstream society. In these instances, individual success stories undermine group cohesion because the latter is precisely grounded on the alleged impossibility of such occurrences. The result is downward leveling norms that operate to keep members of a downtrodden group in place and force the more ambitious to escape from it. (1998, p. 17)

Thus, following the work of Fordham (1996), Fordham and Ogbu (1986), and others (Stepick, 1992; Suarez-Orozco, 1987), the assumption is that social capital for low-income, oppressed groups is really a manner of social control through downward leveling norms. To climb the economic ladder, one must forego the familial and communal associations that presumably generate social capital. Social capital demands norms, and if one is to succeed in a capitalist system, one must fit the regulatory norms that produce inequality for some and wealth for others.

Bourdieu's strength is that he factors into account what Coleman does not. He tries to understand how social capital changes over time in order to come to terms with how inequality functions. In doing so, he avoids Coleman's problem of reducing social capital to logical circularity: If an individual has "A," then "B" will occur; if "B" occurs, then the individual must have "A." Bourdieu also seeks to understand why and how individuals are denied access to social capital. Because he is concerned about group inequalities, he not only seeks an explanation for the dynamics that exist within the network but also how one enters and exits the network.

My concern with Bourdieu is twofold. First, his overly theoretical discourse begs for contextualization. Second, Bourdieu seems to deny agency to individuals. Society exists as a set of unequal relationships that are continually reproduced. In a curious manner, Bourdieu posits that society is composed of networks that are dynamic.

Individuals function in a field which is incredibly powerful. No one ever really learns the rules of the game. The rules change and shift in order to maintain the status quo. Thus, society is dynamic, but its overarching premise is that the status quo must be preserved. Individuals are little more than pawns in ever-shifting currents. And yet, local actors are able to create alternative networks that do not necessitate severing bonds with communal associations. Associations of Black business owners are only one example in the private sector. In higher education, the proliferation of gender and ethnic studies programs demonstrates the potential for local actors to generate new networks that facilitate professional development and career success.

Although scholars of social capital frequently portray Bourdieu and Coleman as theoretical opponents, I suggest that their work actually has significant potential for synthesis. In particular, if one utilizes four epistemological positions to extend the work of Bourdieu and Coleman, then the potential for understanding trust in academic organizations becomes possible. While my purpose here is not to enter into a philosophical exegesis on the nature of knowledge, I touch on these four positions in order to highlight how I utilize the perspectives of Coleman and Bourdieu.

On knowing

One cannot understand social capital as an abstraction. Insofar as social capital depends upon how members interpret and mediate their relationships in networks, it is incumbent on the researcher to conceptualize these multiple interactions. In consequence, who joins and who does not, why certain people are members and others are not, and how individuals navigate their networks are imperative. The result is that analyses that utilize a social capital framework will have thick descriptions that are multi-vocal and extend over time rather than single snapshots of a solitary individual or group.

On power

I agree with Bourdieu that one cannot avoid the parameters of power in order to accurately study social capital. Indeed, understanding power also enables one to understand trust. Power functions in multiple ways. Although one may correctly describe membership and exclusion from organizations such as the Chamber of Commerce as power-laden, not all networks of social capital have power that functions in a similar manner. Mechanisms of social control operate in different ways. Whereas Coleman posits that social control is useful for creating structures of civic engagement, Bourdieu sees social control as leveling aspirations and reproducing inequality. Different networks have different effects and yield different conclusions.

The kind of networks that Robert Putnam (2000) has described—such as bowling clubs, church socials, softball leagues, and the women's auxiliary—function in a manner fundamentally different from a country club or an exclusive private group such as the Bohemian Grove outside of San Francisco. To be sure, one needs to come to terms with the micro-activities that take place within a network, but the analyst cannot stop there. Researchers also must situate that network in the larger political sphere. Of course, low-income individuals have social capital that enables them to function in a particular manner with one another. Social and cultural minorities always have created formal and informal groups with one another in large part because they were excluded from mainstream groups.

The Log Cabin Republicans and Catholics' "Dignity USA" are gay-affiliated groups that have come together to work toward changing larger groups that have rejected or ignored the rights of gay and lesbian people. These groups provide social capital. But these forms of capital are quite different and yield different results from the kinds of analyses that Bourdieu conducted. Rather than assume one or another stance—power exists within networks or it does not—the challenge is to understand how it occurs and how to marshal it for productive results.

On agency

A caricature of the Coleman and Bourdieu positions would posit that either individuals are able to create associational networks in any manner that they like, or that individuals are caught in a tightly woven web of relationships that provides them no room for empowerment and self-fulfillment. The position I work from seeks a middle ground. Individuals are not free to pick and choose their networks as if there are no external parameters that structure their choice. And yet, individuals struggle to change their lives and the lives of others. Oppositional tactics and strategies of resistance yield the possibility of far-reaching reform and change. One is not faced with a trade-off between assimilating to unbending norms or being stuck with the life one has been given. The assertion about human agency assumes that structures exist that coordinate power in society, but individuals also are able to gain control over their lives to some extent and not simply be fitted into a Weberian straitjacket.

On culture

Although a structural analysis of social capital yields several benefits, what appears to be missing is the assumption that individuals and groups construct, interpret, refine, and reinterpret the networks in which they are embedded. Instead, Coleman works from a rational-choice framework and Bourdieu a neo-Marxian perspective. Just as one applauds structural analyses that moved the field away from intense focus on the individual, one also needs to move beyond a focus solely on structure when analyzing social capital. Proponents of structural analysis generally do not dismiss out of hand how individual identity may help shape structures; in similar fashion, a cultural perspective on social capital and trust surely ought not to overlook the importance that social structures have.

However, my assumption is that individuals create structures; structures are not preexisting, rigid entities. They have little meaning prior to individuals giving them life. An array of sociohistorical forces is at work that provides meanings to the participants in those structures and networks, but current contexts also provide new and different meanings from the past. The entrance and exit of actors from a network provide possibilities for redefinition and redirection.

Accordingly, when one wants to understand social capital, many of the points made by Bourdieu and Coleman are critical. To understand organizations and trust, however, one cannot come to terms with the meanings of social capital without a contextual understanding of the networks to be studied. These networks are not loose affiliations that enable any actions whatsoever to occur. Nor are they entirely composed of mechanistic social controls that allow no interpretation or agency. Social capital is more a cultural framework than a structural one. The challenge for researchers is to come to terms with the elements of social capital prior to analyzing a specific network in order to have a scheme from which to proceed.

Elements of social capital

Given the abstract and intangible nature of the term, it will be useful if I define the elements of social capital. My intent is to synthesize the different approaches I outlined above such that when one references social capital, there are four interrelated elements: forms, norms of obligation and reciprocity, resources, and funds of knowledge. One or another element may seem to favor Bourdieu's or Coleman's approach, but taken together, they provide the scaffolding for how to think about a more protean notion of social capital. In order to investigate these elements the focus can be both *internal* and *external* (Adler & Kwon, 2002, p. 19).

Internal focus

An internal focus pertains to the relations an actor has with other actors within the organization or network. How social capital is a resource that links individuals within a network is of primary interest. Coleman observes that "social capital is defined by its function. It is not a single entity, but a variety of different entities having two characteristics in common: They all consist of some aspect of social structure, and they facilitate certain actions of individuals who are within the structure" (1990, p. 302). The intent is to understand how people within the framework come together to work cooperatively so that coordination and cooperation are outcomes. The researcher with an internal focus seeks to comprehend how social capital facilitates the resolution of problems and promotes development of the network.

External focus

An external lens considers the linkages accrued beyond the network. Such linkages occur not only for individuals but also for the organization via memberships in exclusive associations and relationships developed with various external constituencies. From this perspective, social capital is "the ability of actors to secure benefits by virtue of membership in social networks or other social structures" (Portes, 1998, p. 6). An external focus, then, pertains to what the individual accrues due to involvement within the network as well as how the organization relates, interacts, and is perceived by external constituencies. The intent is to understand the benefits and opportunities that an individual or the organization gains through involvement in a network, and conversely, to consider what individuals and organizations lose because they do not have that specific form of social capital. Obviously, individual and organizational analyses differ in scope and approach, but, in order to consider trust formation, one needs to investigate not only internal interactions and perceptions but also those that are external.

An external focus is particularly important for understanding organizational networks, and as I discuss in Part 3, how trust and the public good are linked. Certainly the "public" takes a risk when it trusts institutions with financial resources and operational autonomy. Institutions may be inefficient, and they may utilize their autonomy in self-serving, rather than public-serving ways. How, then, does the public develop trust in postsecondary institutions, and what do these organizations need to do to develop the conditions for trust to exist? Such a question moves the analysis away from the individual creation of networks and toward an organizational analysis that suggests organizational networks generate social capital, which in turn, generates trust. As I discuss in Part 2, the extent and quality of a university's participation in the local community (one element of an organizational network) may generate social capital and public trust.

My intent is to merge the two vantage points of Coleman and Bourdieu. I suggest that they need not be in competition with one another. Adler and Kwon are helpful here:

> The distinction between the external and internal views is, to a large extent, a matter of perspective and unit of analysis: the relations between an employee and colleagues within a firm are external to the employee but internal to the firm. The internal and external

views are not mutually exclusive. The behavior of a collective actor such as a firm is influenced by its external linkages to other firms and institutions and by the fabric of its internal linkages: its capacity for effective action is typically a function of both. (2002, p. 21)

From this perspective, social capital comprises the internal actions within the network as well as the resources and values developed for individuals and the organization outside of, or within, the network. For the researcher who utilizes a cultural framework, the network is a web of relationships that influences the behavior of the web, the organization, and individuals. Simply stated, social capital influences behavior that also influences the networks in which the individual and organization resides. Accordingly, when I consider trust and how it pertains to a college or university, I look not only within the organization but also situate the institution in a larger web of relationships. Trust as a concept needs to be considered vis-à-vis the relationship of internal actors to one another and also with regard to whether societal and civic groups trust the organization. Such a point underscores the importance of understanding how a concept like the public good is defined and how postsecondary institutions enact the term.

Forms of social capital: The form of social capital pertains to the structural aspects of social ties and relations, including the breadth of the network, its depth and intensity, and the nature of social relations. Researchers should map the multiple forms that function within and outside of the network that are both 'real' and symbolic. Assume, for example, that one wants to understand how social capital operates in the governance structure of a small liberal arts college. The organizational chart, bylaws, and a multitude of guidelines and handbooks will outline formalized processes and procedures that provide clues about the existing forms of governance that involve social capital. Whether a faculty senate exists, for example, and what its formalized responsibilities are, provides useful information.

The forms of relationships that the organization has with the populace also matter. Is the college an ivory tower with little interaction in the local community, or does it see itself as a resource for the community such that it attends local meetings and is an active participant? How is "community" defined for business interests, local government, or community-based organizations?

Informal forms of social capital also exist that need to be taken into account. One might track a decision to see not only where a proposal emanated from and how it worked its way through the governance process but also the informal aspects of such a decision. Forms are not only lines on a chart; forms also have a symbolic content that should be studied and analyzed. One need not be a political scientist to recognize that who is involved in a decision and how decisions get made and implemented not only occur through formalized procedures but also through informal push and pull. Who pushes and who gets pushed, who is ignored, provide clues about social capital.

Further, forms not only pertain to structures such as those that deal with decision making, but also with that of information and communication. Who is privy to information and who communicates with whom are vital pieces of data to gather when the researcher tries to piece together how social capital functions. The president who sends email to senior faculty on a regular basis updating them about events that are happening affords the possibility for social capital to accrue with those individuals whereas untenured faculty are presumably left shortchanged. Similarly, when an institution has faculty on its board of trustees so that a faculty representative is privy to all board-related information, one form of social capital occurs. When a board has business leaders as members, different interactions occur as compared to when a board's composition is dependent upon alumni. The point here is not to assume that one form is correct and another is not but to come to terms with the forms that social capital takes in an organization and to understand the sociohistorical forces that have brought such forms forward.

Norms of social capital: This element pertains to the mutuality that exists within a network. Individuals participate in a network because they expect some kind of return. Social capital theorists eschew the idea of altruism. Individuals invest in others because they assume that they will harvest some benefit. Organizations also enter into similar arrangements. An organization joins an association because of the assumption that membership will somehow enhance or impact the organization.

Such an idea is not new. In 1924, Marcel Mauss wrote his classic essay on gift exchange. He posited that gift giving is always reciprocal. An individual provides a gift to someone else because the two parties are involved in a reciprocal relationship. These norms generate goodwill among individuals and produce what rational-choice theorists perceive as civic engagement.

Although I return to all four elements of social capital in the subsequent chapter on trust, the clearest example of where trust is not simply created by, but also helps create, social capital is with regard to norms. Networks that have norms where trustworthiness is strong are likely to generate more social capital than in units where trustworthiness is absent. Norms of reciprocity assume that a culture of mutual obligation to one another exists in the network. In this sense, one initially has an internal focus in order to come to terms with what the norms are, how they function, and what develops for the actors. Ultimately, one investigates from an external focus as well in order to understand the benefits of the norms for the network as a whole and for the individual actors.

In order to avoid the logical circularity of Coleman's position, a key task here is to think of norms as dynamic processes. Obviously, when one studies a small liberal arts college where the norm is one of intense faculty engagement in governance, then one may conclude that social capital exists because of the relational norms between parties. However, an investigation about norms has less to do with simply checking off which network has norms that foster social capital and which do not. Such a checklist is reductionist. A checklist simply illustrates that networks with norms that are "x" have social capital and those with norms "y" do not. Rather, the challenge is to consider how norms are created, introduced into a network, changed, and enhanced or eviscerated. If norms are to be understood, then they must be seen in a diachronic process, rather than a static, asynchronous development.

Resources of social capital: "Any discussion of how social capital affects behavior," notes McNeal, "must take into account both the resources within the network as well as the potential resources that can be drawn upon outside the network" (1999, p. 119). While norms are initially more internally focused, resources might be thought of as primarily externally focused. Resources accrue between internal actors and external agents, and they occur in "real" and symbolic ways. A private school that has access to computers because a board member owns a software company is able to generate a very specific kind of "real" resource. At the same time, symbolic resources also occur with the board member when he or she is able to provide a student with a job, a reference, or career advice. Here, then, is an example of the interaction between internal and external actors that enhances the social capital of the individuals within the network as well as the network itself.

Resources differ for different persons. A child in a public school in South Los Angeles will not have access to either the "real" or the symbolic resources that a child in a private school has. Affluent board members are more likely to be at a private school such as Exeter than a public school such as Manual Arts in Los Angeles. The result is that both "real" and symbolic resources that lead to the accumulation of social capital occur in one location and not another. At times, an attempt will be made to increase the physical resources of a public school like Manual Arts; although the physical resources never approach that of a private school, what is also overlooked are the symbolic resources that reside and increase in the private school.

A second kind of resource is that which occurs within the network rather than between internal and external agents. Coleman points out how "the set of resources that inhere in family relations and community social organization . . . are useful for the cognitive or social development of a child or young person" (1990, p. 300). Examples would be organizations such as the PTA and the Boy/Girl Scouts, or events such as parent-teacher conferences and commencement. Such resources produce social capital.

Again, I caution not to look at communities that have such organization and events and those that do not, and simply to state that only one is rich in social capital. Obviously, in my example, the private school has more social capital than the public school in South Los Angeles. But one needs to consider not simply the objective resource of the meeting or event but also the symbolic resources that are generated by such meetings. A PTA meeting in a low-income neighborhood is not the same as a similar meeting across town. Access to fiscal and cultural resources provides those in upper-income neighborhoods with ways to increase capital for the young that are not possible in low-income neighborhoods. Indeed, how individuals approach (or avoid) such networks influences the nature of social capital. Wealthy individuals look upon schools as avenues for their children to increase their worth. Those who are low-income and minority frequently do not see schools in the same light. A school may be viewed as culturally disruptive from the norms of the family, or it may be seen as oppositional. The result is that families may choose not to participate in what may be thought of as traditional organizations such as the PTA; or if they do participate, the participation is as an outsider trying to protect, rather than promote, the interests of their children.

Social capital is not unimportant amongst the poor and working class. It is not impossible to accrue. I argue for the need to contextualize investigations of social capital. This contextualization ought not only to occur within the network. Researchers must also come to terms with the various contexts within which the specific network is nested.

Funds of knowledge: People who are rich in social capital are able to draw upon a fund of knowledge—shared past experiences to help navigate the network. Knowledge of the culture of the network facilitates coordination and cooperation for mutual benefit. Stanton-Salazar (1997) has used the term to describe socialization, both implicit and explicit, in terms of institutional discourses. Such discourses control interaction between organizational groups. Individuals learn how networks function. Some are able to function effectively, and others are disabled. Because socializing mechanisms are often implicit, one will not find a list of rules on how to create social capital in a network. Instead, an individual must decipher the network's culture, considering his or her own specific history.

Some individuals arrive to the network with sufficient cultural capital to function effectively; in turn, their initial investment of cultural capital increases with the related increase in social capital. Those who lack cultural capital, however, are at an initial disadvantage and must try to catch up even as they begin. Consider, for example, two individuals who begin a career as an assistant professor. One individual had parents who were faculty, grew up on a college campus, attended an Ivy League institution, and associated with peers who attended similar institutions and would attain similar careers. The other individual is a first-generation college graduate, who grew up in a low-income neighborhood, attended a second-tier doctoral institution, and socialized with peers who never went to college. Both individuals arrive at a research university at the same time as tenure-track assistant professors. The professors' child arrives on campus with a fund of knowledge that in turn generates additional cultural and social capital. The other individual has learned about the norms, resources, and forms of social capital that exist in higher education only through undergraduate and graduate school. Clearly, one individual is privileged and the other is not.

One ought not to read such data in deterministic fashion—the privileged succeed and the rest cannot. Nevertheless, the analyst makes a mistake when individual and collective funds of knowledge are not taken into account. The phrase "social capital" ought to generate notions of bank accounts. Some individuals arrive to situations with more capital in their account than others. Some individuals even have multiple accounts. One should consider the varying accounts while also recognizing that capital can be spent. How social capital accrues and evaporates provides clues that enable greater understanding into the functioning of networks.

Yet again, then, the challenge is to contextualize what is meant by social capital. To do so, the researcher proceeds by analyzing the internal and external parameters of the elements that have been outlined. An additional task is to consider the uses of social capital, their benefits, and costs.

The abuses and uses of social capital

Any analysis of social capital ought to function from the awareness of three cautions. The first concern pertains to the ability of "bad" social capital generated by "bad" people. de Souza Briggs has noted, "When we confide distress to a friend or listen as a confidante, social capital is at work, directly serving the person in distress but also renewing the relationship in what will, over time, be used by the speaker and listener. When poor moms share care-giving tasks and rides to church among networks of relatives, friends, and acquaintances, they each draw on social capital" (1997, p. 113). To be sure, social capital has multiple uses by multiple individuals and groups. However, one ought not to think of social capital as always benign such that it is always a "good" or that only "good" people generate social capital. The person confiding distress to the friend could be two mafiosi, and one could substitute the example of mothers with members of a terrorist network who work together to achieve their goal. These, too, are possible examples of social capital. The mafiosi renew their relationship, and the terrorists draw on social capital. A researcher just as easily could investigate the forms, norms, resources, and funds of knowledge of the Cosa Nostra as friends; an internal and external focus might be called upon to comprehend low-income mothers or Al Qaeda.

A second related concern is that social capital calls upon group solidarity. Such solidarity inevitably leads to productive outcomes. Portes cautions, "The same strong ties that bring benefits to members of a group commonly enable it to bar others from access" (1998, p. 15). If one wants to be in a group, there are norms that must be followed. Again, frequently examples have been provided about individuals such as delinquents or criminals. The portrait that is drawn is that when a community enforces the elements of social capital, there will be less delinquency and fewer criminals. As Putnam observed, "Social capital refers to features of social organization ... that facilitate coordination and cooperation for mutual benefit" (1995a, p. 67). While I understand Putnam's rationale, I offer a caution about his examples. Communities can certainly be found where social capital is high, and such strength has facilitated coordination and cooperation for a negative "benefit": Black people are kept out of the neighborhood, for example, or gay people are arrested. I do not wish to reject Putnam's comment. I simply seek to highlight that social capital may indeed generate public goods, but it may also create public "bads."

The final concern is that by always reducing instances of social capital to examples of inequality and reproduction one overlooks the multifaceted nature of the idea. A monthly potluck among friends in the neighborhood may or may not exemplify inequality depending upon the nature of the interaction. But what is certain is that such an event has the potential to generate social capital. Just as I do not want to reduce social capital to an inevitable vehicle to create a public good, or that only good people create social capital, I also do not want to look only for examples of inequality.

Social capital is a cultural construction that exists in networks. The actors within the network decipher the interpretations and meanings that are attributed to the idea and its outcomes. The individuals who seek to understand the network then develop their own interpretations. I portrayed in a negative light the example I gave above of a community that is rich in social capital and arrests gays and lesbians. Presumably, the individuals in the community would not interpret the act in similar fashion. Readers will have multiple interpretations. I simply suggest that individuals bring meaning to a term that I have been struggling to define. I seek to offer it as a vehicle of neither good nor bad.

One key aspect of social capital, and my purpose in introducing it here, is its possibility to generate trust. Putnam notes, "The theory of social capital presumes that, generally speaking, the more we connect with other people, the more we trust them" (1995b, p. 665). One may accept Putnam's assertion without rejecting the ideas of Bourdieu or making any claim to whether the generation of trust takes place in a good or bad community by good or bad people. However, I assume that the creation of trust creates the conditions for risk taking. To be sure, individuals bring their own backgrounds to a situation, but the contexts in which they reside also provide some form of discouragement or encouragement. Richard Sennett notes that "people must draw upon a fund of social capital" to take risks (1998, p. 85).

The primary use of social capital in academic organizations, I suggest, is that it provides the conditions for trust and trustworthiness. In turn, opportunities occur for risk taking and change to take place. Conversely, without social capital, the conditions for distrust will arise. Seligman writes, "Social capital . . . is in essence no more than the forms of associational life based on different types of *confidence* in the workings of the system and its institutional arrangements." Social capital generates goodwill among individuals and groups that facilitate interactions with one another. "The social capital (i.e. confidence) itself rests on different types of unconditionalities which is precisely what is provided for by the different terms of solidarity in its different forms" (1997, p. 80).

Thus, I seek to comprehend how social capital generates trust. The analysis needs to incorporate the elements and internal/external focus I have considered here, and through such a study one may come to terms with how trust gets defined, created, changed, and called upon within academic organizations. Of course, to make such a claim, I need to delineate what I mean by trust, which will be the focus of the next chapter.

CHAPTER TWO

The Grammar of Trust

Trust is an elusive concept that frequently seems to defy definition. Philosophers have debated its meaning, and common usages abound that often equate the term with a moral good. Trust has a positive ring to it. "He inspires trust" implies that the individual is able to persuade people to act in a particular way because the person is trustworthy. Trustworthy suggests that the individual is morally honest. Conversely, when someone says, "I distrust him," the intent is to convey that the individual is deceitful or dishonest. Obviously, given the choice, individuals prefer to be considered trustworthy and to work with someone who is trustworthy.

Simply because someone is trustworthy, however, should not suggest that the individual is moral, honest, or effective. Many criminals of the 20th century—Adolph Hitler, Saddam Hussein, Joseph Stalin—could be trusted by their people to act in a particular way because they were consistent in their immoral actions. Trust, then, does not only mean that an individual may be honest. Trust also implies consistency. What a person says is what he or she will do. Trust in some instances, then, has little to do with ethics or morality, and more to do with actions that meet expectations. Similarly, what does it imply when individuals believe someone is not trustworthy?

Consider the case of American presidents. The moniker of "Tricky Dick" was bestowed upon Richard Nixon; for Bill Clinton, "Slick Willy"—in part because individuals believed they could not be trusted. Yet they also had numerous political and policy triumphs. Jimmy Carter may have been more trustworthy than

Nixon and Clinton, but many will argue that Nixon and Clinton were more effective. Simply because the citizenry trusts someone to act in a particular way gives no indication about whether their actions are moral or reprehensible or whether the individual is capable of achieving specific goals.

When trust is used in isolation from other terms, false meanings can be derived. An auto repair store, for example, that advertises itself as "the most trusted name in town" suggests that consumers should have their cars fixed at the shop because the invoice will accurately reflect the repairs that were done. The mechanic is honest. Such a statement may be contextually important because consumers frequently worry that the costs of car repairs do not reflect the work that is needed and/or actually completed. If a bakery used such a phrase—"the most trusted name in town"—it would not have as much currency as the auto repair shop. In general, bakers are neither trusted nor mistrusted. Trust in the context of the mechanic, however, says nothing about the competence of the repair shop. The mechanics may be trustworthy but incompetent. A number of variables and contexts should be included if one is to judge not only the trustworthiness of the organization but also its quality or effectiveness. If a bakery in a specific town at a specific point in time had been found to use low-grade oil in their cooking because it was cheap, but the oil made people sick, then other local bakers might say they were more trustworthy. That phrase would have meaning. Temporal and geographic contexts matter.

As I noted in the introduction, trust has been relatively overlooked in higher education. There is a paucity of conceptual or empirical work precisely at a time when scholars of organizational behavior have noted its importance. Kramer and Tyler (1996) and others (Elangovan & Shapiro, 1998; Gambetta, 1988; Kramer & Cook, 2004; Luhmann, 1988) have considered how trust enables cooperative behavior to occur. Their assumption is that trust and trustworthiness generate a particular set of conditions for civic engagement and risk taking. Whereas some have pointed out how power, authority, or contractual arrangements might bring about desired goals, others have asked what part trust plays in sustaining cooperation and, in turn, enhancing organizational effectiveness (Sheppard & Sherman, 1998).

The assumption is that people's social motivations play a central role in defining how individuals work together, which in turn impacts the quality of what they produce. A productive work environment, from this perspective, is one where trust exists. Such a premise is particularly important for organizations that need to undergo significant changes. When the status quo is no longer viable and change is imperative, then risk taking is necessary. If individuals are to take risks, then one vital component is that they trust the other individuals with whom they work. Complex organizations where individuals have a high degree of autonomy are also more likely to need trust compared to organizations where work is routine and simple. Trust serves as an alternative to mandates, regulations, threat, coercion, and incentives, which are seldom effective in changing behavior in professional organizations where individuals have a significant degree of freedom in deciding the nature of their work.

Thus, academic organizations appear to be ripe for investigation. They are complex; their organizational actors have a high degree of autonomy. As noted in the introduction, many argue that postsecondary institutions in the 21st century need to undergo significant change. Change necessitates a high degree of risk on the part of the faculty and administrators. But what does one mean by trust in an academic environment? What are the conditions for trust? Who are the parties engaged in trusting behavior? In order to answer such questions, I first outline what I will call the "grammar of trust" and then consider the various levels on which trust occurs. In doing so, I will only touch on trust's conceptual opposite: distrust. Although a great deal of work might be done to elucidate the parameters of distrust (Bigley & Pearce, 1998; Hardin, 2004), I save such a discussion for a later text.

A great deal of conceptual confusion exists with regard to how scholars have discussed trust. As with other complex terms such as leadership, the grammar that individuals use in large part defines how they portray the concept under study. Accordingly, in what follows, I delineate the nine most common grammatical frames that have been used about trust. At times, these terms conflict with one another, and at other moments, the terms complement or ignore other terms. I use the final two frames—rational choice and cultural construction—as overarching language for how to conceptualize trust and suggest why trust, as a cultural construction, is appropriate for analyzing postsecondary organizations. Once I have delineated the grammar of trust, I turn in subsequent chapters, first to organizational trust in general, then in particular to trust in academic organizations. I also consider not simply trust at the individual level within organizations but also how organizational trust operates to impact notions of the public good.

Table 2.1: Forms of the grammar of trust

A repeated interaction
A dynamic process
An end
An exchange
Utilizing faith
Taking risks
An ability
A rational choice
A cultural construction

The grammar of trust

As a repeated interaction

Trust inevitably involves two parties. Those parties may be two or more individuals, an individual or individuals in relation to an organization, or an individual or individuals in a larger social structure such as the government or a religious entity. Further, when public trust comes into play, frequently the idea takes hold between an organization—such as a public college or university—and an entity such as the state government. Although one may occasionally hear someone say, "I can't trust myself," such a comment is in practice impossible. An individual cannot have an interaction with the self. Trust from an individualistic perspective is a cognitive state of mind that involves another individual. At an organizational level, trust is a construction between two or more groups.

The most basic interaction is that between two individuals. A child's relationship to a parent, for example, or two individuals involved in a romantic relationship are perhaps the clearest examples of trust and trustworthiness. At the most elemental level, an infant learns to trust a parent. When a helpless infant cries and the parent picks up the baby, more than a functional act is happening. The infant learns that he or she matters to the parent. The parent is trustworthy. To be sure, there are numerous examples where an infant does not learn such a lesson; a parent may neglect or even physically harm the child. But the infant-parent connection is perhaps the clearest example of trust as an interaction.

Individuals also develop trust for organizations in which they work or interact. Although the organization is an abstraction, individuals who work in or have a connection to an organization come to learn about it by way of their interactions with superiors, subordinates, and coworkers. The organization will have rules, procedures, and symbolic processes that provide individuals with ways to understand how trust functions and whether they should believe that the organization is trustworthy.

Trust also exists for an organization with external constituencies. My example of auto repair stores conveys the previous interactions customers may have had with a shop. Individuals still interact with other individuals within the organization. Trust is built on individualized interactions. However, not all organizations are alike. Some organizations are more trustworthy than others, and as I expand upon in Chapter 3, some organizations need trust as a basic interaction more than others.

To further complicate the matter, public trust has underlying ideas that relate to organizational trust, but the two entities—society and organizations—are not also analogous. A citizen's trust in government is more a belief in an ambiguous idea than a construct that is defined by ongoing social relations. "The consent of the governed" must be attained for a democratic society to function, but such consent is different from individual relations and network interactions that occur with an organization. Russell Hardin (2002) points out that what one needs in a democracy is less a concern for the citizenry to trust in government than for individuals to find its government trustworthy. The idea of *substitutability* is at work here. As Ullman-Margalit notes, "When we express trust in an institution, we express our belief that, even if the present officeholders in that institution were to be replaced with others, the performance of the institution is tantamount to a belief in the impersonality of its performance, in addition to the belief that its goals are compatible with our interests" (2004, p. 77). For those who work from an individualistic perspective, then, such a view of trust is not possible. I suggest, however, that when one looks at a postsecondary institution's relationship to its external constituencies, the development and maintenance of such trust are essential. The repeated interactions individuals and constituencies have with organizations help to determine the degree of trust that exists in the larger society.

Trustworthiness is not so much a matter of the parameters of belief by one party, as in the other parties' ability to enact what was implied. Some may argue that trust may be "impersonal" (Brennan, 1998); hence citizens' trust in democratic structural arrangements is not an interaction because one entity is an inanimate object. We also know that the citizenry imbues entities with meaning by way of individuals. Trust in government decreased through the actions of Richard Nixon and his administration. Bill Clinton's parsing of language—"it depends on what the meaning of 'is' is"—made not just himself but his government less trustworthy. The Catholic Church's unwillingness and inability to deal with priests who were unable to keep their hands off of children caused people to lose faith in the trustworthiness of the people who led the Church, but interestingly, many parishioners did not lose their faith (Mehm, 2002). The results of a 1999 national survey of public perceptions of state courts revealed that African Americans were less likely than Anglos to have trust in the justice system (NCSC, p. 13). Respondents who reported lower incomes also had lower levels of trust in the justice system than those with higher incomes and higher levels of education. These results point out how repeated interactions between individuals and civic entities create an interpretation of trust.

Most often, trust is constructed through repeated interactions. Adam Seligman points out that "for trust to be developed between two individuals, they must have repeated encounters, and they must have some memory of previous encounters" (1997, p. 26). Conversely, however, a single interaction may be sufficient for trust to be destroyed. The husband or wife whose onetime extramarital affair is discovered may never generate the level of trust that existed prior to the interaction. Such a point highlights the delicacy and indeterminacy of the concept. Trust as a repeated interaction may evaporate in a moment's passion, but it is only built over time.

Thus, individuals develop trust through interactions that occur over an extended period of time. One can neither command trust nor coerce someone to trust. Although an individual may undertake a particular action because another individual has power over the person, the individual still will not trust the other party (Luhmann, 1979). A teacher may demand certain behaviors from a student on the first day of school because of the role that each inhabits. In order for a trusting relationship to occur, however, it is most often necessary for individuals to have repeated encounters. And again, these repeated encounters ought not to be viewed within a moral framework. Iraqis came to trust what Saddam Hussein would do by way of the repeated interactions they had with his regime.

As a dynamic process

These interactions have a purpose. Trust is an indeterminate term, yet one with a social function. The specific function varies based on time, locale, and group, but the generic function of trust is to help resolve incomplete information so that an event occurs. Lane (1998) writes, "Trust is a mechanism by which actors reduce the internal complexity of their system of interaction through the adoption of specific expectations about the future behavior of the other by selecting amongst a range of possibilities" (p. 12). Without trust, or its proxy, interactions that lead to a result could not take place.

As individuals interact with one another over time, these interactions lead to an end result. Insofar as the outcomes of human interactions are never certain and are fraught with individual interpretations about the nature of reality, the function of trust is to enable individuals, organizations, and society to reach one or another goal. The individual trusts the other person so that social cohesion will take place. Trust enables expectations to occur about what will happen as an outcome of the interactions of individuals. Trust is a bridge that connects parties who do not function in a causal world where perfect information exists.

A proxy for trust relates to societal mechanisms that can substitute when trust is absent or not yet possible. If the infant-parent relationship is at one end of a trust-based continuum, a legal contract is at the other. Two parties develop a contract such that X is only able to assume the trustworthiness of Y to do Z if a contract is written. If Y does not do Z, then X has recourse to the courts, sanctions, and fines. Again, the function remains the same: to enable a particular outcome, but the processes used to produce that outcome may be thought of as a proxy for trust. At the most absurd level, an infant does not require a contract from a parent to act in a particular way; the infant learns to trust through a series of repeated actions. However, when instantaneous interactions need to produce an outcome and trust between the parties is most likely not possible, a legal proxy will be created.

From this perspective, much of the legal system in society has been created because absolute trust is not possible. Even when trust is a possibility or preferable, there will be fallback legal mechanisms which individuals may utilize. Two individuals may trust one another, for example, but prior to getting married, they will develop a prenuptial agreement in order to ensure that, should anything occur that causes the partnership to end, each individual will understand the fiscal parameters of the relationship. Luhmann (1979) observed that legal regulations are background structures that come into play when trust fails. These structures are lubricants for trust.

As an end

Trust is also an end unto itself. To make such a statement may seem contradictory with a grammar that also defines trust as a process or function. To suggest that the function of trust is to generate trust almost seems tautological. To understand trust as an end, one should consider the notions developed in the previous chapter on social capital. Trust generates social capital and is generated by social capital. Similarly, trust as a function may lead to an end where greater trust has been generated. Such a point is relevant not only to individuals, but also to organizations. The more that the public views the organization as trustworthy, the more likely it will be to have a sustained interpretation of the unit as a public good worthy of support.

A myriad of other ends are important and necessary in social contexts that trust is helpful in creating. But human interaction is not always bound to "if-then" relationships where one action is intended immediately to cause another. Relationships develop over time. The manner in which relationships grow does not always depend upon clearly delineated cause-and-effect circumstances. Individuals come to learn about others in any number of formal and informal ways. To assume that trust is always a functional relationship reduces human interaction to a series of intentional consequences where someone does something only if there is an intended payoff.

As I discuss, although trust may be considered an exchange relationship to a certain extent, it is also true that individuals are not always cognitively aware that their actions are strengthening (or weakening) the conditions for trust. When a leader enters the office on a Monday morning and casually speaks with individuals about their weekends, conveying a genuine interest in their lives, the individual presumably has no stated goal. The conversation was not premeditated, and if asked, the individual most likely would not say that he or she was trying to create an atmosphere where the employees were more productive or had increased trust in senior management. And yet, the result of such a conversation may well be that trust has increased. Nothing more was gained from the conversation than an increase in trust between two parties. Such a point is particularly germane when actions are repeated. The leader who consistently conveys interest and concern with others may be doing so not out of a strategic plan but from a particular vantage point about how individuals should act with one another. The result over time may be that individuals come to trust the leader.

Thus, trust as an end presumes that all of life is not functional. As I develop my own grammar of trust for this text, I want to avoid falling into an "either-or" reductionist mentality where a social idea must be one or the other variable but not both. Those who struggle to define abstract terms such as trust walk a delicate line where we frequently impose either rigidly absurd notions or work from a framework that is so vast that the term under consideration has no meaning. Hence, I reject the idea that to think of trust one must only think of it as a process, and if one does, then it is impossible for it to be an end as well. At the same time, I acknowledge that unless scholars of the term employ a thick understanding for the reader, the term loses any conceptual rigor. As Humpty Dumpty said, "When I use a word, it means just what I choose it to mean—neither more nor less" (Carroll, 1872/1994). Such an assertion may work in the world of Lewis Carroll, but it is futile on terra firma.

Indeed, my purpose in this chapter in outlining the grammar of trust is to come to terms with the manifold ways it has been employed; in later sections, I delineate the conditions and levels in which the grammar is put to use. For the moment, then, consider that in some instances, trust is a function that aids in generating a particular outcome; in other instances, trust is an end where the original intent was not in the production of trust; and in still other instances, trust operates in a cyclical manner such that the process of trust generates trust. The conceptual problem is how trust develops amongst individuals where no trust exists or it has been destroyed. Prior to dealing with that concern, however, I will make the term still more complex.

As an exchange

As opposed to an end unto itself between two parties, trust may also be seen as a utilitarian exchange. The parties are engaged in a reciprocal relationship. Trust involves giving power to someone else that will affect one's interests. In turn, at some point, one party will also trust the other. Kramer, Brewer, and Hanna have written, "The logic of reciprocity-based trust is simple: I will engage in trust behavior because I believe you are likely to do the same" (1996, p. 373). As with the idea of social capital, the assumptions of reciprocity and exchange are rooted in sociological and anthropological traditions. As I noted earlier, Marcel Mauss (1924/1967) wrote in his classic essay about gift giving that the giver always gave a gift with a sense of reciprocity and social exchange. Such a point is useful because it highlights the social interactions involved in trust. It is not simply a cognitive response of one individual. Rather than trust being context-specific, trust transcends a specific event, but occurs through assumptions about the nature of the relationship. Even though one party may enter into such an agreement without a reciprocal commitment on the specific issue, the larger assumption is that the parties are bound together through a sense of mutuality over time.

Social exchange theorists (such as Blau, 1964) have explored the ideas of Mauss further by positing that two parties are involved in an obligatory relationship. Relationships involve interactions and exchanges based on reciprocity and commitment. Again, one runs the risk of creating an example that appears static: How do people enter into an obligatory relationship? Without explaining the roots of how the parties became involved in an exchange relationship, it seems as if trust has existed in a relationship forever—it is unchanging. Of course, such is not the case. Two parties may come together with no history with one another, or an individual may join an organization and have no sense of the exchanges that are necessary or expected. However, there are numerous examples that I will consider where reciprocal relationships appear in incremental fashion such that a gradual expansion of exchange takes place over time. Even though the preceding definition of trust as an end in itself and trust as an exchange may seem to be at odds with one another, I suggest that they are complementary. Trust as an end may create the conditions where two parties are willing to enter into a trusting exchange relationship.

I should also point out that social exchange theory is not presaged on contractual, or formalized, relationships. Although explicit obligations may be delineated, a more routine example pertains to voluntary associations. Because of the voluntary nature of social exchange theory, when a party enters into such an arrangement, there is no a priori assurance that the exchange will be reciprocated or that the initial truster will have any legal recourse. One cannot demand trust. Whitener, Brodt, Korsgaard, and Werner explained, "The exchange of benefits involves uncertainty, particularly in early stages of the relationship when the risk of non-reciprocation is relatively high" (1988, p. 515). Rather than appearing contradictory, when one wishes to understand trust as an exchange, the focus needs to be on its evolution rather than on an isolated moment. Parties need to show trustworthiness; the manner in which this is done is incremental.

As with the previous grammar of trust, exchange theory certainly includes individualized notions of risk and motivation. Individuals and groups come to any given situation or interaction with their own unique histories and beliefs. Whereas one person may well be able to enter into an exchange relationship quickly, others will not. Some will assume that more formalized arrangements should take place. Other individuals will be more amenable to informal relationships. For trust to have an impact on performance and competitiveness in an organization, trust ought neither to be assumed as a constant nor a given. Trust in an exchange relationship is framed by the individual and sociocultural contexts in which it is embedded.

As faith

To carry the idea of individualized notions of trust a step further, trust might be seen as faith in the other party. From this perspective, trust is tied to a psychological orientation that enables an individual to have faith that the other party will fulfill their part of an agreement. Faith, then, is not simply a belief in another individual or group; having faith is an orientation toward how the believer thinks about, and acts in, the world.

Trust, notes Adam Seligman, "is a form of belief that carries within it something unconditional and irreducible to the fulfillment of systematically mandated role expectations" (1997, p. 44). Although Seligman rejects a reductionist view of trust that is entirely dependent upon the individual as the unit of analysis, he usefully points out how trust also must be seen as highly contingent on belief. The important distinction must be made, however, that when I write of faith, I am using it in a manner different from the theologian. The religious notion of faith is virtually always considered in relation to the individual and God, or God's proxy—the Church, the priest, the congregation, or an idea. Indeed, the uproar over the criminal actions of priests in the Catholic Church was not simply that individuals trusted priests, but that they had faith in the goodness of those men because of whom they represented. Interestingly, however, most Catholics were able to make an epistemological distinction such that they saw the priests as wayward men who had broken a religious (and civic) trust, but a faith in God remained absolute. Tragically, many of those who had been abused saw no such distinction; their faith had been destroyed in the church, not simply their trust in the abuser (Dreher, 2002).

Religious faith is also not modulated. One either trusts in God or does not. Such is not the case with trust and faith in human beings. An individual may trust another person in one area of activity but not another—for any number of reasons. A student may trust that the math teacher's proof is correct but not trust the math teacher's views on abortion. A colleague may have faith that a friend believes what he is saying but not trust the intended outcome.

Trust from the perspective being used here, then, has nothing to do with an individual's theological view of the world. Rather, I am speaking of faith between two or more individuals. Such faith is highly conditioned and contingent. When an individual expresses faith to a higher being, the assumption is that the higher being is all-knowing and beneficent. Faith is total and consuming. Humans, in their mortality, are prone to error, deception, miscommunication, misinterpretation, and the panoply of human foibles.

Faith in humanity requires a different standpoint. Faith will not be provided in its entirety, and the response of the one in whom the individual has faith will condition further responses. Whereas a religious view of faith rejects a test-response notion, a human view of faith is dependent upon it. The supplicant who has faith in God does not have faith in the higher being and tests God to see if one's prayers are answered. God works in mysterious ways, goes the saying. The individual or individuals in an exchange relationship, however, act in an entirely different manner. They want less mystery and more clarity. One has incremental faith in increases and decreases based upon the other parties' actions.

As risk taking

Insofar as the interactions in which individuals are involved do not necessitate obligatory actions, the possibility always exists that the one who is trusted will betray the trust that has been extended. Thus, when one trusts that someone will do something, a degree of risk is involved. I have noted that individuals cannot command trust from another, and that trust is a highly subjective undertaking. To have trust in another person is more than having confidence in someone. Confidence assumes that an expected action will occur. If the action does not take place, then disappointment occurs. When trust is betrayed, disappointment occurs. However, the distinction between trust and confidence turns on perception and attribution. As Luhmann suggests:

> If you do not consider alternatives (every morning you leave the house without a weapon!), you are in a situation of confidence. If you choose one action in preference to others in spite of the possibility of being disappointed by the actions of others, you define the situation as one of trust. (1988, p. 102)

With trust, the individual must recognize that a risk is possible where failure might occur—whereas with confidence, no such risk takes place.

Obviously, if a risk is involved in a decision or action, then one may opt not to take such a risk. To take a risk involves making a choice. As I discuss in the following chapter, trust from this perspective is particularly important where risk taking needs to occur and where task requirements are not clearly delineated (Creed & Miles, 1996; Luhmann, 1988; Meyerson, Weick, & Kramer, 1996). An organization that does not need to innovate or succeed by adherence to the status quo may be an example where trust is less important, insofar as expectations and outputs are clear and defined. Legalistic mechanisms or contract-like arrangements also might substitute for trust in organizations where an individual's work requirements are clearly delineated and can be articulated into codified tasks.

Ultimately, any organization's goal will be first to define, and then to accomplish, the goals the participants have set for themselves. A key characteristic of effectiveness, of course, is to secure compliance from the organization's actors to accomplish the goals that have been set. Although compliance may occur in any number of ways—threat, coercion, incentives, or contractual arrangements, to name a few—organizations that operate in dynamic environments where risk is involved and participation is not mandatory are more likely to need to call upon trusting relationships. Voluntarily engaging in decision-making and accepting the results calls upon a form of engagement different from a hierarchical organization. In a hierarchical organization, such as the military, participants follow orders and undertake routinized tasks.

Accordingly, risk plays a critical role in trust. Whether trust is an end, or enables exchange behavior, individuals take a risk. Some theologians will argue that a person's religious faith involves no risk because of the certainty of the Almighty. However, no such certainty exists in the faith two human parties have with one another. Of course, the degree of trust varies by individual, context, and situation. Mayer, Davis, and Schoorman note, "Assessing the risk in a situation involves consideration of the context, such as weighing the likelihood of both positive and negative outcomes that might occur" (1995, p. 725).

Indeed, the context is not only important, but the possible outcomes of the situation also need to be taken into account. If I asked an advanced doctoral student to undertake a lab experiment for me because I had a meeting, I trust the student to do the experiment well. The student assumes that he or she will not make a mistake. Clearly, the degree of risk involved is less with an advanced student than with a first-year student. If the findings of the experiment pertained to a cure for cancer, one outcome is possible. If the experiment were simply a test to see if a particular procedure worked, then another outcome is possible. If I asked that same student to fly me to a conference in an airplane, then I am asking for a much different kind of trust. Risk involves a subjective assessment of the competence of the party to whom one is to trust as well as assessments pertaining to context and outcomes.

As I mentioned earlier, the grammar of trust I concentrate on here pertains to interactions between two or more parties. Similarly, risk pertains to two parties involved in some form of a relationship that hinges on trust. To be sure, individuals may exhibit risky behavior that involves no one else. Because of the lack of another party, no trust is involved.

As an ability

Trust is not something innate to individuals. Not everyone trusts equally. Situations of trust are not self-evident. There are conditions of trust. The call for an understanding of thick relationships takes into account the sociocultural contexts in which individuals reside. One's age, race, gender, class, and sexual orientation all come into play when determining trust and trustworthiness. A stranger in a grocery store may be able to play peek-a-boo with an infant because the infant has not learned to distrust the stranger. But in the early 21st century, most young boys and girls in the United States have been taught that if a stranger speaks to them, they should be suspicious. In the early 20th century or in a different country, the reaction might be considerably different.

Jimmy Carter has spoken of those whose hopes and dreams were repeatedly shattered as having "hopelessness based on sound judgment" (Hardin, 2002, p. 119). And yet, the foundation of a democratic society has to be bound in some way on the ability of the populace to trust one another and their civic organizations. In an ideal format, trust and trustworthiness result in cooperation (Hardin, p. 173). The question then is how to create the ability for trust to occur. Cooperation and reciprocity are important conditions for the creation of trust. Although my focus here is on trust in academic organizations, I do not want to overlook the obvious: individuals create and reside in organizations. Individuals learn about the organization in which they work. They bring individual orientations to the organization and interact with the organization's culture. The challenge, then, is to understand how these very different levels—that of the individual and that of the organization—interact with one another to produce trust.

The adult learns to trust as a means of cooperation. Hardin speaks of encapsulated trust: "I trust you," he writes, "because I think it is in your interest to take my interests in the relevant matter seriously" (2002, p. 1). Trust as encapsulated interest is an ability that is learned over time. The focus of encapsulated trust is not only on future expectations of what will occur but also on past interactions and interpretations. For the scholar who wishes to understand organizational trust, one area to investigate is individual motivations and abilities. To ignore or overlook such abilities is to assume all individuals are similar or that an organization's culture and structure are so strong as to deny agency to individuals.

The grammar of ability also underscores the differences between trust pertaining to individuals and organizational trust. Individuals have histories that make the person more or less likely to demonstrate trust. Although organizations have cultures with distinct histories, the relationship is not so direct or explicit as it is with an individual. To be sure, organizations may have cultures that permeate distrust (as I discuss in Part 2). However, an organization's inability to evoke trust differs from that of an individual who is incapable of trust. The point is not that the grammar is irrelevant for organizations, but that they differ, and in consequence, contextual understandings are imperative.

As a rational choice

A great deal of research on trust has utilized the language of rational choice as its grammar. Sheppard and Sherman, for example, succinctly summarize, "Trust is not an irrational act but a manageable act of faith in people, relationships, and social institutions" (1998, pp. 422–423). The unit of analysis is the individual or organization who exists within a social structure. Rational-choice theorists assert that trust is a subjective assumption by an individual or group about what is going to happen (Dunn, 1988; Hardin, 1993; Morse, 1999). The trusted have incentives to fulfill the trust, and the trusters have information and knowledge that enables them to trust. Thus, by way of a series of complex rational expectations, individuals come to trust others.

James Coleman, a leading proponent of rational choice whom I discussed in the previous chapter regarding social capital, has pointed out the commonsensical idea that "social interdependence and systemic functioning arise from the fact that actors have interests in events that are fully or partially under the control of others" (1990, p. 300). He continues from this observation to argue that the actors are involved in an exchange relationship that helps structure trust because it is in the actors' mutual interests. While his assessment of the nature of social relations goes well beyond the idea that society consists of a set of individuals who act independently from one another, Coleman and other rational-choice theorists (i.e., Putnam, 1995a) assume that conditions can be replicated for trusting relationships to occur irrespective of context and individual.

Trust is a two-party exchange where an individual or organization commits to an exchange before knowing whether the other will reciprocate. The focus pertains to the structure of relationships where the motives for trust are instrumental. The researcher investigates the incentives involved in getting the trusted to do what is obligated and the knowledge needed by the truster to trust. Social obligations, expectations, norms, and sanctions are primary arrangements to utilize in order to build trust. When trust is absent, or does not develop, it is primarily because of the pathologies of the individuals involved in the interactions. When trust exists, it is because the individuals have utilized the structures in a manner that fosters trusting relationships.

A certain logical circularity exists with this approach that presumably justifies, rather than explains, the existing social order. I noted earlier the same conundrum when I discussed the grammar of trust as an end. The question lies less with examples where trust exists but instead where it does not exist. The wealthy have trusting relationships that enable them to send their children to good schools. The children in turn have trusting relationships that enable them to study hard and be admitted to good colleges, where they will develop more trusting relationships, get good jobs, and so on. The poor do not have such relationships. In this light, rational choice is more an explanation of the status quo rather than an examination of organizational and societal power, structures, and functions. Nevertheless, the rational-choice framework has led to useful analyses. Rational-choice theorists react against an overly individualistic or psychological view of life.

Although I disagree with the idea that for trust to exist, individuals need to subjugate their views within existing social structures, a focus on structure is useful in moving one's thinking away from a strictly psychological notion of trust. The language of rational choice usefully points out that structures exist in which individuals are embedded. How those structures function is critical to understanding trust and multiple other phenomena. Rational grammar, curiously, also enables individuals to think about how change occurs. That is, proponents of rational choice may be criticized because of their static view of the world—structures exist preformed and determined. However, one needs to consider, if such an interpretation is correct, whether individuals are able to shape the structures in which they reside or if they are simply passive observers who react to societal forces.

The concern with the language of rational choice when one thinks of schools, colleges, and universities pertains as much to ideological notions of the world as to individual ability to affect change in one's life and work within an organization. Rational-choice theorists hold an implicit assumption that a structure exists. But an explicit analysis that an overriding ideological view of the world is framed within that structure is absent. How one understands different phenomena is by way of an investigation of the social networks of individuals within these structures. The path to change for those who are unsuccessful deals with altering their view of the world and trying to fit within the overarching structure. This view of school failure, for example, will focus more on how to fix the student, by way of the structure—but the structure itself is not flawed. This view suggests the flaw resides with those who populate the school. Thus, one investigates the networks in which a family is embedded and how those networks might be changed in order to improve the lives of the children. Structures from this perspective are neutral. They are not powerful forces that reinforce ideological hegemony. Trust comes about when individuals hold similar views of the world that are in sync with the structures in which they reside.

As a cultural construction

An alternative language, and the one I favor here, is to conceive of the symbolic nature of social situations and structures that individuals construct and reconstruct such that an organization attains a culture. A cultural grammar of trust forces an analysis not only of structures but also the social contexts and histories in which these structures are embedded. Trust is contextualized and understood not only from an individualistic standpoint but also from a vantage point that seeks to interpret how the actors define the individual and how that individual (re)acts within structures such as organizations (Seligman, 1997). From this perspective, the grammar one seeks is to understand the social bonds and shared identities that enable trust to occur. Rather than a predetermined idea that is understood and widely shared by many, trust is a social construction interpreted by the parties involved in the undertaking. The focus is on the internal dynamics within a social organization as well as the forces at work that help shape the social organization. Feelings of shared identity and interpersonal connection need not be shaped to an impersonal and impervious structure but instead have broad leeway for interpretation and reinterpretation as individuals enter and exit social structures and as individuals themselves relate differently over time to their situations.

Whereas the language of rational choice seeks to understand how individuals might align themselves to a structure, a cultural view enables the researcher to see the social organization as much more fluid. Conversely, organizations such as colleges or universities do not bend one way or another but have ideological parameters framed in part by the larger social structure. Postsecondary organizations, for example, are not simply an avenue for upward mobility for whomever so desires it but a filter that promotes some and excludes others. Testing is not only an examination that enables reviewers to determine who knows what about a particular subject; testing also acts to maintain the social order for those who have access to what Pierre Bourdieu defines as cultural capital. The challenge for the researcher is not to develop a grammar that determines how to align individuals with predetermined social structures but instead to develop a grammar that accepts the fluidity inherent in cultures and understands how relationships might be developed that build commonalities across differences and enable agency for individuals.

Unlike rational choice, trust as a cultural construction has no predetermined conceptions of what is rational or irrational, logical or illogical. Meaning occurs within the contexts and situations themselves. Thus, trust becomes a highly contingent concept rather than one that exists through an inherent logic. To work from a cultural construction of trust does not reject the previous grammar I outlined but frames it in a particular manner. From this perspective, trust is a repeated interaction and a dynamic process where it may be an end or an exchange. However, there is no deep structure, for example, to an exchange relationship and how those exchanges take place will vary. Note that I do not say that there are endless variations of exchange relationships, for to say so suggests that two parties are able to develop infinite structures of exchange. The focus of a cultural construction of trust moves away from trying to develop a taxonomy of processes or exchange relationships so that they can be replicated. Instead, the researcher tries to make sense of the specific situation where trust has been called into play.

Faith and risk occur. But obviously such terms have little meaning without understanding the cultural and symbolic processes in which they are embedded. At the most obvious cultural level, it is understood that different people have different definitions of faith and risk. As I discuss in the following chapters, organizations in general and academic organizations in particular will have quite different understandings of what is to be believed and trusted and what is a risk. Simply because an individual believes something is a risk does not make it so; as opposed to Humpty Dumpty, words do not mean anything a speaker wants them to mean. To understand the grammar of risk and faith, the researcher needs to be situated within the culture in which the terms are being used.

Conclusion

Although a cultural construction works in contradistinction from the language of rational choice, I acknowledge that both languages seek grammar that does not use the individual as the unit of analysis. Yes, individuals exist in structures and cultures. One needs to come to terms with an individual's interpretations of reality, but one works from a quite different vantage point when the initial focus is away from a psychological understanding of the individual and toward a cultural understanding of the contexts and social organizations in which individuals live their lives. Trust as an ability, then, is less a psychological examination of an individual and instead a search for how individuals within cultures acquire and change abilities that generate trust.

Trust is a dynamic process in which two or more parties are involved in a series of interactions that may require a degree of risk or faith on the part of one or both parties. These processes help individuals make sense of their worlds and ultimately enable individuals and groups to work toward a common endeavor. It is within their self-interest to do so. Accordingly, I turn now to a more in-depth discussion of the form of trust that concerns me: trust within organizations. I utilize the grammar of trust developed here and work within the language of culture to consider trust across disparate parties in formal organizations.

CHAPTER THREE

The Culture of Trust in Organizations

An organization is a culturally constructed entity. Of consequence, trust is an idea that gains meaning and currency within the culture, especially during times of change. The effects of globalization, for example, are accompanied by uncertainty and complex change. Trust assumes a strategic importance (Lewicki, McAllister, & Bies, 1998, p. 438). As discussed in Chapter 2, to work from a cultural vantage point situates the analysis of organizational trust in a fundamentally different manner from those who think of organizations as preformed entities and trust as a rational choice of actors.

In what follows, I first elaborate on my definition of culture in organizations and consider the conditions of trust within a cultural framework. I then turn to a discussion of the levels, dimensions, and characteristics of trust from a cultural framework. Once I have delineated the parameters of trust in an organization's culture, I conclude how such a framework provides a useful understanding of trust within academic organizations.

An organization's culture

Organizational culture refers to the manner in which meaning is generated, conveyed, and interpreted within an organization (Tierney, 1988). Rather than a search for universal underlying structures or meanings that pervade all organizations, the focus is on the study of individual organizational cultures as unique and autonomous systems of meaning. Although the very notion of "organization" assumes an entity that has boundaries, students of organizational culture pay particular attention to the interactions individuals in the organization have with other individuals and how those boundaries are drawn and redefined. Concerns such as efficiency and effectiveness certainly drive much research about organizational culture; however, the theoretical issues primarily pertain to how individuals make sense of the organization to themselves and to one another.

The basic assumption is that organizational reality is never fully comprehensible because it is always in flux due to the entry and exit of the organization's actors. As I have noted elsewhere, "The culture of an organization constitutes human existence to such an extent that prediction and the ability to reduce organizational meaning to predetermined elements are impossible. Intentionality depends upon the culture's prior histories within which individuals constitute meaning for themselves" (Tierney, 1989, p. 28). Organizational reality, then, is defined not as objective and external to the participants but instead as a process of social interchange that cannot be readily mapped, graphed, or controlled.

Organizational culture ought to be equated neither as a synonym for the history of the institution nor as a proxy for symbols and rituals. Yes, the culture of the organization is in part determined by its history. A college with a 200-year history will have a culture different from a new campus. Similarly, a president's speech at the start of the year, or any number of overt rituals that occur in academe such as Commencement, in part pertains to the culture of the organization. But history and symbolic events are not the sum of the culture. Indeed, culture can not be "summed" up. Culture is not simply a decontextualized taxonomy of functional artifacts such as ceremonies and institutionalized histories. An organization's culture is a complex of traditions, events, and formations that are defined and reinterpreted by the actors. An organization's culture is not a straitjacket that determines human interaction, but the culture also does not allow or promote any actions whatsoever to occur.

At the same time, even though there will not be perfect information and understanding of the organization, individuals need to make sense of their work-world in order to function. If the organization made no sense and was simply chaotic, then it would cease to be an organization. An organization's culture, then, has three primary utilities. First, it provides the organizational members with a sense of meaning and identity. Second, culture shapes behavior; individuals act in one way and not another because of the organization's culture. And third, strong cultures presumably increase organizational stability and effectiveness.

The question thus turns on how an organization's members make meaning. What are those means that enable individuals to make sense of organizational events? My purpose here is not to provide a fulsome exegesis on organizational culture, which I have done elsewhere (Tierney, 1988); however, it is useful to a discussion about trust within organizational culture if I briefly summarize those three dimensions of culture that enable individuals to make meaning: structure, environment, and values.

Figure 3.1: Utilities of organizational culture

Shapes behavior ◀▶ Increasing organizational stability and effectiveness

Provides members with a sense of meaning and identity

Structure

Structure pertains to what organizational theorists commonly mean when they write of organizational charts and lines of authority, but the manner in which structure is interpreted has a dramatic difference. The purpose of studying structure has less to do with generic ideas about efficient lines of decision making and more to do with what the structure of the organization means to those who are external to it and how those within the organization interpret it. I have seen numerous institutions, for example, that have virtually the same organizational structure with regard to promotion and tenure decisions. On one campus, however, the faculty believes the structure is excellent. On another campus, they think it is corrupt and administratively driven. Conversely, some campuses have what may seem to be a cumbersome structure for making decisions about tenure, but the individuals involved in the structure are content. At another campus with an entirely different structure, the individuals are equally content with the tenure decision-making process.

Structure involves the formal and informal aspects of decision making and takes into account not only end results but the perceptions of the individuals involved in the processes and structures. An investigation of structure, then, relies less on a unitary event and more on how structures are formed, changed, and perceived over time. How communication, information, and rules function within the structure also become key aspects to understand. Again, the point is not that perfect information will be conveyed in effective structures and inadequate information in an ineffective one, but rather, what kinds of information are communicated to whom? Similarly, rules are molded by the structure, but they reflect back on cultural norms.

Environment

As with structure, to study the environment in which an organization exists is hardly unique. Rational-choice theorists have long discussed the importance of studying the environment and how to deal with it when developing strategy and making decisions. However, from a cultural perspective, it is more appropriate to speak of the *enacted* environment. An enacted environment is defined by the understanding members develop about the nature of the organization's context (Chaffee & Tierney, 1988; Smircich & Stubbart, 1985). Thus, the enacted environment pertains to those facts that individuals choose as defining the organization's context and, by inference, those facts that they do not choose through selective interpretation and attention. Many individuals in a university, for example, may well think of their environment as the local neighborhood. They focus on better serving that constituency, whereas another organization in a similar setting might have an entirely different interpretation of their constituency.

An investigation of the environment frequently provides as much insight about how the organization's members perceive of the organization as about how the constituents think about the environment. That is, if the members of an organization think of the environment as a "market," one way of thinking about the organization is created; if the environment is a set of political groups whose needs must be ameliorated or met, then another interpretation exists. Do the organization's participants think of the environment as encroaching on what the organization wants to be, or do they think of the environment as partners in defining a mutual future? The manner in which the organization's participants answer such questions offers an understanding about how the actors perceive the institution. Thus, the framework operates from the perspective that the organization is less a matter of objective fact and more a process of ongoing definition and interpretation.

One caveat here is to note that as with all cultural frames, one cannot personify "the organization" as if 100% of the members interpret the environment in exactly the same manner. Actors within the university have many different standpoints on the environment, which may increase dissonance, contest, and the like. By working out these differences, a vantage point develops about how people perceive the environment. These interpretations in large part get defined by way of the values the organization holds and the values the members bring to the organization.

Values

What are the beliefs, norms and priorities of the organization? How do people come to learn and change values? The answers to such questions offer a useful guide to an organization's culture. Values become apparent in the ways in which individuals work with one another and through the overarching goals of the organization. Organizations where individuals are never asked their opinion about the organizational direction, for example, presumably suggest that one value is that those at the top of the hierarchy are the decision makers and those below take orders. An organization that values particular constituents in the enacted environment will presumably be more solicitous than an organization that sees those constituents as irrelevant.

When one investigates organizational values, as with structure and environment, the intent is to understand how the members make sense of their world. In doing so, the researcher's aim is value-neutral. The idea is not to prejudge that one organization has good values and another bad. However, one ought to understand how congruent these three dimensions are with one another. Optimally, an organization's culture is in dynamic equilibrium where the dimensions are in sync even as they are continually reinterpreted and new members enter the organization. An organization, for example, which has a written mission statement that espouses beliefs about the importance of every individual working on a team but has a structure that is top-down is not in congruence. An environment that the members look upon with dread or disdain is hardly in sync with an espoused value of respecting the needs of constituencies. The challenge, then, is not only to understand these dimensions in isolation but in relation to one another.

Trust, of course, may be seen as an organizational value. Some organizations will work explicitly toward developing trust as an integral value and other organizations will neither see it as important nor a value. However, based on the grammar I developed in the previous chapter, trust may also be found in the enacted environment and the organization's structure as well. As I discuss in Part 3, external constituents come to find the organization trustworthy in any number of ways which in part determine how they arrive at a definition of the public good. A structure may be created in an organization that is built on suspicion and another organization may have a structure that the actors interpret as open and trustworthy. Accordingly, I turn to a consideration of how trust is enacted within an organization's culture.

The enactment of cultural trust

In order to elaborate on how trust operates within a cultural framework, I turn now to three key conditions that help frame how trust becomes understood. The first component pertains to how an organization's members come to hold *shared experiences*. How a culture's participants make meaning plays a key role in whether trust is pervasive, fleeting, or absent. Secondly, how one *learns* about shared experiences becomes critical to understand. The socializing experiences of new members, as well as the reiterated interactions and events that individuals have with one another, are the processes that lead to epiphenomenal interpretations of organizational life that enable trust to occur. And third, a cultural view suggests that concepts such as trust are *conditional;* they are never taken for granted or assumed, but when one enters an organization, certain conditions exist that need to be taken into account in order for trust to occur. Larger sociocultural events in which the organization is embedded as well as the historical legacy of the organization and its actors help frame how trust is built, maintained, or destroyed.

Trust as shared experience: Trust does not come about without a framework and language for common understanding. "When I trust you in the sense that your interests encapsulate mine in at least the matter with respect to which I trust you," noted Hardin, "we can, naturally, be said to share interests to some extent" (2002, p. 144). One way to share interests is by common interpretation. Two parties view events similarly when they have mutual objectives in attaining the same goal and see the path to that goal in a similar manner. Trust occurs when both parties share interests such that what is good for one party is also good for the other, or what Jay Dee defines as "shared commitments" (2004, p. 14). Such a view is context-specific. One party trusts the other on a specific issue, but both parties may not have developed a generalized trust.

Characteristics of trust as shared experience

1   Offers a common interpretation of events
2   Fosters shared interests in the organization
3   Allows for the communication of cultural facts
4   Emerges from reciprocity and mutuality that are based in structures and beliefs
5   Cannot be summarized as rational

Common interpretations, however, can never be assumed. Individuals arrive in an organization with their own unique histories and ways of viewing events. Simply because a college president, for example, has concluded that the college is in fiscal jeopardy does not mean that the faculty will come to the same conclusion. A rational-choice perspective assumes that, if the college president presented the same facts that he or she had utilized in arriving at the conclusion, and if the faculty had the same information and interests, then they will view the fiscal outlook of the college in a similar manner. Rational-choice theorists assume that when two people are faced with a choice and share the same information and the same interests and values, they must rationally make the same decision.

Proponents of a cultural framework disagree. As I noted, a cultural view acknowledges that perfect information is impossible and that a multitude of viewpoints exist about a particular issue. The challenge for those in the organization turns less on collecting and disseminating perfect data so that everyone will thus view the information in a similar manner and instead focuses on how to build an organizational culture that incorporates multiple viewpoints and calls upon cultural symbols, rituals, and communicative processes to highlight organizational goals and overriding ideologies. From this perspective, trust develops through the ability of individuals to communicate cultural meanings rather than rational facts.

A second way for trust to come about is, on the surface, a beneficent view where one party adopts another's interests with an overt sense of obligation. Rather than context-specific, this form of trust transcends an event but occurs through assumptions about the nature of the relationship. Even though one party may enter into such an agreement without a reciprocal commitment on the specific issue, the larger assumption is that parties are bound together through a sense of mutuality over time. Kramer, Brewer, and Hanna explain, "The logic of reciprocity-based trust is simple; 'I will engage in trust behavior because I believe you are likely to do the same'" (1996, p. 373). The assumption of reciprocity and trust is rooted in a sociological and anthropological tradition. As I noted earlier, Marcel Mauss (1924/1967) wrote in his classic essay about gift giving that the giver always gives a gift with a sense that eventually some form of reciprocity and social exchange will occur. Obviously, when a person gives a gift to an individual on her birthday, the giver does not expect a present in return. However, a belief system is built up such that individuals understand obligations to others. Such a point is useful because it highlights the social interactions involved in trust. Trust is neither simply a cognitive response of one individual nor a structural response of two individuals who are acting in a rational manner.

On an organizational level, this form of trust also occurs through shared meaning of the culture. If the president concludes that a fiscal crisis is on the horizon, individuals will trust the leader not through rational persuasion but through a culture of reciprocal obligations. When individuals and groups are involved in reciprocity-based trust, multiple factors come in to play. Such a relationship occurs over time within the context of specific situations. Simply because an individual claims a crisis exists does not mean everyone will agree. The individual claiming a crisis has to develop a relationship over time so that the organization's participants are willing to believe him or her. Conceivably, a new leader may have more trust if he or she was elected rather than appointed; another leader may enter an institution with trust "credits" earned elsewhere. The individual also needs to have some claim to competence. The president may be believed if the crisis pertains to the college's finances. However, if the president states a crisis is going to happen because a natural catastrophe is about to occur that will destroy the institution's buildings, presumably the organization's participants will be less likely to trust in the prediction.

Trust is multifaceted and complex, and hence, orchestrating the shared experience is a difficult undertaking. People enter organizations with their own histories, for example, and have to come to terms with the history of the organization. Trust also is absent in some organizations, as I will discuss in Chapter 6. Some individuals have worked in organizations where trust has been absent and are affected by previous experiments. Sometimes trust also is not in people's interests. Collective bargaining, for example, may set one group in opposition to another. Although conflict may result around a specific issue, the long-term interest of one or another group may not be to create trust, but distrust. From this perspective individuals who assume that the way to create trust is to generate faith in a person are mistaken. What I suggest is that trust must be based in structures and beliefs so that the shared experiences of the group generate trust in the organization. Individuals may be conduits for creating that trust. But if trust centers on an individual, then the organization is thrown into confusion—if not chaos—when the individual departs.

The adult learns to trust as a means of cooperation. Russell Hardin (2002) speaks of *encapsulated trust*. Individuals trust one another because it is to their benefit to take others' interests in the matter seriously. Such a view incorporates parts of a rational view but is ultimately inherently subjective. That is, encapsulated trust assumes individuals make rational choices about trust. In part, those choices are framed by the psychological backgrounds of the parties. However, the focus of encapsulated trust is not only on future expectations of what will occur but also on past interactions and interpretations. In an organization, encapsulated trust takes place with an individual entering into a trusting relationship in part because of his or her particular views of the organizational world. The culture of the organization also helps frame that view. The mores of the organization, the symbolic and communicative processes, and a host of cultural artifacts affect how cooperation is likely to occur.

Although stories abound about office rivalries, demagogic managers, and petty intrigue, a significant body of research highlights the importance of cooperation in organizations. This line of research views individuals as decision makers and active agents who are likely to perform better in an environment that exists through reciprocal obligations rather than individualized desires and wants. The research moves, then, from atomistic analyses that center on an individual's rational choices within predetermined structures toward how social connections within an organization are developed, maintained, and enhanced. Other than in highly contractual arrangements where all parties are clear about how each is to respond to different situations, what kind of relationships might be built that engender trust?

Researchers have found that high-performing organizations are ones where hierarchical control and legalistic mechanisms are not the sine qua non of daily existence. Organizations with cultures of lateral alliances and cooperative behaviors have been found to be effective and high performing. Hierarchical commands or political machinations may produce one or another result, but high-performance organizations are ones that reproduce a system for effectiveness over time rather than periodically. Such an observation points out a key precept for the conditions of trust; trust occurs over time with a set number of people.

Academic organizations exemplify the kind of cultural entities where trust has the potential to flourish. A great many people stay in the organization for a significant length of time. Individuals generally interact with one another because of their desire rather than a command. Long-term working relationships are most successful when those relationships embody encapsulated trust. The social context of the college or university has been one that has relied more on a sense of collegiality than a legalistic contract. In this light, trust is an orientation toward the organization and toward one another that cannot be precisely or neatly summarized as "rational." One has faith that because he or she works in the organization and the participants in the organization have a particular history with one another, the organization will respond in ways that reinforce trust.

One of the curious aspects of colleges and universities is that they are organizations with highly autonomous workers—the faculty—who are capable of absenting themselves from a great deal of campus work. And yet, as I discuss in the subsequent chapter, these autonomous workers assume a great deal of voluntary work in their organizational and professional lives that bind individuals together. In effect, academic organizations utilize a human-resource model that assumes workers will be creative and inner-directed, and the workers in turn assume that they have obligations to one another and the organization. The challenge for the leaders is to create and maintain an organizational culture where the conditions for trust flourish.

Trust as learned experience

One can neither command nor coerce an individual to trust. Although an individual may do what a superior wants because the person has power over the individual, or the superior has coerced the individual, trust is not part of the interaction (Luhmann, 1979). A professor may demand certain behaviors from students because of the role that each inhabits. Similarly, if individuals constantly receive messages in an organization that command them to act in one way or another, they may do what they are told, but trust has nothing to do with the interactions. For there to be a trusting relationship, it is necessary to believe that the relationship one has with the other individual is useful, and that the truster has confidence in the other. An element of risk is always involved because one can never be certain that what the trusted is expected to do will be done. But the interactions involved are part of the ongoing social contexts of the organizational actors. Trust is learned.

Trust as learned experience

1 Influenced by an individual's background
2 Affected by cultural contexts
3 Guided by socializing mechanisms that induct individuals into the culture

The infant example I employed in the previous chapter is useful in a discussion about organizational trust in two respects. First, one need not be a psychoanalyst to recognize that some individuals will bring to a situation the ability or inability to trust that has less to do with the particular situation or organization than with the individual's background and history. The manner and contexts in which an individual grew up surely provided environments for learning about trust. A secure familial structure taught one lesson and an insecure structure taught another. If trust exists by way of learned experiences, then the kind of interactions that an individual had as a child taught that child some lessons. Although one may change his or her perspective over time as new experiences occur, a high capacity for trust is based in part on one's history.

Trust is enwrapped in cultural contexts. The manner in which parents treat their children, or how local villages or towns view children, has tremendous variation. Significant differences exist with regard to how different groups view their children's school. The same holds true for class. Mainstream middle- and upper-class families frequently think of school as a place where their child will learn the requisite information needed to succeed so that they can go to college. Interactions with the school are usually frequent and anxiety-free. Low-income minority families, however, frequently see the school as an alien environment where their children learn lessons that teach them to reject their culture, and hence, their families. When minority family members are called to school, it is often because their child is in trouble. Language differences often keep parents away; their only interaction with the school, then, is when their son or daughter is accused of poor behavior. Thus, when a teacher offers a lesson that involves some form of risk, different individuals will interpret those lessons in unique ways—not because one is rational and the other is not, but because one's cultural background has framed the issues in different ways that force diverse interpretations.

At the organizational level, the assumption that trust is learned behavior suggests that one must necessarily investigate the socializing mechanisms and processes that induct the individual into the culture. Academic life is imbued with socializing experiences. Initiates learn a great deal about academe as soon as, if not before, they become recruits—in graduate school. Institutional pecking orders, the importance of research, how one works with one's colleagues, what is and is not important, are all lessons that individuals learn en route to the Ph.D. Although these lessons are frequently implicit rather than explicit, one ought not to overlook their symbolic importance. Similarly, when one arrives on campus as a new assistant professor, the array of experiences that occurs makes an inevitable imprint about the organizational culture. How an individual achieves tenure, what one has to do to achieve it, and the inevitable aspects surrounding departmental politics all teach lessons to the initiate.

Because individuals will interpret events differently, I do not suggest that socialization is a lock-step process that moves individuals through academic life as if they are on a production line in a factory. Indeed, one's past experiences as well as organizational differences with regard to how individuals are treated will lead to differential interpretations. A new assistant professor whose parents were faculty will arrive at the institution with a different set of assumptions than someone who is the first in the family to attend college. In an engineering department, the same kind of tenure process may be assumed for everyone, but the process may be experienced differently based on one's gender. A woman who is the only female in the department may have very different interpretations about what one needs to do to achieve tenure from a male who does not feel at all out of place.

Thus, the combination of an individual's experiences and the organization's socializing processes has a significant impact on what one learns about trust. The culture of the organization provides a variety of symbolic processes that teach individuals. An individual receives one message when a college president says that teaching is important at the start of the school year, for example, and another message when a colleague is denied tenure because of a lack of research. A university where the message from the provost is that individuals should take intellectual risks and the faculty are frequently rewarded when they take risks sends another kind of message. In the former example, individuals learn not to trust what the president says. In the latter, they learn to trust what emanates from the provost. Learning is most often never a singular event, but ongoing and multidimensional.

Trust as conditional experience

Organizational trust, as distinct from individualized and abstract trust, is not only shared by constituents. It is also conditional. Individualized trust is based on a one-to-one correspondence between truster and trustee. Trust in the organization by external constituencies is built over time but is never permanent and always transitory. Organizational trust is not only constituted by the participants' shared beliefs of the culture—it is also conditioned on assumptions about social and moral obligations within the organization. One arrives at an organization with a set of role expectations. Just as individuals may change these expectations in one way or another, the conditions for trust also exist prior to an individual's entry into the organization.

Trust as conditional experience

1   Influenced by assumptions about social and moral obligations to the organization
2   Influenced by the temporal context
3   Affected by the competence of the trusted

If trust is a social construction within an organization, then the researcher necessarily documents the variety of conditions that individuals inherit, change, and create to enable trust to occur. From this perspective, trust is not a preordained quality, a psychological facet of the human mind, a unitary act, or a pervasive and unchanging condition. Trust occurs over time. The creation of a trusting relationship is highly contingent on the social and cultural contexts in which individuals and the organization are embedded.

Such an argument rejects the notion that, if adequate information is supplied to an individual, he or she will be able to find someone else, or the organization, trustworthy. An adequate explanation of trust hinges not exclusively on facts and information but on the conditions within an organization's culture that lead to trust being accepted or thwarted. Trust can be episodic, long-standing, or nonexistent depending upon the conditions at work over time within the organization's culture. An organization, for example, that has a culture of trust may have that trust destroyed in a relatively short time by a new president who betrays the culture. Conversely, imagine a new president who arrives at a university and wants individuals to be trusting—but trust has previously been absent. The president will need to develop a climate for trustworthiness prior to trust occurring. How might such a climate be developed?

Three ideas already have been inferred. First, trust occurs over time. Second, trust depends on the competence of the trusted. Trust cannot occur if the trusted has no claim to do what he or she says will be done. Third, trust can neither be coerced nor commanded. Trust depends upon overlapping and ongoing relationships that exist within social and cultural contexts. Such relationships generate a great deal of knowledge that individuals call upon to determine whether one or another individual is trustworthy. One's race, gender, class, sexual orientation, and the like are personal characteristics that not only impact how the individual views trust but also how individuals come to think about trustworthiness.

Bernard Williams (1988) defines trust as a function of thick relationships. Through "thick relationships," individuals have a rich history with one another that helps them arrive at a judgment on whether to trust the other person. Although trust may occur on political or societal levels with "thin" relationships, I agree with Williams that individual and organizational trust occurs through multiple and overlapping conditions. Face-to-face interactions, communicative frameworks, and organizational processes, structures, and actions help individuals come to terms with whether the conditions for trust exist.

Of course, different kinds of actions are dependent upon the nature of the relationship and interaction. How one comes to trust one's partner in a loving relationship, for example, is surely different from how trust exists within an academic department. Further, as I discuss below, it may be possible to have a campus with a high level of trust within groups, but a low level of trust between groups. The individuals in an academic department may trust one another, for example, but the same individuals and department may not trust their dean. The challenge for someone who wants to develop trusting relationships across the organization is to make sense of the overarching culture and the specific climate that exist for thick relationships to be built. "If we wish to understand trust for real people, what we will have to understand are the capacities for commitment and trust, which must largely be learned," notes Hardin (1993, p. 508). These conditions are not only learned—they are also shared, highly contingent, and constructed.

Organizational levels, phases, and characteristics of trust

Levels of trust

Trust is not a pervasive notion that exists throughout an organization, as if the organization is the only unit of analysis. Three primary levels of trust need to be considered. By "level," I mean the area in which trust occurs such that it becomes a multidimensional social reality for the participants (Lane, 1998). Organizational trust focuses on how individuals in groups come to trust other individuals and groups. Accordingly, in an investigation of organizational trust, the study has to move beyond merely the analysis of interpersonal interactions between two individuals. The manner in which two participants trust one another in an organization has great potential impact for trust occurring at other levels. A simple analysis of two individuals is insufficient. At the same time, to look at trust as if it occurs only at the organizational level overlooks how the participants themselves experience reality and come to trust one another and the organization.

Organizational levels of trust

1　The organization and its external environment/constituencies
2　Between constituents within/to the organization
3　Between and among formal/informal organizational units

One level pertains to the organization and its external environment and constituencies. A second level is that between and among individuals within the organization who function within a specific unit. A third level is between and among formal and informal organizational units. Any analysis of organizational trust must take into account these different levels rather than simply assume that 'trust' is ever present. It might be difficult to build trust on an organizational level if it is absent at the micro-level, but an analysis that only looks at trust at the meta-level overlooks the complex dynamics of trust.

Trust at the formalized unit level is frequently more personal and less abstract. At a college or university, for example, individuals come to equate a department or school as synonymous with particular individuals rather than as an abstraction. Interpersonal trust is the extent of trust individuals share with one another as members of a distinct social group. It describes the extent to which individuals within a unit have a collectively held belief about trust and execute that belief in their orientation, attitude, and workings with one another.

Informal units occur within organizations. They also are areas for the creation of trust. An organization, for example, may have a weekend softball team or a book club that takes place during the lunch hour. As with the formal level, the occurrence of trust in such venues is frequently implicit. Trust is most often not a test where individuals undertake an exercise to see if they can trust an opposing party. Instead, one learns about trust through the multitude of interactions that take place frequently during quite microscopic activities. As I noted above, these conditional, shared, and learned experiences take place at different levels and frequently impact the way individuals come to trust others.

Trust at the organizational level deals with how individuals come to trust, or distrust, the organization in which they work. Obviously, individuals may trust one another at the unit level but exhibit very little trust at the organizational level. Especially in large organizations, individuals may have little data to draw on to define the organization. I suggested, for example, that organizations are cultures that are saturated with meanings, symbols, and interpretations. The units in which individuals spend their working lives provide meaning and context on a daily basis. Indeed, especially for new entrants to the organization, the unit may be the boundary with which they define the organization. Individuals and groups beyond the close-in group are abstractions without meaning or import.

An organization that hopes to develop a sense of camaraderie with the intent of developing high performance has to have individuals who are able to see beyond their individual unit. At a minimum, an organizational culture where individuals trust one another within a unit—but where distrust exists at the organizational level—is antithetical to high performance. Obviously, the opposite is equally true. Although individuals may trust the organization because of pervasive policies that are beneficial, or the organization communicates in a way that individuals interpret as caring and useful, they also may work within a unit where the supervisor is not trusted or individuals have not found one another trustworthy.

Trust also needs to exist across organizational levels and with multiple publics. That is, whereas levels clearly occur within an organization, interorganizational trust is a meta-level that seeks to come to terms with how organizations develop, maintain, and expand trust with one another (Zaheer, McEvily, & Perrone, 1998). As with the previous two levels, one may have quite different interpretations of trust. There may be a great deal of trust within the organization, but the organization does not trust individuals in other groups. Synonymous units in different groups may trust one another but exhibit very little trust in their respective organizations. A union, for example, may have members in two different companies; the members trust one another, but neither trusts the parent organization. Although individuals may trust a university to educate their children, the state legislature may have no faith in the postsecondary institution because they use entirely different criteria to judge trustworthiness.

Two relatively simple points are significant. First, when one seeks to understand how trust functions within an organization, an initial question that needs to be asked pertains to the level of analysis. Trust is an elusive concept that is multifaceted and existent on various levels. To have trust on one level ought not to suggest trust on another level. Optimally, trust will be found throughout the organization such that individuals within a unit find one another trustworthy. The individuals within the organization trust the institution, and the organization builds lasting and trusting relationships with its external environments.

Second, an understanding of whether trust exists at a particular level is inevitably a cultural undertaking. The external environment, for example, is a cultural construct. An organization's participants may not even take into consideration one or another organization because they are seen as unimportant and irrelevant, whereas a similar organization may interpret its environment quite differently. Similarly, the reasons that individuals come to trust one another within a unit will vary dramat-ically across units depending on the culture and the unit's members. Communication varies based on the sociocultural contexts of the unit. How it comes to interact with the larger organization is as much a cultural construct as anything else insofar as there are no preordained rules and structures about how organizations must inter-act with subordinate units. The point here, of course, is not that "anything goes," as if all individuals are free to act in any manner they so desire. Instead, the culture of the organization needs to be investigated across levels if we are to come to terms with how trust operates in the organization.

Phases of trust

Just as a meta-level examination of trust in an organization would be insufficient, the assumption that trust is one-dimensional is also mistaken. Trust is not a static phenomenon but a dynamic one (Rousseau, Sitkin, Burt, & Camerer, 1998). When an individual enters an organization, the conditions for trust presumably are not set in metaphorical stone. They change over time depending on a number of interac-tions at different levels. Insofar as trust is dynamic, to define trust at a particular point in time is fruitless if the intent is to portray trust as a predefined quality of the organization. Some will liken defining trust to nailing gelatin to the wall—an impossible task not only because the substance lacks a solid physical property but because the walls (the organization's actors) change as well.

However, one way to conceptualize trust is to think of it as a variable dimen-sion. Trust is part of the social capital of organizations. Trust might be seen as being created, maintained, or dissolved. The creation of trust occurs with individuals at specific levels who are actively or passively building trusting relationships and deciding if their counterparts are trustworthy. Such a point is particularly germane for an organization's leaders. If one were to equate trust with capital, an individual may arrive to a position where the position is replete with capital. An individual also may come to a position with a particular reputation that also provides capital. One ought not to assume, however, that within an organization, trust simply exists. A new person may have to work actively toward creating trust. An individual may also unknowingly engage in trust-building activities.

Similarly, and perhaps with greater rapidity, trust may also be in decline. Indeed, as I will discuss in Part 2, individuals continually report that the creation of trust takes a great deal of time, but its diminution may occur in a matter of months. The betrayal of trusting relationships and the creation of distrust may per-vade an organization to such an extent that the culture becomes dysfunctional. Thus, trust's dimension is not linear as if it were a symbolic bucket that is empty and grad-ually fills. Rather, trust occurs in different dimensions at different levels.

Perhaps what is most typical, however, is the functioning of trust under relatively stable conditions. The arrival of new entrants always brings new conditions and the potential for instability as individuals interpret the culture differently from others. Even in a dynamic environment, the potential for stability always exists. In suggesting that trust occurs in phases, I portray trust less as something that exists within static structures and more as a dynamic property that is defined, worked out, and redefined as individuals come together in the organization. Far too often, however, researchers portray trust in a snapshot when it is fleeting and evolving.

Characteristics of trust

What are the characteristics of trust? What are those aspects that might be investigated? Creed and Miles note, "Characteristic based trust is based on norms of obligation and cooperation rooted in social similarity" (1996, p. 18). Common characteristics provide an inclination to trust, and diverse characteristics do not so much defeat the possibility of trust, as need acknowledgement as challenges to overcome. An organization where individuals enter with common expectations and views of how to behave and what constitutes high performance is more likely to foster trust than organizations that are highly diverse with regard to expectations, definitions of excellence, and standards for work performance.

Occurrences of trust

1 Through communication
2 Within organizational/structural relationships
3 From antecedents that affect current configurations of trust
4 Through the consistent behavior of individuals
5 From perceived individual integrity in actions and language

---

I want to stress that, when I write of characteristics of trust, I am not suggesting that individuals single-handedly carry specific traits with them that enhance or destroy trust. A checklist of trust behaviors does not exist. An organization's culture circumscribes characteristics such that a specific behavior that an individual might have employed in one setting will be unsuccessful in another. How groups enhance trusting behavior where everyone knows one another will differ at the more macro-organizational level. Nevertheless, within an organization's culture trust occurs not only on a level or a dimension but also as a characteristic in five specific ways. If one were to investigate trust in an organization, what are those cultural characteristics that ought to be reviewed?

The manner in which individuals and groups *communicate* with one another is one characteristic (Gilbert & Tang, 1998). Particular communicative styles are not as important as the idea that communication plays some role in the development and enhancement of trust. Communication takes on various guises. Formal and informal communication takes place as well as speech and literacy events that involve oral and written behaviors.

Many traditional cultures were primarily oral in their communicative strategies. Thus, if a culture based on literacy scripts interacted with another that utilized speech, the potential for trust was lessened. Similarly, some units view written communication as bureaucratic whereas the sender of the message may consider such events as an efficient way to communicate important information. Both groups may well make judgments about trust. The group that views the communicative event as bureaucratic may have less reason to trust the message's sender, whereas the sender may think that trust has been enhanced. Thus, just as one needs to delineate the level and phase on which trust is being enacted, one also needs to look at the communicative strategies employed to engender trust.

A second characteristic is the *structural relationships* involved in an organization. Although structures evolve and change, they also help determine the nature of relationships and how they are to be perceived and utilized. By "structure," I do not mean the level on which trust is being enacted. Structures are also something more than simply what is on an organizational chart, although that is one example.

As I noted at the outset of this chapter, structure is a central aspect of understanding culture. Just as structure provides a clue to how the organization's participants interact with one another, structure also is a characteristic to study in order to come to terms with how trust functions. In some organizations, a manager may have an open-door policy where virtually anyone is welcome. In other organizations, a strict chain of command exists, where a subordinate speaking to an individual at the top of the command would be grounds for dismissal. How structures are set in place provides a clue about trust. Individuals may exhibit high levels of trust in offering ideas to their superior in one organization, whereas in another organization the same behavior would increase suspicion, rather than trust.

Obviously, as with the remaining characteristics, structure and communication overlap and support or contradict one another. A dean who says she has an open-door policy but never communicates with the faculty sends conflicting messages that may result in a decrease in the culture of trust. A CEO who believes in a strict chain of command and communicates only in formalized manners may enhance unit-level trust, whereas a unit-level manager who seeks out individuals in order to gain their ideas may also demonstrate (by communicative and structural strategies) trusting behavior.

Third, in any analysis of trust, *antecedents* exist that inevitably impact how trust is currently configured, portrayed, and enacted. Far too often snapshots of trust capture how a group trusts at a particular moment in time. As I noted above, however, trust develops over time. An organization with no examples of trustworthiness is surely different from one where the structures and communicative processes are viewed by the organization's participants to exemplify trust. A new organization with no antecedents to draw upon is different from one with a conflicted past.

Thus, diagnosing trust at a particular level demands that the antecedents be examined from the participants' perspective. Insofar as trust involves risk, understanding an individual's action involves determining preexisting conditions. It is surely easier in some ways not to take a risk. Although trust is but one of many factors involved, the situation that led up to the action must be studied in order to come to terms with the trust aspect of risk taking.

Consistency is a fourth characteristic. I suggest that not only is an understanding of the antecedents of the context important, but also how consistent individuals have been in their relationships and interactions with one another. Behavioral consistency pertains to the ability of individuals to behave in a consistent manner over time, across situations, and with multiple constituencies. Rules may be a factor in the development of consistency. Whitener, Brodt, Korsgaard, and Werner (1998, p. 516) explain that "these conditions primarily reflect qualities attributed to the trustee by the trustor." The belief that an individual, a unit, or the organization itself is reliable and predictable is a key characteristic of trusting relationships. How such reliability gets enacted in large part depends on the culture of the organization. The American military, for example, is rule-laden and, yet, dependent on trust. The military may punish someone for acting or speaking out of rank without permission, not because it is untrustworthy behavior per se, but because it constitutes a failure to follow rules. In this light, the organization may not presume that an individual can make the right decision in a given situation, hence the need for rules and the need to trust that individuals will abide by those rules.

Such rules in another organization with a different culture would be entirely inappropriate. Indeed, when organizations fail to trust, they run the risk of creating an alienated workforce. Over time, failures of trust undermine individuals and organizations. Hopeless or alienated employees may ultimately not count on trust, and in doing so, they will be unwilling to take risks for the organization. The willingness to be vulnerable—to accept risk—in part depends on individuals and units having a sense of how a particular individual or organization acts over time. Erratic or contradictory behavior is less likely to induce the conditions of trust whether it is on a subunit level or organizational level.

The antecedents and consistency of a situation highlight why simply looking at one moment in which an individual communicates with others or only the structure that exists at that moment will be insufficient. A department chair, for example, who speaks at the start of the school year about the importance of involving everyone in the workings of the unit but eventually cancels all meetings and arbitrarily makes decisions, is clearly not consistent. If previous department chairs have said and acted in a similar manner, then the antecedents of such behavior are only further confirmed.

Integrity is the final characteristic. Individuals in organizations constantly make attributions to individuals' behavior. The ability to do what was promised and to tell the truth is not merely a matter of consistency but also one of integrity. Behavioral integrity pertains specifically to what individuals say and what they do. However, I wish to stress yet again the cultural ramifications of this characteristic. Culture reflects a group understanding of words such as integrity. An individual's actions could be perceived as situational integrity—present in one situation but not another.

If one were to try to understand integrity, then, other characteristics are important, as well as a basic understanding of the organizational culture. Integrity is defined by existing communicative codes and structural relationships. Structures, for example, that exist to monitor and control employees assume a lack of integrity. Communication that emphasizes rules and the consequences of breaking rules in an organization is quite different from an organization where such discussions are irrelevant or downplayed. An individual who assumes a role in which the previous person embezzled money and disrupted employees' lives has a different challenge from a person inheriting a job from a person who personified integrity. Customers are likely to view the integrity of the bakery different from that of an auto repair shop. And, as I discuss in Chapter 9, the integrity of public postsecondary institutions differs in the early 21st century from that of a half century ago.

A brief review is in order. I have argued that a cultural view of organizations affords a more useful tool to study trust than a rationalist framework. I suggested that in order to study an organization's culture three broad categories come into play: structure, environment, and values. Underlying these categories is not the assumption that pervasive, firm meanings exist but that the participants within the organization interpret structure, environment, and values in manifold ways. Culture is the search for understanding those interpretations.

I then pointed out that to look at trust within a culture three conditions need to be examined: trust as shared experience, as learned experience, and as conditional. The conditions focus on how people learn about trust and how to trust one another in an organization. I then pointed out that trust occurs on different levels, and that trust ought not to be thought of as a static, preexisting dimension. Instead, I argued that a more fine-grained analysis will examine a specific level of trust and come to terms with the organizational phases of trust. Such a point is particularly important insofar as one's focus may be to understand notions of the public good at the meta-level of the organization or to understand the challenges to be faced at the micro-level within a unit of the organization. I finally turned to various characteristics of trust. I do not intend to develop a checklist or list of attributes of trustworthiness but instead to point out the kinds of characteristics that need to be examined from a cultural perspective in order to come to terms with trust in organizations. I now turn to a specific kind of organization that is my primary focus for the remainder of the book—a postsecondary organization.

CHAPTER FOUR

The Cultural Conditions of Academic Work

In the preceding chapters, I considered problems pertaining to the creation and maintenance of trust in academic organizations. I now discuss what I define as the *cultural conditions* of academic work. As I have noted, I am writing from a cultural framework that assumes organizational reality is defined by the sociohistorical parameters of the organization, the interpretations given by the organizational participants, and current environmental conditions that frame organizational life. I noted in the introduction significant environmental changes that currently influence academic life. However, those changes will be interpreted and acted upon in different ways based on the culture of the organization.

I have outlined in previous work (Tierney, 1988, 1989) my definition of a cultural perspective for analyzing colleges and universities. Just as a traditional anthropologist will seek to come to an understanding of the various terms in a traditional culture, such as kinship and mythology, so too will a researcher who wishes to decipher the culture of an institution try to understand its mission, strategies, and leadership. Both traditional and organizational researchers also seek to understand basic aspects of a culture such as communication, rituals, ceremonies, socialization, and history.

An additional way to understand an organization's culture is to focus on a specific angle of the organization. How do particular individuals or a specific subset of members conduct their work? A traditional anthropologist, for example, might look at the work of women or the work of a particular caste within a culture; those scholars concerned about the organizational culture of colleges and universities might focus specifically on the cultural conditions of academic work. Using this perspective, I am initially less concerned about the mission of the organization, how the participants choose one or another decision-making strategy, or who is considered to be a leader and what that entails. Those issues and others may eventually be of interest. First, however, I elaborate on the conditions for work in a postsecondary organization and the interpretation of those conditions.

By "academic work," I do not mean the decisions that take place throughout a normal workday or the myriad of activities that occur in administrative life. Academic work, for the purposes of this book, refers to the raison d'être of academic institutions—the creation, transmission, and refinement of knowledge. Academic work may be in the classroom, in a laboratory, or any number of locales, but the faculty are its principal conveyors. Students (and frequently the broader public) are consumers of knowledge. My focus here is more on the producers of academic work insofar as without them, consumption would be impossible. A student may certainly gain a great deal of knowledge outside of the academy or may even participate in the creation of knowledge. Faculty, as they are currently configured, may eventually become secondary or even irrelevant to knowledge production. Yet, at present, academic work's chief architects are faculty.

Faculty have four cultural frames from which they work (Becher, 1987; Clark, 1987; Tierney & Bensimon, 1996). The faculty are socialized as "professors" as opposed to the myriad of other professions that exist. Faculty are also defined by the nation in which they work. Being a professor in the United States differs from being one in France, Australia, or elsewhere. Most importantly, faculty become attached to their discipline. The mores of being a chemistry professor, for example, differ from those of a professor of classics or business. Finally, a professor becomes socialized to the culture of the campus on which he or she works. Indeed, these four cultures are consistently played out on a campus.

Accordingly, this chapter investigates faculty work. A hallmark of academic life in the 20th century is the involvement of the faculty in formal and informal decisions that explicitly or implicitly impact the organization. The assumption has been that faculty work, in part, involves creating an organizational structure conducive to the ability to search for truth and the production of knowledge. In this book I do not assess the relative success or failure of the faculty in doing so but instead consider how networks for social capital have been constructed, changed, or destroyed. These networks primarily reside in two domains—that of the organization, and that of the discipline. In what follows, I discuss the parameters of these domains and consider the formation of social capital.

Social capital and academic work

I previously defined social capital as the actual or potential resources developed within a network of more or less institutionalized relationships of mutual acquaintances. The institutionalized relationships of academics are conducted primarily in two arenas—on their campuses, and in their disciplinary or professional associations. My interest here is to delineate how social capital is built within these networks such that the networks become stronger (or weaker). The networks are either voluntary or obligatory insofar as some activities of an academic's life—such as teaching a class—are mandatory and part of an individual's formal contract; there is also a wide array of activities either on campus or within a disciplinary association in which an academic need not participate. Both kinds of networks, however, have significant resources that enable individuals to create social capital. Presumably, less involvement in networks generates less social capital, which in turn suggests fewer possibilities for the conditions of trust to exist. When trust is absent, those in the organization are less likely to take risks, innovate, or engage in discussions about how to reform the organization. I now discuss institutional and disciplinary networks where social capital might occur and/or be built.

Table 4.1: Campus-based institutional networks

ELEMENT	EXAMPLES
Obligatory networks	Teaching
Formal structural networks	Senates or assemblies, departments, divisions
Informal academic networks	Reading groups, informal decision-making venues

Institutional networks

Obligatory networks

Faculty have one primary task that they generally must do: teach students. In many respects over the last century, the task which has changed the least is the manner in which knowledge is delivered to students. How one does research, with whom one is in regular contact, what one expects of a postsecondary institution, how funding is formulated, and a host of other organizational artifacts have undergone a significant change since World War II in general, and over the last generation in particular. However, the lone professor standing in front of a class of students still remains the basic instrument of teaching. Two models predominate—either the lecture or the seminar. One would be foolish to assume that a generation from now, these two models will remain as the only ways faculty teach students. Distance learning, the Internet, videoconferencing, and ways not yet imagined are more than likely to transform teaching similar to the transformation of research. Once the teacher no longer needs to be in a classroom, standard assumptions about academic life will be called into question—and then changed. The credit hour, the semester or quarter system, and the concept of the academic year will all undergo transformation.

My purpose is neither to bemoan nor to celebrate the portending changes. However, when I look to the past, one consistent issue relates to the seemingly innocuous obligation the faculty have. Whereas most employees in organizations in America have set time schedules and an array of tasks to perform, such is not the case with faculty. Although faculty have checks and balances such as tenure review, they have a much higher degree of autonomy afforded to them than most employees. One unique area, however, is teaching. Faculty sign a contract that delineates how many courses they must teach. Although they are generally able to negotiate what and when they will teach, the majority of individuals must conform to certain norms. When asked, for example, "When do you want to teach this semester?" very few individuals are able to respond by saying, "I'll do the first five Sundays beginning in November, and then have two intensive weeks, break for a month, and wrap things up during the first weekend of the new year." Individuals respond by functioning within a cultural timeframe: "I'd prefer teaching classes on Tuesdays and Thursdays in the afternoon." The negotiation on both sides falls within cultural constructs of time: "I'd like you to move one of those classes to Mondays and Wednesdays, but you can choose morning or afternoon."

The result is that faculty participate in a loosely affiliated institutional network that nevertheless ties them all together. Unlike other organizations that have no annual beginning or end, colleges and universities have an academic year that is significantly demarcated by different time periods. The school year begins in September and ends in May. Midterm exams, finals, a summer recess, and the semester schedule all bind faculty in some way that develops a commonality and bond. Different professors, of course, have vastly different schedules and calendars. Some individuals have sabbaticals. Other faculty in professional schools such as education may have the bulk of their teaching duties occur on the weekend or in the evening. However, the culture of most traditional colleges and universities still remains within the temporal timeframe of an academic year. The consequence is that individuals have the possibility of working within a social construct of academic work.

One unexplored irony of the current changes pertains to how individuals fit within a professional culture. A professor may rarely, if ever, visit other classrooms or teach courses with other faculty. Teaching is a remarkably individualistic and solitary endeavor. The classroom door shuts and the individual teaches. Nevertheless, once the door closes, there is little variation. Indeed, when that door shuts and opens, when students are examined, when the professor is able to relax, and when he or she must feverishly grade papers are more similar than different. Of consequence, there is a great deal of unexplored conformity when many critics who want greater academic accountability are trying to tighten up the system. However, what is little understood is that the changes that are taking place may possibly have the opposite effect. What it means to "teach" may be remarkably different.

What do such changes suggest for a faculty accumulation of social capital? When the cultural construct of work is revised, one result is that the current network responsible for cultivating affiliational relationships will be lessened, if not cease to exist. It is entirely possible that new networks will arise or be created; it is just as likely that no such networks will develop. If social capital is important, then academic leaders need to attend to the ways that networks can possibly be enhanced. When a network evaporates or disintegrates, others must take its place.

Formal structural networks

Social capital assumes that networks exist or are created by affiliations that develop in multiple ways and derive from numerous forces. Throughout the 20th century, one characteristic of American higher education pertained to the concept of shared governance. Although the creators of the idea of shared governance—scholars such as John Dewey and Arthur Lovejoy—had more instrumental goals in their advancement of the idea, shared governance also has been a fountainhead for the creation of social capital. The vast majority of colleges and universities have some form of academic senate or assembly where members participate in the governance of the institution. The faculty governing body also has a wealth of committees that call upon individuals to participate in such issues as the creation of retirement policies, the refinement of general-education requirements, and the implementation of standards governing human-subject research.

A traditional postsecondary institution also has as its building block a department or division. The chair generally comes from the faculty, who have some say in the chair's appointment. The department faculty typically create a major and recommend the requirements for graduation. Additional faculty committees oversee and approve the recommendations of the departmental faculty. As with the senate, the department has regular meetings where attendance is required. Faculty think of their intellectual home as the department insofar as most of the decisions that impact their daily lives occur within its boundaries. Who teaches what class on what day and time is usually determined in departmental meetings. Whether an individual teaches upper-level undergraduate classes, graduate seminars, or introductory lectures are matters for departments to consider. Whether to hire a person of one intellectual persuasion over another is usually a departmental decision.

Of course, policies such as summer salaries, office hours, institutional support for computers, or requests for new faculty positions are frequently determined not at the departmental level but at a school or college level. Yet again, those who participate in the making of those recommendations or decisions are typically faculty on committees of a school's faculty council. Policies travel up and down decision-making lines. Some suggestions derive from faculty meetings in departments and others come from a school's council.

Three observations are obvious to anyone familiar with how shared governance functions in academe. First, I am not making any comment from my vantage point about the effectiveness of shared governance. As with any example pertaining to social capital, a member's involvement in a particular activity focuses on the nature and ramifications of the involvement rather than whether their involvement helps a group achieve a particular goal. The critical point here is not whether one or another governance structure is effective but rather how participants perceive governance structures. I accept that such an observation is a conundrum. The premise of this book is that those who work in academe need to be better organized to cope with the significant changes that postsecondary institutions face. For performance to improve, individuals need to trust one another. Outcomes matter. But rather than a cause-and-effect relationship where one model leads to good outcomes and another model does not, I suggest that the cultural interpretations that individuals bring to their participation in the organization play a critical role in eventually improving outcomes.

Second, shared governance does not suggest that the faculty are the sole, or even primary, decision makers in an institution. For my purposes here, I am not so concerned with what should occur with regard to the proper role for faculty and administrators in decision making but rather with what the faculty perceive actually takes place. Many will say, for example, that the administrative role in decision making has increased considerably over the last generation to the detriment of faculty input. In consequence, decisions have become more corporate and less collegial, more based on the bottom line and less on academic quality. Whether such assertions are true is certainly interesting and debatable, but my concern is what these changes portend for the nature of academic work and the creation of social capital. If faculty find that their role is less, then presumably they will have fewer avenues to social capital and be less willing to participate in a process that they perceive no longer considers their voice as worthwhile.

Third, although I have mentioned terms such as "academic senate" and "departments" as if they exist in all colleges and universities, in the panoply of postsecondary institutions, different terminologies and arrangements undoubtedly exist. Some organizations have no senate and others will not have departments or even divisions (Tierney & Minor, 2003). Nevertheless, throughout the 20th century, an enshrined hallmark is that faculty have some role in the governance of the institution. The unintended result is a wealth of formal structural possibilities for social capital to occur. Although much of this work comes under the guise of "service" and is usually the least formally appreciated aspect of academic work, I submit that it also has been the social glue that holds postsecondary education together. An individual is much more likely to be feted by his or her peers for the quality of teaching rather than for service on a committee. Research is generally held in much higher regard than either teaching or certainly service; individuals are sure to be recompensed at a higher rate for a stellar article rather than distinguished service on a committee.

Nevertheless, the multiple structural affiliations of academic life within the organization create immense possibilities for social capital. The vast majority of individuals who participate in shared governance on a campus do so not because they must but because they accept voluntary participation on a committee as part of a faculty member's obligation. In turn, there is the implicit recognition that the agenda a committee might have is not the only outcome that occurs. The interactions within the social networks of shared governance contribute to a shared understanding of the organization. Involvement in governance is also a social regulator and a norm that communicates to the members of the organization certain beliefs about the community.

I will turn in a later chapter to how trust originates and develops, but one's active engagement in voluntary associations clearly has the potential of building trust. Although in Chapter 1, I criticized Coleman's tautological approach to social capital, where access to social capital begets social capital, such a concern is less important within academic organizations. Yes, the potential exists for an in-group to participate in shared governance to such an extent that other faculty feel excluded or disempowered. Some individuals will believe that it is in their interest not to participate, not to help generate social capital—and hence, trust.

The challenge for those who work in academic organizations is to generate capital and overcome the concerns, fears, or objections of those who are reluctant to participate. The avenues for participation in shared governance are considerable; more often than not, the challenge turns less on individuals not being allowed to participate in governance and more on the fact that not enough individuals are willing to be engaged. Such an observation, of course, raises significant issues about the possibility for the creation of trust. Low social capital suggests low levels of engagement, which in turn leads to disempowerment and low levels of trust.

I concur with Bourdieu's analysis that networks are constantly (re)created with the caveat that many networks also exist over time—their purposes may not change.

An academic awards committee may year after year decide in the same manner about who should get an award for distinguished service at an honorary convocation. A commencement committee may function in the same manner every year as they decide how to formulate graduation exercises. Within colleges and universities, Bourdieu is substantially correct. Library committees of a generation ago concerned themselves primarily with the kinds of acquisitions that needed to occur and were relatively noncontroversial; in the 21st century, library committees have probably renamed themselves something akin to "information technology committees." The Head Librarian is now the Chief Information Officer and may not even be a faculty member. How to deal with the revolution in electronic journals, the dilemma of print texts, and a wealth of other issues have made such committees confusing and frequently confrontational. Because of the complexity of the issues, faculty in the humanities may perceive the issues from one perspective and those in computer science and engineering from another. Some faculty will interpret these shifts as going to the heart of academic life, while others see the institution as simply keeping up with the times. Therefore, participation on such a committee means something different from participation on its forerunner of a generation ago.

Similarly, faculty governing bodies take up not only different issues over a period of a few years but also occasionally confront heated issues. Curiously, such controversies have the potential to increase social capital, but the outcomes of the confrontation could also have the result of depressing further faculty engagement. As I will elaborate by way of a case study in Chapter 5, at one institution a majority of the faculty interpreted certain decisions made by the trustees as an attack on tenure. Many of the most distinguished professors who otherwise would not have participated in campus-level governance became involved. They acted as a group in support of the formal faculty governance structure. Their participation was not out of self-interest; as prestigious faculty, they had a multitude of possibilities and were relatively insulated from the decisions of the trustees. However, they had a sense of what academic work entailed, and the challenges the trustees put forth brought their interpretations into question. Such an issue galvanized voluntary participation and presumably increased social capital.

I need to emphasize the voluntary nature of participation in formal structures of shared governance. One of the more different aspects of academic life is that the academic has very few obligations that must be met at a specific time and in a specific manner. As I mentioned earlier, one must teach. But what one teaches is more a judgment call by the teacher rather than a prescribed set of rules and procedures. One history professor may choose a certain text in teaching early American history, while another may choose an entirely different text without anyone raising an objection. Similarly, reviews for tenure, annual reviews, and post-tenure reviews are all judgments on the worth of an individual's work, but unless the individual has seriously transgressed academic norms, there are very few sanctions or mandates that will be put into play. Some individuals over the course of an academic career will be more involved in formal structures of academic governance than other individuals, but it is just as likely that other individuals will have found different means to participate in the cultural work of the academic. My point here is simple: one makes decisions about participating in formalized governance structures. Frequently the decision has little to do with improving one's career.

When one volunteers to participate in shared governance, there can be several reasons. Those who reach the upper echelons of academic governance may harbor desires to become an administrator, and one or another individual may join a governing committee because of concern over a single issue. However, the vast majority of individuals commit themselves to participating in the humdrum day-to-day committees of their college or university as a voluntary obligation to their institution and as a desire for their own particular engagement. Participation on this level is in large part a way for the individual not only to identify as an academic but also to claim allegiance to the organization. Unlike Bourdieu, then, I suggest that when individuals participate in formalized governance processes, they claim a form of agency that enables them not only to voice their concerns but also to change the policies and structures of their work. Tenure and promotion standards, for example, are policies that faculty have the potential to change if they are involved in governance processes. Although one may not always be successful in any change effort, the point here is that without involvement, change is impossible and agency is denied.

Perhaps the clearest examples about the generation of social capital pertain to those issues that go to the heart of academic life. Although many faculty may only have a dim recognition about the intellectual roots of academic freedom and its relation to tenure, the vast majority of individuals recognize the importance of tenure and promotion. Most faculty see involvement in the multiple levels of review that occur when a candidate is considered for tenure or promotion as an academic obligation. There are, of course, always individuals who dismiss their duties or others who have a private agenda, but in the bulk of research conducted about the manner in which faculty are reviewed, scholars have pointed out how much time and effort faculty spend on such an activity. The engagement in such a process is one example of the stimulation of social capital at work. Individuals participate in a common undertaking that develops mutual understandings of the organization and binds people closer together.

An additional example pertains to faculty grievance committees. Although the committee may not meet very often, when it does meet, the topic frequently goes to the heart of academic life: whether an individual's tenure should be removed. The cultural meanings that faculty have given to such an action demand a committee with intense faculty involvement that may stretch over the course of a semester or even longer. Some individuals have compared such an action to a trial where testimony is taken, witnesses are called, and the faculty grievance committee act as judges and jury. Such a committee, again, is a cultural artifact of academic work. The "product" of the committee is not merely a decision about whether a professor's tenure should be maintained or revoked but is also an associational undertaking that increases social capital for the larger community as well as those who are engaged in the process.

Although I previously mentioned that my purpose in this text is not concerned with whether senates and their counterparts are effective, it is imperative that those who participate in the process do not see their work as useless or irrelevant. If senates have tasks that never get completed, or if the president frequently overrides faculty decisions about promotion and tenure, then those who have participated will undoubtedly question the worthiness of the process and their investment of time. Indeed, the most common complaint from individuals in regard to formal organizational structures is that it is a waste of energy. At the same time, individuals pointed out in a recent survey (Tierney & Minor, 2003) that they were relatively content with faculty input into governance on their campuses—but participation was much broader than simply a senate. The most basic level of participation and where individuals find the most satisfaction is at their local, departmental level. There are also multiple other venues for participation that deal with specific issues such as promotion and tenure or in informal arenas.

Informal academic networks

Academics have multiple affiliations within the university that may either pertain to their intellectual pursuits and interests or to their personal lives where they use the institution for the support network. As in the larger society, individuals are frequently unaware of the numerous engagements they may have with others when they are informal. Nevertheless, these informal webs of affiliation may have just as much possibility for generating social capital as formal networks. And just as there is frequently not an explicit agenda or goal to informal meetings, the growth of social capital is usually implicit and inferred.

The most typical informal networks are those where faculty participate in decision making but not through formalized structures such as the senate. A provost may gather together a group of senior faculty, for example, whose input she solicits regarding the strategic plan. A quasi-formalized structure might even be created whereby faculty work with the provost to develop the plan. However, the group has no formal authority. No one appointed them they have a finite task, and when their work is done, they will go out of business. An additional example might be a president or dean who has a "'kitchen cabinet'" of faculty on whom he relies for advice and opinion. The cabinet may be a loose network of faculty from throughout the campus who meet with the president for drinks once a month. Their agenda may be entirely open and they may never be expected to make a decision. Certainly, with both examples, the president and provost have a particular goal in mind, irrespective of social capital, but the potential for social capital to be increased also exists.

Faculty also may come together for a reading group that advances their research interests. Some individuals, for example, may desire to develop a new Ph.D. program that has a unique angle, where the faculty believe it is in their best interest to read a particular group of texts. Other individuals may be working on a problem that will benefit if individuals all read a particular article or book that the faculty then use as an initial text to discuss and debate. Some departments will have lecture series where they bring in outside speakers. Although the lectures may be open to everyone, they also may be seen as central meetings for the faculty to the extent that everyone attends. Small institutions or schools and colleges within an institution may have a similar series that revolves around a particular topic or theme that the faculty wish to emphasize. A school, for example, that emphasizes urban issues may bring in a series of speakers who are recognized as urban experts. The expectation is that faculty will attend the meetings and that they will have some new understanding about how they might organize themselves to focus on a particular initiative.

Teaching is also an area that may have informal networks. Individuals may have a discussion group about feminist approaches to pedagogy or how to build a more inclusive classroom. An interdisciplinary group of faculty may come together to consider ways to collaborate across academic units. A center for teaching and learning may appoint faculty fellows who are recognized for their teaching; they may simply meet on occasion to discuss issues of pedagogy. Another group may come together around a specific topic such as the worth of student evaluations, but it is little more than a reading group that tries to understand the strengths and weaknesses of the issue. The point here, of course, is that some faculty are genuinely intrigued and interested in pedagogical issues and use their interest to create informal associations where a by-product is the increase in social capital.

Ceremonial occasions also punctuate life at a postsecondary institution. Although a wealth of activities exist which faculty may decide, one by one, to attend, there are generally activities where the expectation is that the faculty should be in attendance. Again, attendance is not mandatory; no one will check to see if a particular individual has participated. But cultural norms often point to what kind of informal activities necessitate faculty involvement. Graduation ceremonies, holiday events, and honorary convocations are the kind of activities that fit as informal networking events that have the potential to increase social capital. I am well aware that some individuals dread holiday events and others do not consider convocations worth attending. However, networks are not all-pervasive to the extent that everyone must attend. The nature of social capital and network formation is that numerous avenues exist, and ceremonies are but one kind of network. Some faculty, for example, actually enjoy the annual holiday party, and they will use it as an occasion for getting together with acquaintances until the next event, which may be a spring party held by the dean. Examples such as these are not unlike church socials or family get-togethers where a preponderance of individuals gathers for a potluck or the holiday picnic. True, someone's Uncle Harry may avoid the party. But these individuals, like faculty who avoid such informal get-togethers, presumably have other possible ways to increase their social capital.

Indeed, personal interests that are outside the domain of academic life may occur within the organization because that is where many individuals spend a great deal of their time. A Bible Studies group may be a loose-knit affiliation of faculty who have no other concern than reading the Bible together over a lunch hour. A gay men's group might have a similar common interest and gather for monthly potlucks. Sometimes a school may start a faculty-student softball league that plays games on Saturdays. A faculty squash group may exist for faculty who use the gym in the late afternoon. I have even known of a faculty bridge group who play bridge on Friday afternoons, while another group meets regularly in a local bar on Fridays to unwind.

All of these examples are voluntary associations that have goals other than the accumulation of social capital, or they may actually have no intent other than relaxation. Nevertheless, I suggest that these multiple institutional venues are significant forums for the creation and accumulation of social capital. Although an observer such as Bourdieu may be justified in claiming that some venues privilege some over others—who meets with the President in the "kitchen cabinet," for example, as opposed to a gay men's potluck—I also maintain that virtually all faculty have the potential to immerse themselves in numerous networks. Inevitably, some networks lead to more privilege than others; however, all networks have the ability to create and maintain trust.

Indeed, a campus full of associational networks not only has the potential of increasing social capital for those directly involved but also for other members of the faculty. A tennis club or teaching center may have no additional benefits to those other than the individuals directly involved in the activity. However, committees such as promotion and tenure or even a faculty senate also have the potential for increasing the social capital of faculty beyond those who are direct participants. Individuals generally pass in and out of committee work. Someone is on the senate one year and then stops out for a year, later joining the promotion and tenure committee. Although the benefits of capital may be particularly germane during the year of involvement, simply knowing that such committees exist that directly go to the heart of the nature of academic work has benefits to the larger community. A community bereft of such networks puts at risk not only those who are participants but also the community itself.

My assumption is that involvement in these networks has the potential of increasing trust in an organization's culture. Although a lack of involvement may not doom the career of an academic, it is potentially harmful for the organization. An individual may be a perfectly good teacher or researcher yet be isolated from the rest of the organization. Indeed, the image of the "lone wolf" often permeates academic discussions. The assumption is that academics just want to be left alone to do their work. I do not doubt that in some cases such an image is correct. And in most cases, academics demand some degree of personal autonomy and time to themselves. However, faculty find multiple networks in which they participate. Individuals engage in some of these networks because they have a sense of social obligation to one another or to a larger abstraction such as "shared governance" and what it means to be a member of the professorate. Individuals participate because they enjoy one another's company, feel that they will benefit in some manner, or simply want to be connected to the organization and their colleagues. These networks are not only useful but necessary for trust to increase. An organization without opportunities for social capital is an organization at risk.

Intellectual networks

Traditionally, faculty at four-year colleges and universities hold a terminal degree and have a particular intellectual home. Even those who are in newer fields, or hold interdisciplinary degrees, have some way of thinking about, and studying, particular phenomena. One's intellectual training and background provides rich possibilities for the creation of social capital within disciplinary and professional networks. An interesting paradox of these networks, however, is whether an increase in disciplinary social capital results in an increase in organizational social capital. Putnam (2000) looked at social capital as a way to increase civic engagement and was unconcerned about the specific locale. His assumption was that, regardless of the network in which an individual joined, civic engagement was likely to increase. Thus, a bowling league, a parent–teacher association, or a political party all provided ways to increase social capital, which in turn increased civic engagement.

Table 4.2: Discipline-based intellectual networks

ELEMENT	EXAMPLES
Regulatory networks	Professional disciplinary associations
Formal networks	Peer review, discipline-specific conferences
Informal networks	Electronic communication

Social capital within an organization, however, functions in a different manner. I stated at the start of this chapter that a faculty member has four socializing cultures. Two of those affiliations are primary—the institution and the discipline. Although involvement in professional associations such as the American Association of University Professors (AAUP) is possible, membership in such associations is maintained by a distinct minority of faculty. When individuals are surveyed about those forces that impact them most significantly, the discipline and institution are most frequently mentioned. Campus-based and disciplinary affiliations are not divided but instead are meshed together. A scholar increases his or her social capital in the discipline where he or she is located—on a campus. Disciplines and professions are nongeographical and temporal. They are located in the cultural DNA of an academic. Whether an increase in social capital of the discipline helps increase the social capital of the organization, or if it is in contest with the campus, is an unresolved question that many find of interest. However, I do not find the answer to such questions to be important. True, some faculty will affiliate more with their discipline than with their institution, but such an observation is a "social fact." The challenge on a college or university campus is not simply to acknowledge the fact or to somehow seek to change it; instead those on campuses ought to seek ways to build capital in a manner akin to how individuals acquire social capital in their church groups but also in their local communities. Accordingly, I turn to the various networks that exist on and off a campus.

Regulatory networks

Members of a discipline or profession frequently join an association. Although any association has multiple activities, those that are most important pertain to intellectual regulation. At the most serious level, such an activity refers to formal investigations of academic fraud or wrongdoing. Some years ago, for example, David Baltimore, a respected scientist and subsequent president of the California Institute of Technology, was accused of a serious breach of ethics that forced multiple scientific reviews that eventually exonerated him (Kevles, 1996). The American Anthropological Association recently conducted an investigation into a series of allegations about scientific misconduct of an anthropologist who conducted research about the Yanomami in Brazil (AAA, 2002). In this instance, the disciplinary committee that investigated the charges consisted of senior, respected members of the profession who were chosen not because of their institutional affiliation but because of their disciplinary standing. The American Historical Association also commented on the work of one of its members after questions of veracity arose regarding his award-winning book (AHA Council, 2001). Although similar investigations may occur on a campus about a specific individual charged with intellectual fraud, there is usually heavy reliance on the findings of the disciplinary committees.

On a less volatile level, but similarly important, members of a discipline are frequently called upon to judge the quality of candidates considered for promotion and tenure. At virtually all institutions where research is taken seriously, there are external letters that assess the adequacy of a candidate's research. Although some letters have become standard and may be dashed off in a relatively brief time period—the ubiquitous letters of references, for example—letters of review for promotion and tenure are another matter. An institution's review committee generally sends a great deal of written material for a reviewer to assess. Letters do not simply attest to the quantity of a candidate's work but also to the quality of the ideas. The assumption is that those in the discipline are closest to the intellectual work of the candidate and know best how to judge the worthiness of the work. Letters frequently run to numerous pages that comment on the adequacy of the ideas and methods of the candidate.

Interestingly, networks of regulation may tear asunder the fabric of the discipline while at the same time increasing social capital. Associations have the potential of splitting apart when investigations ensue over matters of academic fraud where the case is not clear-cut. Similarly, when candidates with a particular viewpoint are continually denied tenure and promotion, they may form a splinter group that focuses more centrally on their issues and concerns. Feminists, for example, who found that traditional disciplines such as history, political science, and law were unwelcome professional homes, created their own intellectual associations in a manner similar to individuals who have recently created an association that looks at popular culture. While these permutations may create surface-level tension, they are also examples of the ecology of networks and social capital. Rather than being denied agency, individuals came together and created a new branch of an association or an entirely new association, thereby generating new potentials for social capital.

Formal networks

Disciplinary and professional associations have an array of committees and boards on which their members participate. Virtually all of this work is voluntary. Associations have elected boards where candidates run for a term in a manner akin to an academic senate. Peer-reviewed journals have editorial boards on which individuals are appointed or elected for specific terms. Conferences have committees that organize meetings. New initiatives develop where members are invited to serve.

On a secondary level, numerous members of an association act as reviewers for journals, conferences, and grant submissions. External agencies such as the National Science Foundation will turn to particular members of an association to review proposals that fall within their intellectual domain. Again, the assumption is that those who are best able to judge the quality of an article, a conference paper, a research proposal, and the like are those scholars who are members of the submitter's intellectual area. Individuals may certainly turn down requests to do a review, but participation in such activities is an example of civic-minded academics who increase their social capital. Whether such participation is decreasing and why is an issue that has provoked considerable discussion but no firm conclusion and warrants formal study; for now, I simply point out the degree to which individuals have opportunities to participate in a voluntary manner in their associations.

Informal networks

As with informal networks at a college or university, academics also create informal networks within their disciplines and professions. Over the last generation, the opportunity for such networks has increased dramatically with the advent of the Internet. A generation ago, individuals may have only seen one another at an annual meeting and corresponded through postal mail; the times have changed dramatically. Academics are now able to correspond with one another instantaneously. A team of researchers from throughout the world may work with one another simultaneously through a videoconference. Messages about a particular intellectual problem or question are put on disciplinary email lists where multiple communities might be able engage with the issue rather than only a handful of scholars.

Whereas a decade ago I may have reviewed a colleague's draft of an article on an occasional basis and over a relatively leisurely time period, I now receive email attachments daily with requests to read and comment within a greatly shortened time frame. The Internet also appears to foster informal communication that would have been unheard of only a few years ago. Graduate students, assistant professors, and numerous other individuals and groups have much less hesitation in contacting senior colleagues via an email message than in previous ways such as by phone or in person. Any senior academic who is research-active and has meager computer literacy has undoubtedly seen his or her associational inquiries rise dramatically over the last generation. Indeed, it is not uncommon for individuals to receive fifty email messages a day, many of them discipline-based requests.

Previously, informal networks were relatively stable and closed. A young aca-

demic rose through the ranks and developed friendships and intellectual relationships with peers, staying in touch with one's dissertation advisor. The individual had
a meager network which gradually expanded. Today, networks are multiple, expansive, and quick. Networks may form and reform within the space of an academic
year where someone has an interest, joins a group online, and then moves on to
another group. The implications for this revolution in communicative networks for
social capital are twofold. First, as opposed to Bourdieu's analyses of power inequalities with regard to individuals' ability to network and develop social capital, the possibility now exists for neophytes and new members of a discipline or profession to
have rapid access to networks. I certainly do not wish to imply that, as soon as one
joins a discipline, his or her networks will be as extensive as senior members. At the
same time, to overlook the changes that have taken place, and are likely only to
increase, is to miss a significant change in the cultural conditions of academic
work.

Second, and perhaps as importantly, these changes may well have an opposite
effect. Although the potential for increasing social capital is vast, it is also not unlike-
ly that individuals may suffer from communication overload. Whereas the concern
for social capital on campuses is that individuals feel that their participation is irrelevant, the concern here is quite different. When individuals solicit advice from a person, the request is usually sincere. Although the Internet has created a great deal of
conversation amongst colleagues and friends about minor daily activities, it is
equally common to receive messages that demand some form of response in a
timely manner. When an individual adds up all these messages, he may well at some
point decide to opt out. These are, after all, voluntary associations. The ironic
result of an increase in the potential for network formation would be an actual
decrease in social capital. When individuals within the organization receive too many
stimuli one response is to shut down and withdraw. Fragmentation and the impov-
erishment of trust result.

Conclusion

What I have attempted to portray in this chapter is the multiple potential networks
that exist for faculty which enables the creation and production of social capital. The
primary arenas are twofold—on the campus and within one's discipline or profession. Networks, of course, are not static. They change over time based on membership and current demands. My concern is that within both arenas, the potential exists
(if it does not already occur) for the lessening of networks, the decrease in social capital, and the insolvency of trust. Ironically, at the same time, there has been an
increase in the venues for social capital because of the vastly expanded potential of

electronic means of communication. Indeed, what remains an open question is how the Internet, videoconferencing, and websites influence social capital formation. Adults have learned to adapt to technological changes, but their norms remain face-to-face communication. Younger generations will have entirely different technological norms; in consequence, how they interpret network formation may be at odds with the current interpretation of communicative interaction and engagement.

My concern focuses on two questions. First, if the traditional academic community is disrupted for any number of reasons, then on what, if anything, will faculty develop affiliations and attachments? If traditional avenues for participation in the organization are now seen as superfluous, how might the organization be less fragmentary and more cohesive? If the discipline is no longer seen as an intellectual home but a burden, then to what—and with whom—will the academic create attachments?

Second, the notion of "faculty" itself is also under consideration. The portrait of the full-time tenure-track academic who spent his or her career in one or two institutions is a vestige of the past. As I mentioned above, how one teaches and how one constructs the "academic year" is equally under redefinition. The more common portrait today is of a part-time non-tenure-track professor who has no particular identification with a campus and few opportunities for sustainable networks. The individual may be involved in an electronic discussion group, but the form of intellectual networks akin to what existed in the past is destroyed. I have outlined a straightforward analysis of the cultural conditions of work and detailed the multiple opportunities for networks and capital formation. Insofar as the old mechanisms no longer seem sufficient, we must now consider the mechanisms of socialization and the inherent changes at work.

PART TWO

Enacting Trust

CHAPTER FIVE

Networks and Trust

To provide a context for my admittedly abstract terms from Part 1, I offer a portrait that highlights how trust operates at one institution, with particular regard to faculty involvement in governance. The data were collected by way of a case study in which 31 individuals were interviewed over the course of one academic year; these individuals were asked about their perceptions of the role of the faculty in the governance of the university. In addition, a variety of documents were read and analyzed, and follow-up interviews took place via the Internet and by phone. I do not suggest that trust operates in this manner in all locations. Instead, I offer an individual portrait in order to be able to advance the notion of trust in academic organizations. In subsequent chapters, I offer contrasting data that demonstrates how trust is culturally conditioned. I first present the data, and then focus on how it highlights the relationship of trust to social capital, institutional networks, and culture.

Prairie Home University

Prairie Home University (PHU) is a large public institution that has over 30,000 students and 1,500 faculty. The institution is well respected for its focus on academics and has a faculty who take teaching, research, and service seriously. The state has a history of support for public education; although the budget for the university decreased over the past decade, the perception of PHU remains positive. PHU has a history of successful shared governance. Senior administrators serve on the Academic Senate, and the faculty and administration have a tradition of working together to solve problems. The senate and its executive committee are well funded and adequately staffed with a suite of offices and five full-time employees. Most importantly, the culture of the university expects and rewards faculty involvement in governance.

When asked what advice faculty would give to a new president, a consistent theme emerged. "He has to get to know the faculty. Don't go around us," offered one. Another added, "We would never hire someone who was uncomfortable with the tradition around here of consultation." A third said, "He had better take governance seriously. Someone from a radically different kind of place would have a pretty steep learning curve," and a fourth concluded, "Embrace the governance structure. It's the way we do things." A final person said, "See the faculty as an ally. I know that's not the way it is at other places, but here we all see the need to get along and work with one another."

Similar kinds of comments occurred when individuals spoke about faculty involvement at PHU: "We expect leadership from the faculty. You have tenure, so use it." A second person contrasted his experience at PHU with other institutions: "We have a stronger governance system here than at other places. Faculty expect to be consulted, and by and large, we are." "Don't get the wrong impression," said another, "This is not a democracy without flaws. Faculty have their typical turf battles and we avoid difficult decisions. Faculty still make the process slower than it should be. But if you're interested in faculty engagement, I'd say for the kind of institution this is we are aware of what's going on." A fourth person concurred: "Faculty are never satisfied. They will always say they want more consultation, but when I look at other places, this place is far better than most and it functions pretty well." In an interview with two individuals, one said, "Some issues are perennial and you wonder why we keep repeating ourselves," and the other summarized, "But it goes to the heart of involvement. Faculty feel they can speak up on anything, and they do."

One example of faculty engagement pertained to a search for a new president. When the current president took a job at another institution, the PHU board of trustees created a search committee that contained relatively few faculty. "They made a mistake," commented one person. "It creates bad faith. There are fewer faculty on this search committee than the last one." Another person explained, "It was a misstep on their part, but off the record I've heard from the chair and understand why it was done. They'll still take our voice into account." A third person concurred, noting: "There is a growing consensus amongst the faculty about who we want, and we have been quietly writing letters to the search committee. Senior faculty and university professors also have written. I don't know what the outcome will be, but I'm

sure we'll be listened to." A fourth person added, "The board knows to avoid conflict, so I'm not sure why they created a committee with so few faculty, but we also
have used informal channels, and I'd be surprised if they chose someone out of step
with the faculty."

Three points arise in the responses to the presidential search committee. First,
although the interviewees viewed the structure of the search committee as important, they also were not overly concerned that the structure did not meet their expectations. Rather, the culture of the organization is what mattered. The means of
communication and the shared belief that they would be heard enabled the faculty to focus on whom they should hire as president rather than on the structure utilized to make that decision. Second, not all voices are equal. University
professors—campus-wide endowed chairs with tenure—have an important role in
the organization. When they express an opinion, the expectation is not that what
they say will be agreed to, but that they, as faculty, will be heard. Third, a presidential search is an unusual case. A college president is ordinarily a key actor in creating and maintaining (or destroying) the conditions for trust. Here, then, is an
example in which the culture has created trust through shared and learned experiences, so that even when the president is not involved, trust thrives.

This example also demonstrates the importance placed on socialization. Indeed,
one key concern of the faculty is that individuals new to the organization have different expectations and obligations. One person stated, "I suppose it's common
everywhere, but the younger ones seem less involved; they want to focus more on
their research or have national ambitions." A second noted, "There's increasing pressure to increase our research standing, and you can't do everything. It takes away
from service. It's not a crisis because there are still many of us involved, but I wonder if that will change." A third continued, "When crises erupt people come out of
the woodwork, but in the meantime everyone goes about their business. I'm not sure,
though, if we're in a new ball game. Everyone seems so busy, and governance takes
so much time. We should streamline the process." "If I were to make a prediction,
I'd say that faculty will be still involved in 10 years at the department level," said a
department chair, "but less so at the university level. It's not that they're uninter-
ested in university politics. It's that there's no time, so you make choices." Another
interviewee agreed: "I think there has been an erosion of faculty governance. It's
nothing overt, or a power grab, it's just the times."

The nature of socialization at PHU is primarily implicit and informal.
Individuals do not go through training and there is no manual for what is expected of a faculty member. However, there are numerous lessons that are implied and
internalized. As one individual commented, "It's quite natural for faculty to work
in administration for a spell. There's a lot of coming and going from one to the
other." The individual went on to explain that such interaction was common and

that it contributed to trust between faculty and administration. Another individual concurred: "I was in the administration once before, and then I went back to the faculty, and now I'm back again. It gives me useful perspective." Again, it not only provides individuals with useful perspectives but also shared experiences that enable trust to develop.

PHU is an exemplar for trust and trustworthiness. The institutional norm is for the faculty to shift back and forth between administrative and faculty positions. I do not, however, suggest that all institutions should have such a standard. Rather, the perception of such shifts is what is of interest. Consider, for example, the following quotation from a faculty member at a different institution:

> A few years ago I took a turn as a dean. During the summer I packed up my books in boxes and as I was taking them over to the administration building, a professor who I know rather well bumped into me. I thought he was going to help me with the boxes. Instead he told me, "I just want you to know that as long as you're in that building, you're one of them. I won't be talking to you." I thought he was kidding. You know what? He wasn't! He didn't talk with me until I finished my term and moved back to my faculty office. (Tierney, 1989, p. 118)

Clearly, at this institution, the perception of faculty movement into administration is quite different from PHU. The point is not that faculty need to avoid administrative life at one institution and undertake it at another. Instead, the challenge is to understand how similar actions are interpreted in different cultures and to consider what one might do to improve the conditions for trust and trustworthiness.

A related example pertains to faculty appointments. The pervasive assumption at PHU is that a senate committee will vet virtually all committees on which faculty serve. "Shadow committees, or kitchen cabinets that have formal power, won't fly around here very well," explained one person. "If a president just appointed individuals to important committees without the senate's input, that would be seen as a real problem. It's just not done." "We expect leadership from the faculty," commented a second person. "For a president to handpick people for an important committee would be a sign that he doesn't understand our culture."

Of course, individuals do not see the organizational world in the same way; PHU is not an academic utopia where everyone trusts one another. However, the comments reflect common perceptions about the nature of faculty governance. Indeed, when queried about what an indicator of effective governance might be, one respondent said that "the administration [should be] managing in a way that reflects academic values." Another person noted, "The extent to which academic community is strengthened would be an indication [of effective governance]." A third person stated, "These are all indirect effects—faculty involvement, the way people are socialized, the way they see their role here—but I think that most of us believe that when faculty are engaged with the goings-on around campus that the place is just more effective in fulfilling its mission."

"This place is overgoverned," complained one person. "On what campus is there too little governance, too few committees?" asked a second individual. She continued, "We need to streamline things here, but because we are inefficient does not mean we are ineffective." A third person noted, "Governance today is often silly. The issues are so complex and we don't have the time to attend to them, so we may take a quick pass at something and then defer to the administration, but there's been an erosion of faculty involvement. It's not at the breaking point, I don't know when that is, but we're heading down that road—everybody is." Another person noted, "Governance is ailing here. Discussions aren't as robust as they used to be. I think the fight we had with the board a few years ago exhausted people. That left a mark because it was a time in the history, at least in the time I've been here, where you really felt that they were out to screw you. We won. But it left a bad taste. It violated the culture." Another respondent summarized these issues: "It all comes down to time. Maybe the people who trained me felt like I do now, but I don't think so. I find myself in a race, and governance isn't a good use of my time if I am to accomplish what they want me to do—to get grants, publish, move the university in a position of prominence."

The comment about the "fight with the board" warrants elaboration. Some years ago an aggressive board raised questions about tenure and the work of the faculty. The manner in which the questions were raised, and the consultants who were brought in by the board, created a great deal of consternation on the part of the faculty. Faculty considered creating a union and a great many public comments were made by faculty about how the board had overstepped their authority and misunderstood the culture of PHU. The backlash against the board was virtually unanimous—senior and junior faculty as well as the most respected professors of the institution spoke up against the perceived derogatory comments made by the board. The result was that the board backed down and the chair resigned. On the one hand, the contretemps showed the importance of faculty governance and how they had trusted one another; on the other, such a serious conflict has left wounds that are not yet healed.

How one defines effective governance has more to do with cultural markers pertaining to the nature of faculty-administrative relations than with typical "bottom line" indicators one might find in a business. "Do the faculty trust the administration, or is the administration arbitrary in their decision making?" asked one individual. Conversely, a senior administrator noted, "I have to be sure I can speak confidentially to the executive committee and its chair. Sunshine and open meetings are fine, but I have to be able to be frank. It's a marker of effectiveness because it says we can get things done because we trust one another." A third person stated, "The administration needs to be open to conversation and discussion of major policies, and they have to respect faculty governance." Another person added: "I like benchmarking and comparative indicators. How are our graduation rates? How do we measure up? But those are less important than the nature of relations that have been built up between the administration and the faculty." Again, one respondent summarized the situation:

> I know if I just say we [the faculty] have to be perceived as a stakeholder that it's not enough. Simply being invited to the table doesn't mean governance is effective, but think of it as an entry card. You can't be effective where there's no communication and everybody is watching out for his or her back. I've worked at a place where everyone distrusts one another and it's not good.

When I asked individuals about the future, I was interested in how their view of the future correlated with their present perceptions. Although many of the previous comments forecast a troubled future, they also highlight a culture in which the faculty are engaged citizens of the university. "We will be more managerial in five years," commented one person. "The kind of 'Mr. Chips' world that has existed is probably a thing of the past." "Collaborative relationships with the administration have to continue, but I don't know if they will," said another. A third said, "The apple cart could be overturned. I'm not sure if that's a bad thing, but I know that what we have now is working." A long-time member of the faculty said, "I hope we streamline things. Every 20 years or so we should abolish committees and think through what we do. But I hope we maintain our core, the academic values, the belief in what we're doing and one another." "One thing that all these committees have served to do," explained another, "is to let us get to know one another. Otherwise we're just isolated within our departments and disciplines. University citizenship helps us see the whole rather than the part. It won't work if we lose that." Another added, "We have resisted the corporate model even though our committees might seem bureaucratic. I'm not sure if that will remain. I'm not sure if consultation and trusting one another will be what we're about in the future."

Discussion

I turn now to a consideration of how the ideas delineated in Part 1 relate to the comments by the actors at PHU. I first situate the discussion of trust and then return to Chapter 1's analysis of social capital and network formation. I then analyze the forms of the grammar of trust individuals utilized at PHU with particular emphasis on the cultural construction. I conclude with an analysis of the networks utilized by the actors and the implications of their usage for the creation and maintenance of trust.

Locating trust at PHU

My focus at PHU was more on the internal aspects of trust rather than on the organization's relationship with external constituencies. To be sure, as a public university, the institution had to prove itself trustworthy of public monies and engender civic support, but the issues that arose in the interviews had little to do with problems that existed in the external environment. By and large, PHU had the support of the public and the citizenry viewed the institution as a cherished public good. Indeed, the institution had long-standing support in the community; relations with legislators, pertinent constituencies such as schools and civic groups, and the local community also were generally good.

Although the relationship with the board had been tempestuous a few years prior to the case study, the rift seemed to have been resolved. For example, the faculty were able to communicate with the trustees about whom they thought were good presidential candidates. Ultimately, the board chose the candidate who the faculty supported. Although such an action could be seen in a political light as little more than power politics and the strength, for example, of a faculty union or senate, individuals did not paint such a picture. Instead, they pointed out how the university's constituents were able to work with individuals external to the organization in a manner that conveyed trustworthiness.

The data focus much more on the internal dynamics of trust. Of note, even though the interviews came at a time of presidential succession, the culture of the organization was such that trust existed on multiple levels. On some campuses, for example, a significant transition such as the hiring of a new president or provost might create a sense of instability in individuals to the extent that they will withhold trust, adopting a "wait and see" attitude. After all, how can an unknown individual be deemed trustworthy? However, PHU had a culture that in part assumed the trustworthiness of roles rather than in the charisma of an individual. At other institutions, however, a new president or provost may be viewed with suspicion not because of what he or she may have done elsewhere but instead because of the role that was to be inhabited on campus. Although the interviewees were not romantic in their notions of trust within the university, they also recognized that their relationships existed on firmer ground than the shifting sands of presidential succession and who would inhabit the office. In large part, these relationships are due to what I have defined as social networks; to this I now turn.

Social networks and trust at PHU

In Chapter 1, I noted how the *forms* of social capital play a role in network development as does the presence or absence of *norms of obligation* and *reciprocity*. Finally, the *symbolic resources* that exist within and outside of the network also needed to be examined for their interpretive and "real" value. At PHU, structures of governance are such that they induce trust. Indeed, on this campus, the formal forms of social capital play more of a role in network development than do the informal forms. Recall, for example, the comments made about the need for a new president to work with the faculty in governance and the need for committees to be vetted by the Academic Senate. As opposed to some campuses where faculty governance is more an affiliation of informal groups, and the president or provost has a great deal of leeway in committee appointments, the opposite is true at PHU. An individual who did not take governance seriously would find a hard time at PHU; the culture is such that involvement in formal governance structures is mandatory and seen as a norm. The result is that trust is fomented in the culture of the organization rather than in individuals. Such a point is useful for the continuity of trust. As I noted in the previous chapter, formal structures and wide participation do not ensure good governance or the creation of trust per se. They are necessary conditions but are not guaranteed to ensure equitable processes for all. However, without such structures and participation good governance becomes an unachieved goal and the development of trust that much harder.

Indeed, norms of obligation are ingrained and embedded in the culture of the organization. The manner in which these norms are played out is through primarily formalized structures, although as noted with the presidential search committee, informal processes are also called into play. The interviewees pointed out the importance of "frank communication" and "open conversation." Tenure was not simply a sinecure for an academic or a means to search for truth in one or another academic discipline. Instead, tenure was a right and privilege that obligated the academic to participate in the life of the community. Repeatedly the interviewees spoke of faculty as "leaders," especially those who had the most important honorifics of the university—endowed chairs.

Forms of social capital also might be seen by way of the communicative structures employed within a culture. Again, at PHU, there was an emphasis on formalized structures that were circumscribed by a sense that "people know one another." When individuals spoke of the future, they expressed concern of losing what they had—that new faculty would not become involved in the organization and that people would use the university as a way station en route to another academic outpost.

One point worth noting is that symbolic and "real" resources were also in sync with one another. It would be odd, for example, to have a situation where members express support for a particular structure and not point to it as a potent organizational symbol of importance. But when it came to deciding about the amount of fiscal resources to devote to the structure, the individuals were penurious. As I will elaborate in Chapter 9, consider the stark differences between the resources devoted to the military and education on a national level, for example. The citizenry point to the military as a critical resource and Congress provides sufficient funding for individuals to carry out their work; at the same time, individuals point out how important education is, but teachers are underpaid and schools often lack basic resources such as books, computers, and (in inner-city schools), functioning toilets. Clearly, education as a public good does not garner the same support as the military.

In terms of building social capital, it is critical that adequate symbolic and "real" resources be provided. At PHU, such resources exist for formal faculty involvement in the institution. Individuals are symbolically compensated for their volunteer work by way of other individuals expressing their support and admiration. The structures of the faculty such as the senate are staffed by full-time individuals and receive funding for the myriad of activities that they undertake.

The result is that the conditions exist for the creation and accumulation of social capital. The formal and informal structures of the organization support communicative networks that not only enable individuals to come together when a crisis erupts but also facilitate interactions for renewal and support. Individuals see themselves as members of a community and, in doing so, commit themselves to involvement. Such a commitment is not simply a voluntary undertaking devoid of self-interest. Instead, we should understand that by involving themselves in the university and identifying themselves as "faculty," they are creating a situation that will advance their own self-interest as well as the organization.

Although I am trying to understand the conditions for the creation and maintenance of trust on an organizational level, I also previously noted that the presence of social capital ought not to be seen simply as a "good," as if social solidarity is without any negative consequences. As with other large research universities, there is a sharp differentiation between tenure-track faculty and the rest of the employees at PHU. Faculty do, indeed, feel a sense of ownership of the organization that leads to the creation of social capital. However, the assumption at PHU is that the category known as "faculty" comprises the ones who provide leadership and direction to the university in concert with senior administrators. Student affairs personnel and the burgeoning cadre of academic staff are frequently ignored or thought of as something akin to second-class citizens by the faculty. I did not focus on those individuals—one can attempt only so much in a focused case study—but it appears through secondary interviews and document analysis that those groups also have their own networks that lead to social capital development. Nevertheless, when one looks at a concept such as organizational trust, of necessity one needs to consider not only how a particular group creates its own social capital but also what the consequences are for other related individuals and groups. The point is less that social capital formation of one group inevitably leads to inequality and exclusion of other groups, but that when one investigates network formation, the analysis not only needs to be on those involved in the formation, but also those who are excluded or ignored.

At PHU, most observers would conclude that useful networks exist as a baseline measure. The presence of networks does not presume that trust will occur, but without it, I suggest that trust most likely will not be in evidence. Accordingly, I now turn to the various forms of the grammar of trust developed in Chapter 2 and employ them at PHU.

The grammar of trust at PHU: I previously noted that trust might be conceptualized as a distinct grammar, depending upon the situation—such that trust might be seen as an example of faith but may not have been seen as an end to itself. At PHU, however, the manner in which trust might be conceived is by way of overlapping definitions. Trust, for example, was a *repeated interaction* and a *dynamic process.* The interviewees pointed out how trust came about over time through numerous examples rather than a singular incident or major event. As I explained above, I was more intent on understanding the dynamics of two parties—faculty and administration—and what stood out in how these two parties repeatedly interacted with one another in ways that created trust. The rule-based behavior of the organization created a dynamic that demanded interactions between the two groups, and the dynamic was one of respect that took place over time. "It's in our organizational DNA," pointed out one person.

Many of the interactions were also purposeful. As a dynamic process, individuals worked with one another in discussing, debating, and implementing one or another policy pertaining to educational improvement. Expectations were built up over time that any issue being considered was worthy of discussion. Although obviously not every topic would be approved, the vast majority of times individuals approached a particular issue with a modicum of good faith—in the process and the individuals involved in it.

In any organization where representative government exists, the dynamic process also serves as a proxy for trust. Individuals ceded the right to other individuals to take up one or another issue with the expectation that the discussion was based on trust and goodwill toward the whole. In effect, the structures acted as lubricants for trust.

Conversely, trust at PHU was also an *end.* I pointed out in Chapter 2 the seeming tautology where trust could simultaneously be a process and an end, but consider the comments of the interviewees. The networks that had been built assumed frank and open communication by the faculty. The community was one where individuals knew one another and the assumption was that people should be involved. Socialization was implicit and informal, but it nevertheless existed, and what new recruits learned was that the community was important. Faculty went back and forth over their careers from the professorate to the administration and back to the faculty. Although such actions lead to additional consequences, one end is that trust became part of the social fabric.

I noted in the previous section how trust can also function as a reciprocal *exchange*. Faculty at PHU frequently cede the right to the administration to make decisions, but they do so in part because they also recognize that the administration will ask them for advice or to make a decision on other issues. The administration recognized that the faculty not only had particular expertise on an issue, but that they had a right to proffer an opinion on whatever issue they so desired. The faculty saw the administration more as colleagues than as opponents—a viewpoint that is increasingly rare on many campuses. The result was that a great deal of open communication existed between both groups because they trusted one another.

As with any culture, when norms are violated, the observer gains the best perspective about the meanings individuals give to actions; what is implicit is frequently not discussed but assumed. Thus, when the Board of Trustees some years ago tried to mandate new requirements pertaining to faculty work, the faculty rose up in protest. Their protest had as much to do with the policies trying to be ham-handedly implemented as with the betrayal of trust. The exchange had been broken.

PHU is also not a unionized faculty. Although a handful of individuals over the years tried to create a union, they were always resoundingly defeated. However, when the board tried to implement new policies, a union vote was again put to the test. If the exchange could not be based on trust, the faculty decided, it would be formalized by way of a union contract. The board backed down, some regents resigned, the faculty did not unionize, and the fabric that had been torn asunder was gradually stitched back together. The parties recognized that trust was in their mutual interests.

An additional interesting observation about the PHU faculty pertains to the grammar of *faith*. Obviously, the vast majority of faculty had little, if any, experience at the institution prior to their faculty appointment. As with most research universities, there is a bias against hiring one's graduate students for a faculty position. Although some individuals may have been undergraduates at PHU, most were not. Consequently, individuals arrived to the institution with their own notions of trust based on their own interpersonal foibles and strengths as well as their graduate school experiences and previous employment socialization.

Thus, in some respects, the creation and maintenance of trust is no small feat: individuals continually enter and exit the organization and recreate its culture. The norms of the culture, however, assume that individuals will cede some of their individuality to the organization. In doing so, individuals have faith in the larger tenets of the academy and in the manner in which those tenets are enacted at PHU. That is, individuals assume that academic work has value and that basic precepts such as academic freedom, a search for truth, and more typical needs such as a salary and adequate working conditions will be provided. In Chapter 2, I suggested that trust as faith is highly conditioned and contingent. Faith neither exists as a simple test-response scenario nor as part of a complex epistemological belief system; rather, faith grows or recedes based on the ongoing interactions individuals have with one another in the organization. Thus, when individuals enter PHU, they find an organization that revolves around faith in the system. Over time the neophytes also come to gain faith when they learn how the organization functions and that when, for example, the administration says that it values faculty opinions, they actually mean it.

All of these interactions presuppose that individuals engage in trust as *risk taking*. In some respects the other side of faith is risk. Individuals have *faith* that a particular action will take place in part based on previous interactions and interpretations. But faith is not certainty that an action will occur. Organizational faith always carries it with the need to take a *risk*. Consider the manner in which the faculty proceeded with the search for a president. When the board constituted a search committee that structurally provided for fewer opportunities for faculty input, the faculty did not offer a vehement protest. They made their concerns known, but they also had faith that their voices would be heard. To proceed in such a manner was a risk. The board could have ignored the faculty. In part, the ability to engage in risk-taking behavior was because the conditions for trust had been built up over time and the parties mutually recognized that a culture of trust was in their interest. Indeed, in the next chapter, I will offer the opposite example: a board creates a search committee and faculty are excluded; the result is commotion over the number of faculty seats on the committee. Faith is nonexistent.

Trust is also an *ability*. I proffered the poignant comment by Jimmy Carter in Chapter 2 that hopelessness is all too often based "on sound judgment." The opposite is to create the ability to trust where risk taking is based on sound judgment. Russell Hardin's notion of encapsulated trust is useful here: individuals recognize that trust has useful payoffs for all parties. The faculty trust the administration because the faculty believe it is in the administration's interest to take them seriously. Trust from this position is learned over time. Finally, as should be evident, I consistently work from the idea of trust as a *cultural construction*. The importance of the case study of Prairie Home University is that individuals make meaning. The challenge of the researcher and reader is to try to make sense of these constructions. As I will show in later chapters, individuals interpret actions in manifold ways. These interpretations occur by way of the individual interactions within an organization's culture.

The culture of trust at PHU

The portrait I am painting is one of a relatively stable and consistent culture that encourages network formation that in turn engenders the conditions for trust. How does a stable and consistent culture come about and how is it maintained? I previously noted that, in order to determine if trust is evident, the three primary parameters of a culture to investigate are the members' *shared experiences*, the extent to which the culture enables *learned experiences*, and the *conditionality* of the culture.

On a surface level, one may assume that similar organizations will share a common language and way of doing things. Traditional four-year colleges and universities, for example, in general all have a system of tenure and promotion that is more similar than different. Further, the tempo of academic life remains remarkably consistent even with the advent of distance learning. The academic year begins around Labor Day and ends in May. Summer term is still a time when significant numbers of faculty and students are absent from campus. Midterms, finals, commencement, homecoming, and a host of other terms are easily understood regardless of whether the institution is in California or Vermont or if the professor is a historian or engineer. However, to assume that all institutions are similar because of such surface-level comparisons would be akin to stating that all traditional cultures are equally similar because they also have seasons, ceremonies, familial patterns, and rituals of socialization. The challenge is to understand not simply how organizations (or traditional cultures) have surface-level similarities but to understand the unique aspects of a culture that enable members to interpret daily life from similar perspectives.

Therefore, at one level, PHU is similar to its peer institutions. What enables the organization's participants to develop trust, however, is the degree to which they share collective interpretations that recreate themselves over time. Consider the advice the members gave to a new president. Individuals consistently pointed out that the faculty saw themselves as engaged in governance, the faculty and administration were allies, and a key aspect of faculty life was to be involved in the life of the university and to speak out when warranted. Such advice will not be heard on all campuses. Indeed, at many institutions, faculty will eschew involvement in governance; faculty will view the administration with suspicion, if not hostility; and speaking out on campus matters will either be perceived as a waste of time or potentially harmful to one's career.

As with many other colleges and universities, PHU has long-term members who share a high degree of autonomy—the faculty. However, the experiences that these individuals shared were generally actions that helped create a culture of trust. Individuals spoke about the need for faculty input on the creation of committees and how frank and open communication was assumed. The movement back and forth from the professorate to the administration enabled individuals to see the organization from more than a single focus. Ironically, on many campuses, there is often a resignation that faculty do not see the full range of challenges that confront the organization. "They have tunnel vision," one person once told me and mixed his metaphors: "They can only see the trees of their department rather than the forest of the university." The result on many campuses is to keep faculty involvement in governance to a minimum and to increase administrative prerogative and power. At PHU, the opposite occurred. Over time the culture fostered engagement, and in doing so, one can reasonably assume that faculty were able to see the academic forest.

When I write of shared experiences, a reasonable question is to ask how people learn about these experiences. Indeed, at PHU, senior faculty worried over whether new faculty would be as engaged as they had been. Perhaps such a concern is common, somewhat akin to individuals recalling what they had done "when I was a boy" and lamenting that the new recruits have an easy time of it. But such a concern at PHU also implicitly recognized that a common way of participating in the life of the university actually existed, that individuals had to learn about it, and that it was not permanent, but transitory, conditioned by the interpretations and preferences of the new members.

Interestingly, socialization at PHU was informal and implicit rather than focused and explicit. I have visited a college, for example, that has a unique style of teaching. They assume that new faculty—regardless of rank and age—will not know how to teach in a way consistent with the mission of the institution. In consequence, all new faculty co-teach during their first year with experienced faculty in order to learn a key cultural aspect of the organization. At PHU, individuals learn from watching others; learning in part involves understanding when a cultural code has been violated. When the board seemed to violate a central tenet of academic life, for example, the faculty became involved on multiple levels. One reason for vetting appointments on committees with the Faculty Senate is to solicit involvement from a wide cadre of individuals rather than a narrow swath of "the same old faces."

The result is that faculty at PHU arrive with broad assumptions about academic life and they fill in the canvas based on what they experience and how they interpret those experiences. A "how to" manual is obviously absurd at such an institution; instead, faculty get to know one another and in doing so, the university. Trust permeates the culture of the organization rather than being carried by a charismatic individual.

Consider how different the socialization experience is at PHU as opposed to other institutions such as the military or a business. The military has a strict code of behavior. Individuals learn explicitly how to behave or face the consequences. A business frequently spends a portion of its resources on training and renewal. Even in organizations that encourage personnel involvement in decision making, there is rarely the assumption that the workers actually own the organization and should provide direction and guidance. At PHU, however, faculty arrive with fundamental assumptions about their role in academic life, and they find a consistent message. Such consistency enables trust not only to be maintained but also to evolve as new members arrive. A rupture, or revolution, of course, may always occur insofar as human activity is conditioned rather than predetermined. However, the cultural conditions of academic life have created a web for PHU that has balanced stability with change and enabled trust to flourish.

The cultural conditions of academic work at PHU

I made a distinction in Chapter 4 between what I termed "institutional networks" and "intellectual networks." Although they do not need to be in competition with one another, there is an increasing tendency to see them as such. Interviewees at PHU commented on how newer faculty were more likely to be concerned about their disciplinary affiliations rather than those currently at the institution. At the same time, up to this point, even those individuals who are most respected for their disciplinary knowledge—distinguished university professors—saw as part of their responsibility to be involved in the life of the university.

If institutional networks occur by way of organizational structures that help create norms of obligation and reciprocity, then PHU is an example of a university with plentiful opportunities for social capital. I noted earlier how much of this analysis is circular: networks create social capital that in turn creates a sense of trust that enables more investment in social capital so that network bonds become stronger. In many respects, such an observation is not unlike how capital functions in a capitalist economy: an individual earns capital, invests it, and the investment provides greater returns, which in turn are invested and so on. In this light, networks constitute and are constituted by social capital. Two questions arise. Does a bad investment ever occur, and what happens if a bad investment happens? That is, surely social capital simply does not increase as if organizational networks are an ever-expanding economy. Surely, boom and bust cycles happen similar to what takes place in a capitalist economy. I also noted earlier that, as Bourdieu would observe, not everyone succeeds. Those who are on the margins—academic staff, for example—may have their own economies, but they are marginal to what exists in the mainstream.

As I will later discuss, networks are by no means deterministic and self-generating. To the contrary, they are fragile and capable of being destroyed in a relatively short time or gradually over a number of years. Humans create and sustain networks. In consequence, individuals are just as capable of destroying them as maintaining them. A hiring committee can never be certain of the kind of individual they hire for president; a judgment will be made on an individual's past track record, references, and responses to questions in an interview. To a certain extent, yesterday can be a useful predictor for tomorrow—but it certainly is not absolute. PHU could have assumed they were hiring one kind of president or provost and discovered that they did not. They also could have hired a president who went against the grain for one reason or another or had the sense that faculty should be involved in governance or that the faculty voice could be rejected.

The board might have created a search committee with fewer faculty members on it for the simple reason that new board members felt that PHU had too much faculty voice. Indeed, public boards of trustees are perhaps the most unstable structure in postsecondary education at the present. Individuals join boards for any number of reasons; their desire to become more centrally involved in the affairs of the campus is greater today than at any time over the last 50 years. Whether such involvement is good or bad, I will save for another time, but one result of board involvement could be that faculty engagement lessens. The PHU board could have ignored the faculty both formally and informally and hired someone who explicitly rejected the ethos of faculty governance.

To be sure, such an action might provoke a reaction. What I hope to have demonstrated is the relative strength of networks at PHU. Trust involves a mutuality among parties that is embedded not in transitory structures or individuals but instead in the culture of the organization. Just as the faculty were able to coalesce and fight what they saw as attacks on faculty by the boards some years ago, they certainly could have come together and worked against an administration that sought to override faculty authority. However, whenever such actions arise, the possibility exists not only for success and evidence of further network development but also for failure and the dissolution of the network. Investment in the stock market may generate additional income, but it also may dissipate it. And with its dissipation, obviously, comes the erosion of trust.

If formal faculty networks erode, it is also possible that informal institutional networks may erode as well. A desire to attend voluntary ceremonies, holiday events, and the like may evaporate insofar as the culture is no longer seen as supportive. At the same time, one must remember that networks exist on multiple levels. The organizational networks may be diminished whereas departmental networks might increase. Faculty may lose trust in the central administration and fail to work with them on organizational issues, but an increase in trust may occur at the departmental level on issues germane to the particular set of faculty with whom one works on a daily basis.

The other danger for network erosion comes from competing networks; the PHU faculty expressed such a sentiment about new arrivals. The intellectual networks of the academy are in large part out of the hands of institutional leaders. Whether an intellectual network increases or recedes has little to do with what an institution does. Thus, intellectual networks have the power to influence what takes place on a campus, but institutional networks are relatively powerless to stem the development of disciplinary affiliations.

As with the vast majority of postsecondary institutions, PHU faces the retirement of a significant number of senior faculty over the next decade. If PHU follows the trend of virtually all postsecondary institutions, the hiring patterns will be twofold. On the one hand, new tenure-track faculty will be hired from graduate schools and other institutions. On the other hand, there will be a smaller percentage of tenure-track faculty as part-time faculty are utilized as a cost-cutting measure. The result will be a larger percentage of individuals who have less interest in, presumably, institutional networks. The new tenure-track faculty will be more involved with intellectual networks, and the part-timers will have few networks to call upon. Although it is certainly true that the tenure-track faculty may recreate what currently exists and maintain a high level of involvement with institutional networks along with their intellectual networks, such a development is by no means assured.

What will be the future, then, for PHU? Just as no one can predict the future with precision, an equally significant mistake would be to assume that an organization's conditions are unchanging or it is impossible to orchestrate any action whatsoever. PHU is an example of an organization where trust is in evidence and the culture has nurtured trustworthiness. But as conditions change, perhaps a more focused consideration might be given to how to socialize individuals into PHU. A formalized system of socialization for new tenure track faculty might offer a way for individuals to learn not only about PHU but also the import of the institution's networks. The point, of course, is not simply to maintain and enhance productivity, although that is surely a useful goal.

In addition, for the foreseeable future, the institution is where the academic will spend his or her time. While noninstitutional affiliations will continue to arise and expand, the college and university will also remain as the locus for the vast majority of faculty. Insofar as the campus will be the intellectual home of individuals, more consideration might be given to finding ways to increase the social capital of the organization in order to enhance the potential for trusting environments.

Finally, I mentioned three other groups at PHU. Student-affairs personnel and academic staff have their own networks, but they appear to be second-class citizens, marginal to the organization. They need to be given ways to enter into meaningful participation in the university. Part-time faculty do not even have organizational networks; they are hired in a manner akin to day laborers and go home when their job is done. If they are going to become a more significant cadre of the organization, then they need to be socialized into the institution. To ignore the entry of new workers into the organization is to place the institution at risk insofar as networks will be nonexistent, social capital formation will not take place, and trust will be absent.

In turbulent environments the status quo will not hold. PHU finds itself with a healthy culture that has functioning networks and a wealth of social capital. The challenge is to adapt these networks to a changing environment so that social capital formation increases and trust is maintained. Such a challenge is most likely a test of the common bonds of affiliation. In what follows, I offer a contrasting portrait of an organization without networks, social capital, or trust.

CHAPTER SIX

The Dissolution of Community

Dysfunctional University (DU) has experienced an unprecedented level of acrimony over the last decade amongst the faculty, administration, students, and Board of Trustees. DU is a large public institution that has followed the well-traveled route of numerous other public institutions: from a 19th-century small college to a technical institution and finally to a university with over 20,000 students and 1,000 faculty. Although the institution is not a member of the AAU, DU has earned a reputation for a decent faculty and a reasonable level of student competence. The sciences, engineering, and professional fields such as business are stronger than the humanities, arts, and social sciences. Over the years, DU has taken pride in college athletics, especially football, and a significant portion of the state looks fondly on DU as a local institution—although that fondness has more to do with sports than with academics.

DU does not have any academic or cultural distinctiveness other than being a well-regarded regional institution with a good football team. Over the last generation, strategic plans have come and gone, as have university presidents. Fund raising and capital campaigns have not compared to what major public and private institutions have attempted, and the campus has the traditional look of a public institution that is not receiving sufficient funds from the state to maintain an infrastructure that is up-to-date, much less cutting edge. Indeed, state support for public higher education has always been modest; the citizenry have paradoxically looked suspiciously at DU as an elitist campus with a significant concentration of faculty who are outsiders, while at the same time, they have supported DU's success on the gridiron.

The saving grace—some might say "curse"—has been the football team. The one area where DU has a claim to excellence has been on the football field. College sports have played an important role in the institution for much of the 20th century. Many would say that the "brand" of the institution is known as "Football U." Rivalries are intense, and autumn Saturdays bring thousands into town. The alumni have a fierce loyalty to the university more because of the winning ways of the football team than for faculty accomplishments or university outreach to the state. DU has played well in its conference and has a vast following in the state, with the alumni, students, faculty, and especially the Board of Trustees.

At the same time, the institution faces the typical pressures most, if not all, of higher education faces in the 21st century. Deferred maintenance is a constant concern. Growing demands from different constituencies call for increasing some areas and downsizing others, all of which necessitates fiscal resources. Technological changes point toward a radically different infrastructure for information than simply a singular structure known as a "library," but DU lacks the capacity to keep pace with premier institutions. Football at DU, as with most other institutions, does not generate vast sources of revenue for the entire institution, and often is not even a revenue center.

For over a decade, there has been a considerable amount of dissension and disagreement between primarily the faculty and the Board of Trustees. Although faculty on most campuses often have but a dim recognition of what the Board of Trustees does, or even who the members are, the DU board has become "public enemy number one" to the faculty. The feeling is mutual. The board finds the faculty to be an annoyance who do not understand their proper role in the governance of the institution. The senior administration, for the most part, has found itself caught in the middle of these warring factions, such that one president was fired and another resigned under pressure. The events that have erupted over governance are useful as a tale for understanding what occurs when trust is absent. In what follows, I tell that story; the data was obtained through interviews with 29 individuals. As I discuss, although everyone consented to be interviewed, I have never undertaken a case study where there was so much hesitancy and fear about speaking with me, in large part because the interviewees felt the board might exact retribution. After outlining the culture that exists at DU that enables such fear to exist, I then turn to a discussion of locating trust in a dysfunctional situation and what such a culture implies for institutional well-being. The moral of the tale can be told at the outset: little good comes about in an organization when trust is absent.

The board reigns supreme

"It all starts with our problem with the board," explained one professor. "The chair runs DU like it's a plantation, and the faculty are the slaves." "There's a climate here unlike other institutions," commented another professor. "It's based on fear and intimidation, that if you speak out, you'll get in trouble." One individual contradicted himself by saying, "It's not something I think about when I get up in the morning. Sometimes you can overdraw the problems. But then you hear things, and you just can't believe it. It's hard to shake off when you go home at night."

Over the last 20 years, when I conducted a campus case study, I occasionally heard a professor complain about the fear of speaking up and confronting one or another disagreeable policy. On some campuses, more than a single professor has spoken about their fear of the administration and often one person on a campus— frequently the president—comes in for a great deal of criticism. But I have never experienced the degree of concern I encountered at DU. Some individuals would not speak with me because it was too "dangerous." One individual said to me, "I'm only speaking to you because I've been told you're an okay guy and this is confidential." I had been told beforehand that I could not tape the interview. Others spoke about threats that had been made by a board member or someone related to the board. One person mentioned late-night anonymous phone calls suggesting that the person stop being so vocal. A senior professor only agreed to meet with me if I spoke with the individual off campus. Another arranged the meeting in a secondary office when the campus was virtually deserted; the individual told me I should not go to the person's main office because the department chair might see me and the professor would get in trouble.

I received agreement to do interviews at DU only after considerable delay. Although I had not gone to DU to do a case study of the contretemps between the board and the faculty, the view was that an outsider could provoke further problems. Indeed, my visit was not announced—why should it be?—but individuals were still concerned that they might be seen with me. The point here is not really whether these individuals had any basis for their fear. I am more concerned about their interpretation of their campus culture. Their perception of DU's culture was the opposite of PHU. Whether they had any basis for their fears is one matter, but the larger concern is that trust clearly was absent. What had happened for such a climate to develop?

One outspoken professor complained, "It's ridiculous. People hesitate to speak out. There are examples of where people's merit raises have been influenced because they spoke up." "The climate has just gotten steadily worse," said another, and a third added, "They fired the president. I think that's what just did it. Many of us thought if they can fire him, what about us?" "The board just pushes us around," said one person over dinner and another person chimed in, "We're nothing special. They push everyone around." "To say that the board is heavy-handed," added a long-term faculty member "is an understatement. We are a public institution and we are supposed to have public meetings, but the board meetings are a sham. Everything gets run out of the chair's office."

The chair of the board was seen to have the rest of the board in his pocket. Roughly a half-dozen of the board members either worked for the chair's company or for the chair. "He appointed them," said one individual, "or actually he got his friends in the legislature to appoint them." "This is cronyism at its worst," said one person. "A board member votes on a contract to have something fixed, or some construction project, and then months later you find out his brother or cousin got the contract." "The conflicts of interest are common knowledge," explained another. "It's an open point of discussion in the local press. But he's just defiant. He could care less." "I think he [the board chair] is kind of prickly," explained the president who would ultimately resign. "He thinks he's acting in the best interest of DU. He went to DU and it's just his background, really, not to be pushed around. He feels if the faculty push, he'll be dammed if he doesn't push back."

"How did it start?" asked one professor rhetorically. "There's probably not one thing, but it's just kept coming. Ever since he got on the board." (The chair has been a member of the board for over 20 years.) Another added, "It predates him. Isn't this really bigger than us, too? The people who get on the board just don't always make sense." Although the individual's comment has a modicum of truth, it is also apparent that DU is unique. The vast majority of postsecondary institutions do not have a palpable fear on the part of the faculty of the board. Indeed, when faculty express concern or anger, it is usually with their administration.

The board chair cared passionately about football; a losing football season was cause for angst and action. NCAA violations had been numerous. Football coaches had been fired, and the board chair often appeared to be the one directing who stayed and went in the football program. A coach appeared to have been fired not by the president but by the board chair. A president appeared to have been sent to meet secretly with another university's coach to see if he would be interested in taking the job of the incumbent; the result of the meeting was that the president resigned. For their part, the faculty criticized the lack of institutional control of the athletic program and worried that the president had lost control of the university.

When the president announced one January that he would become president of another institution in the fall, the board immediately removed him from the presidency and told him to move to a smaller office. They appointed an interim president and then gave that individual a contract without conducting a search. When that president resigned after improprieties that led to a faculty sanction, the board appointed a member of the board as president.

Other allegations pertained to perceived shady business dealings of the board and improper fiscal matters that benefited the chair's company. The chair also appeared to have a great deal of political influence with the legislature and the governor. He backed governors with significant financial donations, and members of the legislature often appeared to be his disciples; they gained public office, it was claimed, because of the far-reaching influence of the board chair. Cross the board chair and your political future was in jeopardy.

The board also made decisions pertaining to areas such as admissions, tenure, and curricula that many individuals see as typically within the domain of faculty. "The board intrudes in large, egregious ways," noted a campus leader. Although shared governance is undoubtedly a nebulous area where the parameters of authority frequently conflict from campus to campus, what appeared different at DU was the degree to which the board insinuated itself into the decision making of the institution rather than the administration. Issues such as "grade forgiveness" or standards for admission might receive the imprimatur of a public board, but the bulk of the decision lies in the delicate decision-making minuet of the administration and faculty. "Program mergers and program eliminations have come from the board," said one individual, and another added, "Sometimes I think they are simply whimsical—they use no data to make a decision, and at other times it's pure retribution. They don't like someone and his program gets in trouble." At DU, it is the board that delved into these matters with vigor and developed policies in which the faculty frequently had little, if any, say before they were voted on by the board. It is the board who set faculty salaries, and some will say they even decided on the raises of particular individuals. "I wrote a book and won an award one year," lamented a professor, "but I also had spoken out. I did not get a raise and others did."

Most of the board's decisions took place with little apparent controversy on the part of board members. Although the university was forced to adhere to open-meeting laws, when the board met the sessions were rarely controversial and votes were virtually always unanimous. It seemed to many observers that board members met behind closed doors in violation of open meeting laws. The result was that various news agencies sued the university for violations of such laws. "The board is insular. There's an unwillingness to debate issues which leads to paralysis," commented a senior faculty member. One individual who supported the board made a similar comment, "They [the board] feel victimized, victims of the faculty. In the board's mind they are trying to do what's right, and they are always criticized, no matter what, so they hunker down." One person elaborated:

> What's ironic is that if they did some of these things out in the open, it would not be terrible—but it would be open to debate. The chair has a particular vision for the university as a public institution. I think it's the wrong vision, but there's no vehicle to discuss it. When you couple that with the actions that I think are illegal or unethical it

makes for a poisoned atmosphere, just plain toxic.

Others also commented on the board's view of the university. "We're a polytechnic to them," said one person, "I really don't think they see a role for the social sciences, much less the humanities. History—who needs it!" A second person noted, "In one breath they want us to be like Silicon Valley and in the next they want us to be a community college offering trade courses. You can't do both, but they don't understand that." A third person said, "Their view is irrelevant. Even if they had a great vision, they're unable to enact it because it's so corrupt." A fourth asked, "None of them have graduate degrees. Do you think graduate education is a priority?" A fifth summarized, "Football is the extent of the vision. A winning season means we're successful. Somebody could win the Nobel Prize and our quarterback could win the Heisman. Who do you think would be more important?"

The result of the contretemps was not only a sense of bad feeling between the two bickering factions. A university does not simply come to a halt when the faculty and board do not get along; students still attend classes and teachers still teach. However, the processes of governance and decision making come unglued. During the fall festival, several students conducted themselves in a manner that was insulting to minority students. Although the actions were obviously objectionable, the Faculty Senate's various committees had virtually dissolved because of the overwhelming obsession with matters pertaining to the board. They did not give attention to the students' behavior. "Our committee structure has stopped," said one person. "I know what they [the board] do is a pain, but life goes on. We should be making decisions about academic things, but the senate doesn't even function that way now. It's like all that matters is the board, all the time."

The faculty had become unable to focus on anything other than the machinations of the board. However, high-performing universities have faculty who take ownership and pride in their programs and curricula. Simply stated, it is hard to take ownership for a product where the individuals have little, if any, input. "The committees are defunct," summarized one individual. The result was that, as one professor observed, "This is a comfortable place for mediocrity. People don't focus on quality. If too many suggestions come from someone about changing this or that you get the sense that you should shut up and sit down." "I like teaching," commented another. "I think we do a pretty good job in the classroom. But it's not a point of emphasis for us since so much else is going on."

The university also ran afoul of external authorities. As I shall elaborate on in Chapter 9, trust develops not only within an organization but also by an organization with external constituencies. The accreditation association for DU conducted investigations and came to conclusions that cast the institution in a negative light. The constant conflict and the perceived inappropriate actions of the board placed the institution under constant scrutiny by the media. Alumnae also began to question the board's actions. The perception that the board chair was using the institution as a personal fiefdom made the public goodwill for the institution evaporate.

Another by-product of the ongoing controversy was that recruiting and retaining faculty had become more difficult. Hiring of senior faculty was often made more difficult because the problems were often on everyone's mind. Unlike some institutions where faculty were on best behavior when trying to recruit senior professors, nothing got swept under the rug at DU. "On the outside, you wouldn't notice anything," one individual explained. "We look like a typical campus. It's not like there are shoot-outs in the street. But the faculty feel battered down. A 'how are you' provokes a long response. It scares off some individuals." Salaries also had not kept pace with the rest of the nation. "We're not competitive. So you end up asking why people would come here?" stated one person. Another individual added, "It exhausts others. Faculty increasingly either leave or retire." A final person noted, "It's not very mysterious what's happening. The climate is poison. Salaries are low. People who are valued can go elsewhere, so we lose some of the best and brightest."

The response by the faculty and other constituencies to these various perceived assaults and threats was multiple and ongoing. "Keep a low profile and you won't get shot," advised one individual. A second person said that he gave advice to new faculty that is generally good advice for all new faculty—yet even the advice had a DU twist: "No assistant professor should serve on any university committee, especially the senate. Don't raise your head. Don't stick out. Just stay in your office, teach, publish." The interesting comment here is that generally such advice pertains to time. Individuals believe that early-career faculty should spend their time in areas that will improve their chances of getting tenure. It is a truism that research counts more than service at a research university. However, the individual's caution had less to do with suggesting activities that increased a candidate's chance for getting tenure than with avoiding activities that would get the candidate known by the board.

Although individuals expressed a fear about speaking out, many did. "It's absolute warfare," said one person. "They think they can wear us out," said another. "We're like in a death match with them. This won't end until one of us is gone. Is it possible to function without the faculty?" asked a third. "He [the board chair] has to go," said a fourth. "He's intemperate, vindictive, and a power monger. There is no alternative to his leaving." A fifth said, "It's the old saying, you can't teach an old dog new tricks. He is what he is and he's unrepentant. It's a standoff."

Students boycotted classes. Faculty made presentations publicly and privately to elected officials. The student government and nine other campus groups voted no confidence in the board or called for its members to resign. The Faculty Senate repeatedly passed resolutions that expressed no confidence in the board, its chair, and most recently, expressed concern over the president's lack of autonomy from the board.

Unlike many campuses where the senate is composed of a select club of faculty and the premier research faculty frequently absent themselves from the meetings, at DU participation is widespread and deep. "I suppose one thing you could say is that this has brought us together," lamented one individual. "The divisions you see on some campuses between the humanities and the sciences or the professions are less evident here," explained another. "We're like people in an abused relationship, unfortunately," said a third. "We stick together." "We have battle fatigue, though," said one person, "I was involved, but you just can't keep doing it. I'm doing the minimal to get by."

One interesting point is that the faculty in general and the members of the senate in particular have more access to senior administrators than on many other campuses. Unlike many large campuses where the academic vice president or one of his or her minions deals with the senate, at DU it is not uncommon for the senate president to confer regularly with the president. The board, in an effort to make amends after a particularly vituperative moment, agreed to let a faculty member sit on the board. Although the result did not produce any visible change in the way the board operated, it was evidence of a structural change. Indeed, structural change frequently appeared to be on the minds of faculty, administration, and even the board.

"I've been here over 20 years," said one person. "The voice of sanity on campus has been the senate." "The senate is like other groups that rise and fall based on the leadership, but overall it's been very courageous," said another. "I admire anyone who leads the senate," said a third. "It's tough having to deal with the board." "We lobbied for a long time to get someone on the board; it's a significant step," offered a fourth. "A faculty place on the board doesn't solve problems, but it moves us closer." "Expand the size of the board, dilute the power of the few," said another individual. Eventually the faculty position on the board was seen like much else: "One person can't overwhelm the others. It's a sham."

Other individuals pointed out that the senate tried to rectify problems, but it was impossible. "Sure, they pass resolutions. We feel good after venting, but what's been accomplished?" "This place is incredibly centralized, and all the power is with the board. It's old-style management. Old style is a mistake, but when the people who wield the power are also corrupt, it leads to what you see now," commented another individual. "The senate has held people's feet to the fire. Good for them," said another person. "But I don't see any change. I think sometimes faculty want to feel that they're in the right, even if we lose. It's not strategic. I don't know what I'm suggesting, but I'm not sure if passing another resolution will do the trick." "The problem is not only with the board," added an additional person. "Sure, they're horrible. But shouldn't there be some clever solution we've come up with, a new way to get things done or something, which would have gotten us out of this by now?"

Two individuals I interviewed supported the board, but even they were circumspect. "In the 1970s, we had a board that rubber-stamped everything. They were not hands-on and we just rocked along. New members have new ways of acting. This board focuses on the bottom line. They may do things the wrong way, sometimes, but their decisions are right." The other board supporter made essentially the same point: "The board is not sensitive to the way they do things. But the board has bent over backwards to make this a better institution." The argument here, then, was that the board used to be provided with information that they wanted to hear and unpleasant news was kept from them; with the arrival of the current board chair 20 years ago, the role of the board changed. They may have been clumsy in their decision making, but they made the right decisions.

Obviously, the vast majority of the faculty felt otherwise. As I discuss below, I also question whether one consistently can make right decisions in the wrong way. To be sure, in any organization where lines of authority are as obscure as in a college or university, a leader is bound to make or implement a correct decision in the wrong way at some time or another. The problem, of course, is only amplified in an organization when those who are involved in decision making believe that the processes are frequently as important as the outcomes themselves. However, one must pause when confronted with a situation such as DU. An occasional gaffe in the way a decision was made that nevertheless generates a positive outcome will usually be overlooked, but as I have discussed here, the board's actions are not perceived as occasional. Instead, the community looks at the board's work as remarkably consistent. It is not simply that on occasion they wielded a blunt instrument when a scalpel would do; rather, the board consistently acted without regard to process or outcome—other than, for example, trying to increase the winning ways of the football team.

Discussion

I do not wish to delineate the problems that exist at DU in order to come up with a consultant's brief about what changes are needed. Indeed, as with any case study of an organization's culture, solutions to conundrums such as those listed are not self-evident or causal. Although virtually everyone will agree that the campus has been engulfed in internecine battles for the better part of a decade, solutions to the problems are not widely shared. Or rather, some solutions may be agreed upon by a large swath of the community, but the suggestions are not really solutions. They are simply acts. Many agree, for example, that the chair of the board should resign. Others will suggest that the appointment criteria for membership on the board need to be overhauled. Whether I agree with such suggestions is moot; the larger issue is that simply a single action, or a series of acts, will not repair a culture that has disintegrated into mistrust. Trust is not in need of repair, as if some part needs to be replaced in an otherwise healthy structure. Trust is absent. What, then, does Dysfunctional University tells us about trust and organizational culture?

The absence of trust at DU

Unlike PHU, the focus was on the relationship of the faculty to another key constituency—the Board of Trustees. However, the broken relationship between the two parties was much more pervasive than simply a constituency argument where one group does not get along with another. Indeed, the Board of Trustees is not merely one constituency among many, but in many respects, it is the key group of any public institution. If a board functions effectively, then they are the key spokespeople for the university that will generate public support. DU's board did not fulfill this role. Instead, the majority of their effort pertained to managing internal relations. The result was that, because the relationship had become spoiled, trust was absent at all levels.

True, faculty may have come together and learned to trust one another as they fought against the board, but my focus here has been more than simply whether individuals trust other individuals. Rather, as a cultural construct, my intent has been to explore how trust's presence or absence impacts the organization's culture. The absence of trust at DU affected numerous aspects of organizational life. Committees had stopped functioning. Discussions about the future seemed futile. The retention and hiring of faculty had become difficult. Any sense of nurturing the idea that the university was a vital public good for the state was lost as the board became preoccupied with internal affairs.

Although trust may have been in evidence at some point in time, the repeated actions, or perceived actions, of the board for over a decade had enabled trust to evaporate. As I previously noted, organizational trust is unlike trust between two individuals on several levels. One individual may no longer trust another because of a single act. Individuals may learn to trust one another based primarily on their singular interactions. In organizations, however, individuals enter and leave. There is often not something akin to a romantic tryst that diminishes the trust of one individual for another. Instead, as with DU, what takes place are repeated actions over time that gradually remove one perception of organizational life and replace it with another. The result is that the faculty ended up at DU forming alliances with other campus groups to overthrow the board, but in doing so, they learned that trust was not part of the organization's culture.

Curiously, as with PHU, presidential and provostial succession played very little role in the increase or diminution of trust. Or rather, the individuals who inhabited those roles neither helped nor hindered the case for trust. Insofar as the board had dictated the terms of how people were chosen for senior-level positions, trust had been eradicated from the organizational framework such that whoever inhabited the role of president or vice president was irrelevant. Unlike many campuses where the arrival of a new president may provoke suspicion about whether the individual understands the culture of the organization, at DU such an individual is precisely what the faculty desired. They did not want a president who was perceived to be in the pocket of the board; rather, they wanted a search to be conducted that emphasized traditional characteristics of a president. In their collective consciousness, the less a new president was like the culture of DU, the better he or she would be perceived. Ironically, then, in order to rebuild the culture of DU, a first step would be to make it act like the vast majority of other institutions rather than accentuate the unique style of governance that presently existed.

We ought not to overdraw the problems that existed at DU. Just as organizational trust is not akin to individual trust, the lack of trust exhibited at DU is not analogous to the lack of trust in a state or society. The institution is, after all, a university and not a totalitarian state. Unlike the Soviet Union under Joseph Stalin or Iraq under Saddam Hussein, individuals did not fear daily for their lives. They did not mistrust family members. The complete lack of trust exhibited in a totalitarian society presents a unique set of challenges for anyone who overthrows such a regime. When a child has learned to no longer trust a parent, or neighbors eye one another suspiciously, trust will not simply spring up when the regime is overthrown.

Clearly, no such similar conditions existed at DU and it would be ludicrous to make such an allegation. However, even though individuals may be able to work with one another and alliances have been built across groups and constituencies, the culture itself was spoiled. People were able to go about their work, but any semblance of group cohesion toward organizational improvement—other than the overthrow of the board—was virtually absent. Any sense that the university was a vital resource to the state was lost in the ongoing battles within the university. Presumably, if a significant change was to occur, the resumption of trust is not something that will automatically reappear like daffodils after a winter's cold. Whether trust exists or is absent, it needs to be nurtured; the absence of networks needs to be resuscitated and over time, the reinvigoration of organizational trust will be possible.

Social networks and trust at DU

Obviously, the *forms* of social capital impede trust at DU. The formal meetings of the board have been interpreted as a charade where the trustees act out what they have decided in private. A residual effect of the pervasive influence of the board is that other than the University Senate, very few forms of deliberation function. Committees have stopped meeting. The issues in the senate itself are almost exclusively concentrated on how to deal with the board. An additional form of social capital is the AAUP chapter that some of the faculty have joined. Although the form is a useful example of a social network, once again the focus of the chapter—and its increase in membership over the last decade—can be directly attributed to the contretemps with the board. The meetings revolve around what kind of suggestions might be made to the senate to stymie the actions of the board. Although many individuals appear to participate in the senate and the AAUP, it is equally plausible that no one has to attend any meetings.

Unlike PHU where the culture is one of involvement and the norm is to participate in governance, the culture at DU is more one of trying to figure out how to respond to the pervasive influence of the board. Recall the comment made by the individual who said that assistant professors should not get involved in the academic life of the community. Another person posited that he had grown tired and dejected and just wanted to be left alone. Although one is sure to find such a comment on any campus from a disgruntled individual, the sense at DU was that such a feeling was pervasive. The portrait one gets of DU is of a Durkheimian anomie—individuals felt alienated from the organization in which they worked. The result was that few norms of obligation existed beyond the obvious—teach at the appointed time, and the like. Norms of obligation had been obliterated. Since the board appeared to be vindictive, individuals also got involved by taking a perceived risk. Unlike PHU, where communication was a given, individuals at DU were aware that if they spoke up, they might not get a raise. They could even incur the wrath of the board.

Again, I do not want to overstate the case; to an outsider, an individual's hesitation or ever fear to participate in an activity because something might happen may appear absurd. But universities, for all of their vaunted political rough and tumble, are actually quite genteel. Individuals do not regularly yell at one another. Most individuals go quietly about their work and participate in the array of academic activities if they perceive them to be worthwhile and not particularly vexing. At DU, however, the perception was that such involvement was always vexing and never worthwhile. The result was the absence of any norms of obligation.

Another way to think about norms of obligation is to consider how individuals are socialized into the organization. What did new recruits learn? What funds of knowledge and cultural resources were available and at the disposal of new individuals? They learned to keep their head down and mouths shut at DU. They discovered that speaking out will get an individual in trouble. Teaching was not of central concern and research was not as important as at other similar institutions. The topic of conversation was not on how to make the institution better in terms of academic quality but only with regard to overthrowing the board. Norms of obligation, then, were not a communicative vehicle to ensure that individuals learned to work with one another to improve the organization. If anything, the reason one met individuals from across campus was to become a quasi-coconspirator in the overthrow of the board.

I am suggesting that DU was an organization bereft of norms of obligation and suffering from a dearth of social capital formation. Funds of knowledge and cultural resources were absent. Networks were not in evidence other than to lobby for the removal of the board. As I noted in the previous chapter, I am not suggesting that simply because networks exist trust will reign supreme. However, as is evident from DU that when networks do not exist, there is little chance for trust to develop. Networks are the frameworks that enable social capital to be accrued, which enables trust to flourish. DU's networks had evaporated—with them, trust.

The grammar of trust at DU

Unlike PHU, where the various forms of grammar demanded elaboration, there was very little grammar to deconstruct at DU because trust was not in evidence. Trust, for example, was neither a *repeated interaction* nor a *dynamic process*. If anything, what occurred was the repetition of interactions that promoted mistrust. The only dynamic process that existed was a never-ending tension between the board and faculty that created organizational dysfunction. Trust was also virtually never an *end* unto itself. Insofar as networks did not exist that promoted trust, interactions revolved around a sense of disengagement and/or mistrust. Just as all organizations have cultures, so too do all organizations have processes of socialization. To say that socialization exists in an organization is saying little more than that members learn about the organization. Of course they do. The question is not if socialization exists, but what individuals learn and if that learning promotes trust. At DU individuals learned to avoid activities where trust was an end and to eschew engagement with one another.

Certain forms of the grammar of trust highlighted their absence at DU more than others. Trust, for example, was in part an *exchange* at PHU. At DU, the opposite was more likely. The two primary constituencies had no desire for any exchange whatsoever. The assumption by the faculty was that whatever the board did had ulterior motives and that the basic premises on which they operated flew in the face not only of trust creation and expansion but also of minimally acceptable ethical standards. The board similarly recognized the right of the faculty to participate in shared governance in only the most minimal of ways. The board assumed that it had the prerogative to insert itself on any number of issues, and of consequence, the faculty's influence was to be minimal.

The result was that the grammar of *faith* was entirely absent. The faculty turned to legal mechanisms such as appeals to external authorities such as the

AAUP, the accreditation association, and the state legislature. The faculty recognized that the AAUP could not exert any direct influence and that the legislature was not likely to be helpful insofar as the chair of the board extended influence far beyond the campus. The accreditation association was able to play a useful role in bringing about possible changes but not in enhancing trust. Ultimately the faculty's perception was that whatever the board said could not be trusted. The faculty exhibited no faith in the board and assumed that the only way out of a perceived abusive relationship was not to assume that efforts at reform would ultimately work. Instead, their stance became that the only effective change would be in the form of a completely new board leadership.

The result was that individuals were unable and unwilling to engage in *risk taking*. I noted earlier Russell Hardin's idea of "encapsulated trust," where individuals were willing to take a risk because they acknowledged that it was in their interest to trust the other party. The opposite was true at DU. Individuals did not believe that the board operated in the best interests of the faculty or the university so they were unwilling, even unable, to engage in any risks. Trust, in effect, had been lost as an *ability* of the organization's participants. Although I am working from a *cultural* framework of trust, *rational choice* is also at work here. Indeed, it would have seemed irrational for the faculty simply to accept the actions of the board. Faculty were not only socialized to the mores of the organization but also to their discipline; many of the actions that the board engaged in ran counter to a professor's sense of self. Faculty are socialized in their disciplines to expect that they have some say in the direction of the institution, especially over academic affairs. The actions of the board seemed whimsical at best, and at worst, capricious, vindictive, and unethical.

At its base DU is a story of meaning construction run amok. Over a series of years, the faculty accumulated a consistent interpretation of how they were valued by the board and what the board found to be most important. The interactions of the board and faculty created a consistent culture. Unfortunately, that culture was much closer to an academic version of *Lord of the Flies* than what I presented in the previous chapter pertaining to PHU.

The culture of trust at DU

At PHU, I outlined how the members' *shared experiences* and *learned experiences* contributed to their interpretations of trust. I also commented on the *conditionality* of the culture which brought about and maintained networks of social capital. Recall that I previously mentioned how surface level examples may be more similar than different in academe, and that I emphasized earlier in this chapter not to overdraw the distinctions at DU. That is, the university is not a battlefield, and like PHU and countless other institutions, the school year begins in the fall and ends at commencement. Faculty are more in evidence during the academic year than in the summer, and tenure is still the process the faculty use to evaluate one another. The faculty are organized by departments, and the organization has the typical trappings of administrators—department chairs, associate deans, deans, and the like.

Outwardly, DU's organizational structure is also not very different from countless other colleges and universities. All campuses have a board that is not that different structurally from DU. Institutions have presidents that boards choose, and board members of public institutions frequently are appointed by a governor or the legislature. Although a typical response to organizational crises is to develop a structural response, the problems at DU are more cultural. Certainly, the structure of the organization might be modified in a manner to improve the flow of communication or make decisions more effective, but unless the members of DU concentrate on its culture, any structural change will be moot.

The inability of the organization's participants to develop trust is a cultural dilemma that must be faced rather than a structural one that must be adjusted. Clearly, individuals have shared experiences, but those experiences are not interpreted as building trust. Similarly, what members learn may be similar lessons, but the experiences do not necessarily engender trust. Such an observation, although hopefully obvious by now, is a useful commentary on the dynamics of organizational culture. Far too often individuals interpret the analysis of culture in organizational life from a unitary perspective that is flawed. Culture is often viewed as a "good" that exists through symbolic events such as graduation ceremonies. What we have seen at DU, however, is that culture is not necessarily a "good," and that its sweep is vast. Cultures can be dysfunctional. What members learn about the organization neither promotes trust nor quality. Culture is also something that inhabits all human interaction within the organization. Rather than a series of artifacts or events, culture is the multitude of interpretations that the actors bring to the organization as they work their way through the day.

One point that surely can be made about DU is that members have received a systematic message from the board. Cultures may be strong or weak depending upon a multitude of influences and conditions. Just as an organization's culture may be primed for high performance, cultures also may provide consistent signals and messages that the members interpret in a similar manner. The culture may be inconsistent and fragmented and may make little sense. Although such a culture may not be primed for high performance, DU is an example of a strong culture; unfortunately, it is a culture that has been spoiled by a series of messages that have provoked suspicion, antipathy, and mistrust.

The cultural conditions of academic work

Socialization occurred informally, of course, but it was consistent. That is, new members did not receive a formal introduction into the machinations of the board or a discourse on how the board functioned vis-à-vis decision making. Instead, socialization was informal—members learned through the actions of the board and then attributed meanings to those actions. At DU, individuals learned about the culture from others through ongoing consistent actions. Insofar as the university did not exist in a vacuum and individuals have multiple academic identities, the faculty constantly compared what took place at DU in relation to what they perceived to be common at other institutions. Thus, as I have suggested in previous chapters, culture is conditional. Individuals make interpretations about the organization based not only on the interactions they have within the university but also based in part on their understanding of other organizations and what is perceived to be "typical."

Cultural norms, then, are violated not only when someone transgresses long-standing behavior of the organization's culture but also when members violate norms about how the organization should function. On the one hand, when someone blithely skips a ceremony that the college or university's participants have imbued with deep symbolic meaning, then we might say that the individual has violated a cultural norm of the specific institution. On the other hand, when a group acts in a manner such as the board has done at DU, the violation is not something that goes against cultural norms because they have become the norm. The transgression is conditioned on how DU is seen in relation to other similar organizations.

DU also has a particular dilemma that places the faculty in something of a metaphoric catch-22. In part because the institution has been consumed by the crisis of the commons over the last decade, the faculty in large part are not considered to be leaders in their disciplines. Although such an observation is undoubtedly true at the vast majority of institutions—how many faculty can be considered leaders?—the result is that their natural affiliation would normally be to the organization. However, unlike other institutions, there is a disincentive to be so inclined. If the faculty were more like faculty at premier institutions, then one might reasonably surmise that they would place their emphasis on their disciplinary home outside the institution rather than the organizational one. Such an emphasis is impossible, however, given the current climate. Stellar faculty will not be attracted to a hostile environment. And thus DU finds itself in a bind.

What will be the future for DU? The temptation for the faculty will be to engage in negotiations in a manner akin to an initial peace conference: discussions about the shape of the table will preclude cultural considerations. Indeed, at some point a search process likely will commence to find a new university president, and I suspect one point of contention will be the number of seats the faculty have on the committee. Such a concern is not surprising. Yet consider how the faculty at PHU reacted with their own presidential search. Rather than have the search stall because of inadequate faculty representation, the faculty moved forward and used multiple avenues to ensure that their voice was heard. Such avenues are nonexistent at DU, and because of the lack of a common grammar of trust, the faculty will be unwilling to work with the board except in a legalistic manner.

Although structural and formalized mechanisms are useful, my sense is that if they are the only methods employed, change will not occur. To be sure, personnel changes at some point will occur with the board. Hopefully the new members will act in a manner in keeping with the most effective university boards. But simply by adding new members, the serious problems that exist will not be resolved. Trust has not merely been chipped away at in the organization—it has been obliterated. In large measure, for trust to be reinvigorated within DU's culture, the participants must invent new ways of communicating with one another within the culture. Accordingly, I now discuss a different institution where the focus will be on communication.

CHAPTER SEVEN

Communication and Trust

In the previous two chapters, I offered examples of institutions where trust either works well or is absent. One similarity in both cases is the degree to which communication played a role in the development of trust. When I speak of communication, I do not merely mean dialogue by actors pertaining to formal organizational activities. Rather, communication pertains to the multitude of manners and processes employed by an organization's actors in formal and informal ways that enable meaning to occur. As with the idea of trust, I am not suggesting an essentialized notion of communication whereby the view of communication is that it is somehow good irrespective of its usage and interpretation. As demonstrated at Dysfunctional University, communication clearly existed in manifold forms. Unfortunately for the participants at DU, however, the messages received and interpreted depressed trust.

I now offer an analysis of an institution I shall call "Salon University" (SU) for the manner in which communication takes place. I visited Salon over the course of three days, interviewing 27 individuals. I also followed up with additional phone calls and off-site interviews, and examined various documents such as the institutional strategic plan and campus newspapers. Unlike PHU and DU, however, the point of my analysis is to enable a consideration of the interrelationship of trust and communication on a university campus. An elaboration of the communicative codes employed in trust creation, maintenance, enhancement, or destruction enables in particular a better understanding of the cultural conditions of academic work, with which I will conclude the chapter.

Salon University

SU is a private institution that originated in the late 19th century. The undergraduate population is slightly over 6,000 students and there are about 4,000 graduate students. Less than 10% of the students are Hispanic or African American. Most students are full-time; a majority come from the surrounding area, although the institution increasingly draws clientele from throughout the United States. Over two-thirds of the undergraduates live on campus. They have close to 2,500 faculty in approximately a dozen schools, including medicine. Over the last decade, the reputation of SU has steadily increased, as have the national rankings of several of its schools and departments. SU thinks of itself as an elite research university where teaching is valued and a commitment to the region is honored.

The current president has been in office for only a handful of years, but he has held previous presidencies. He is popular with the faculty and students and, as I shall discuss, is very visible on campus. His Board of Trustees resembles that of other major private universities, with over 50 members, many of whom are industrial, business, and political leaders. Similarly, the faculty have a senate akin to that of other large universities. The senate largely focuses on topics that pertain to academic matters or faculty rights and responsibilities. Although the Faculty Senate is not in disrepute, it also is not looked on as a central vehicle for decision making, or an organizational body that is thinking strategically about the future of the university. The university runs on a form of revenue-centered management (RCM) where individual deans control their own budgets. Subsequently, the central administration is relatively poor because it is not a revenue center. Although decentralization has several benefits, one consequence is that a strong organizing direction from central administration is relatively difficult to achieve. A new administration has tried to be more aggressive in setting a university agenda.

"I want to work with the senate," noted the provost, "They have a critical role to play as a representative of the faculty." Although the provost's comment appears to reflect the import of the Faculty Senate, he went on to say, "Senates can get lost on trivia. You have to energize them. I want them to get on board with our plans. If they're going to focus on minor issues that are tangential to moving SU forward, then their role will be marginal."

Others commented that the senate's role was not significant. "People who get on the senate," said one person, "are single-issue folks. They've got an ax to grind." Another person added, "They act like a trade union, so most of us don't get involved." A third person said, "I don't see anything wrong with the senate. I don't know that much about it, frankly. It's just not for me." A fourth person summarized, "I guess I'd advise a young person to stay away from service on the senate only because they should be publishing. But if someone else at a later stage of their career wanted to get involved, I guess that's fine. It seems like a waste of time, but some people seem to enjoy it."

Another individual noted that even at a quasi-honor convocation, the faculty did not show up: "The president came to the first meeting to hand out research awards to outstanding faculty and only about half of those called were in attendance." Another professor said, "There is a general belief that the senate is a moribund institution." A former senate member commented, "There isn't even a roll call or attendance taken. You can be a representative and never go to a meeting. No one would know or care." A former leader of the senate said dispiritedly, "Sometimes when folks are elected for a three-year term they will resign, back out, or give up before their term is up."

Ideas currently tend to come from the president and provost. "It's pretty clear what they want to do. They're always talking about it," commented one person. "Graduate education is a priority," said the provost, "as is the establishment of residential colleges, enhancing interdisciplinary work, and figuring out financial aid. Those are the priorities we need to focus on." None of those ideas emanated from the senate.

Graduate education is a useful example of how ideas and decisions get communicated. The previous provost created a committee of faculty members who studied the issue and recommended that the university create a stronger graduate dean. Not surprisingly, the new provost heard from the deans that such a proposal was an outlandish idea. They believed that a graduate dean had no money with which to work and that graduate education should be the responsibility of the individual deans. In short, the deans wanted to protect their fiefdom. The provost then created a committee primarily composed of the deans to study the issue and make a recommendation to him.

As with what happened at DU, the senate's role was to push for committee representation rather than to lobby for a particular stance. Although the atmosphere at SU is virtually the opposite of what I presented in the previous chapter, the concern over seats at a table is similar. While the stakes were much higher at DU, SU's senate appeared to be in a similar position. A senate leader mentioned as a goal, "I hope for more representation on committees that matter. I want us to be in the room when decisions are made."

When a representative body argues over who is on a committee or not, they implicitly imply that appearances at the table and in the room matter. However, more often than not, simple representation neither evinces trust nor brings about the desired result. Representation at the table may be a useful symbol, but it is a process, not an outcome. Far too often faculty confuse the two, assuming that simple representation is sufficient. Such confusion is most likely to occur when trust is absent. From this perspective, seats at a table are seen as akin to legal contracts where two parties are bound to one another. The difference, of course, is that representation assures nothing. On the positive side, individuals at SU frequently called for greater representation, but it was not in a confrontational manner. That is, individuals did not say that there was a conflict over intellectual property, for example, and they wanted to argue with the administration once they got in the room or at the table. Indeed, no issues seemed to be primary for the faculty. Similarly, the interdisciplinary centers, residential colleges, and proposals about financial aid were not projects where the senate had a leading voice. What, then, were the priorities of the senate? The answer was by no means clear.

"I'm not sure what their issues are," commented one person. The provost noted, "I think they're struggling a little with getting and maintaining an agenda." A senate leader commented, "We have so many committees of the university and of the senate that it's not clear what our cohesive message is or ought to be. And the university is decentralized as well, so sometimes it seems like we don't have our act together as a faculty, as a university community." "The deans have power, and to a varying extent the faculty in the schools," said another person, "but not faculty across campus, unless it's informal." "It's a rat race, academic life. I'm not complaining, but when you ask about 'a faculty agenda' it's just too removed for me. I do my work and I enjoy it. But I never really think about the university as a whole. A 'whole' what, I wonder?"

The individuals' comments were also reflected in a faculty satisfaction survey. Faculty were satisfied with their work and their work environment. They felt appreciated and did not have too many complaints. By and large, they were optimistic about the future. When asked about the future, most respondents offered quite positive portraits: "We'll be a better university in five years," said one and another added, "We're on our way. There's a can-do attitude right now." A third pointed out, "Faculty didn't like the previous president very much, but they respected his ability to raise money. In the long run, that has probably put us in very good stead." A fourth summarized, "I like coming to work, and I sense my colleagues have the same feeling."

Not everyone was as optimistic, of course. "I'm never really sure if they [the administration] want to hear our opinions, or if we say something they don't like we'll get our heads chopped off." "You can speak up, you just won't be heard," explained another. A new faculty member commented, "When I first got here, I was asked to be involved in governance because they thought I was peculiar in that I spoke my mind." By and large, most individuals felt that SU was an easy place to voice opinions. The larger concern was for the faculty to not merely develop a host of opinions, but a cohesive identity and sense of strategy.

"Why do we need a voice?" wondered one person. "They're doing a good enough job." Another person commented:

> The problem, if there is one, with the kind of question you're asking has more to do with the way we communicate with one another than with bad relations between us and the administration, or between the senate and the president, or things like that. We don't seem to know what's going on. When we find out, we're generally fine with it, and I'm too busy to care very much, if you want to know the truth. But if you're asking are the faculty really involved in governance in the way things run around here, the way we set a direction here, the answer has to be no, not really. I don't see that as a problem. What worries me is that we don't know what's going on so we have no way of entering the conversation.

Others commented on the lack of printed material. "Sure, we have 'Pravda'— the university's officially sanctioned news of the university's propaganda office—but there's really very little communication across the faculty." Another added, "It's a sad fact that if I want information about the university, I have to go to the student newspaper. There's very little else in thoughtful commentary—not that the student newspaper is thoughtful!" A third person added, "Sometimes there are email alerts, but those are just what they are—alerts about something, not a thoughtful comment about where we're heading." When I summarized these comments to another individual, he responded, "They're essentially correct, but I say 'thank God.' I haven't time to read endless attachments that argue some point about general education. Communication is at a level it should be."

The senate, for its part, had no newspaper, and they did not utilize the airwaves. Indeed, there was no faculty-run communicative vehicle on campus that everyone received. Although many did not see that as a concern, others pointed to a potential problem with regard to university improvement: "If we're to move forward, then people have to buy into where we're moving. Part of this has to do with education, educating people about where we're headed. Don't you need to communicate to do that?" A second person added, "I suppose we're doing what needs to be done to get better. You can feel it in the air sometimes. But this is more like a game of razzle-dazzle than some clear thought-out strategy that gets communicated on a daily basis." A third person noted, "People like to say that we have 'Pravda,' but I think that's not true. Sure, they put out the news they want us to hear. But we're kidding ourselves if we think we're clear about what we're doing, what we value. Watch a politician running for office. The in-phrase right now is 'on message.' We're not."

What is interesting is that most people did not make such comments as an indictment of the university or the administration. The university's participants generally appeared upbeat and positive about the future. Unlike DU, the board was never mentioned except in passing. The comments about the administration were cordial and respectful. Even the previous administration, although not universally liked or admired, did not come in for overwhelming criticism. One senses, however, that most people were more engaged with their own specific work and did not have a sense of the "commons." Unlike DU, no one had destroyed the commons, but no one seems to have cared for nurturing it very much either.

One primary vehicle for binding people together is by way of communicative strategies that help explain to newcomers and "old-timers," internal and external constituents alike, what the university is about and where it is heading. Such explanations had not taken place at SU. Such a strategy is more than a simple message delivered at the start of a school year or a single document that lands on every desk and is never discussed again. Communicative strategies that work are those that are systematic and well thought out, and continue to be delivered long after their initial launching.

"We have a good alumni base," said one person, "but it's not intensely loyal." Although the institution's participants applauded SU's relationship with the community and region, there was not a stifling sense of history that one finds on some campuses. "Some alums get angry over something, and we always have to contend with the region," explained one person, "but I don't think it stops us as an organization." A second person said, "We're not at odds with the region, really. I suppose if we wanted to go in some radical direction the natural conservativeness of the region might grow concerned, but it's much more implicit than a straitjacket. And the region is changing too." Another person concurred: "This is a place today where someone who wants to do something new will not be stopped by somebody saying, 'That's not the way we do it here.' There's a cumbersome bureaucracy that slows things down, but not our history." Sports also did not dominate at SU. The institution was more a campus in the present than one that looked with nostalgia about the "way we were" and tried to recreate that portrait. The strength of such a climate is that the university had the potential to face the future unshackled from the past; the weakness is that no overriding ideology seemed to guide where they were heading. There was no pervasive understanding of a comprehensive goal advanced by either the administration or the faculty.

As with any new leader, the president had been quite aggressive in trying to get to know the faculty and listen to their ideas and concerns. "The previous president never met with the senate," recalled one individual. "This one goes to the senate meetings and meets with the senate president." "He's created these salons around campus," added another person. "It seems like he holds them all the time, getting to know people." A third person said, "I like the idea of a salon, very trendy, and useful too." "We never saw the previous president," summarized a fourth individual, "This fellow is an Energizer Bunny. He's all over campus, in the press, in town. His salons are a success. It's pretty clear what he's trying to do."

"The president feels communication is essential," explained one person. The dean of the faculty commented that "the president and provost are both very active on campus and want faculty to take greater responsibility for the university." Another person noted, "His first few months here seem to be focused on getting people talking—not just to him, but to everyone. The salons are not just him giving a long-winded talk. I think he's smart enough to know faculty wouldn't attend. What they don't recognize, perhaps, is that in holding these things, he's getting people to think about the future and his vision for it." The president's style also permeated to his senior staff. The provost whom the president inherited left; the president chose a management team largely molded to his liking. Consequently, the new provost is also quite visible. "He's more approachable than his predecessor, I suppose," commented one person about the provost, and a second added, "He's also more visible; his style is to call faculty in for meetings and luncheons." "I think it's genuine," said an additional person. "He and the president are raising their visibility, but it seems right, that we need that right now. Who are we and where are we going, they seem to be asking."

"The president's rhetoric is one of inclusion, and by appearances they are more involved—but he's making his own decisions. That's not bad because he's trying to be clear, to get the vision out there," explained one person. Another person had a slightly different interpretation, "Governance is irrelevant here. Yes, we need a senate, and yes, the president recognizes that, and the provost. But I don't think really good universities, and that's what we want to be, function through formalized decision making. People get a message, grab it, and go about their business." A third person agreed: "Aren't there always messes that the new guy has to clean up? Either he inherits them or they just appear." "But this guy's response is less on the organizational chart and more on the feel for the place, the design," said another. "It's trying to get out a sense of who we are."

"It's an organic process," said a longtime faculty member. "Dialogue is expanding and there appears to be mutual support." "We need to rewrite the strategic plan and it's on the agenda," said an administrator. "But they feel before they do that there's some groundwork to cover, some invigoration." "We have to communicate with the faculty about the strategic plan," confirmed the provost. "This won't be something done in private." "It's got to be more than a survey of the faculty. It's not like the last administration was horrible, but understanding the needs of the faculty was not a priority with them. It should be now."

At the same time, communication in any organization is difficult and abstruse. As one individual commented, "I get the sense that improved communication will likely take place through individuals, not structurally across units." A second person laughed, "Is communication ever good at a university? Don't faculty always say it's bad, that faculty morale is low, things like that? Isn't that pretty predictable? But we rock along." Although the individual's comments have a degree of veracity, I suggest that communication is not simply a tap that can be turned on and off—or when an administration turns it on, there is sufficient communication and when it's off, there's none. Rather, what I argue is that the procedural aspects of communication are critical for the development and enhancement of trust. From the perspective of the faculty at SU, individuals make the mistake of focusing on communication as a structural entity that has a singular function. Instead, an organization's participants need to think of communication as a cultural undertaking that takes place over time and consider whether the effects of the processes and interpretations of communication decrease or enhance the conditions for trust.

Discussion

Clearly, the participants at SU trust one another more than at DU. My point, however, has not been to suggest that insofar as trust exists at SU that it is akin to what I portrayed at PHU or on another campus where trust is in evidence, as if all cultures where trust presides are similar to one another. An organization's culture is unique and the manner in which trust manifests itself (or does not) is peculiar to the organization. Indeed, these case studies are portraits at a point in time. As I noted in Part 1, organizational trust takes time to be created, and it can be destroyed slowly in organizations as it leaches out of the institution by inequalities of power, poor communication, anomie, and the like. But it also can be destroyed relatively quickly if structures and policies appear arbitrary and self-interested and individuals do not attend to the culture. Accordingly, one ought not to be surprised if, in a handful of years, a return visit to DU revealed that trust was still not in evidence, but it was being created—whereas at PHU or SU, trust had been rent asunder. Case studies are unique portraits aimed at revealing the specific ways a culture functions at one institution.

The lineaments of culture, however, are similar. Communication plays a central role in fomenting or depressing trust in all organizations. My purpose has been to highlight a university where communication might be portrayed in order to consider how communication relates to the ideas discussed in Part 1. I turn now to a discussion of how trust might be located via communication at SU and the role that social networks play in trust's formation. I then work through the grammar of trust and consider communication's role in the creation and advancement of this grammar, concluding with how communication helps create shared experiences.

Locating trust at SU

To speak of trust and communication necessitates an understanding of the contexts that circumscribe meaning. Linguists have defined "situated meaning" as an understanding of the specific context that is transformed and negotiated by rules of speaking, which reflects the actors' relationship to, and attitudes toward, one another and the issues under consideration (Hymes, 1974). Although rules exist in any institution, they are particularly important in an academic organization populated by highly verbal participants who frequently seek to understand underlying structures. Thus, we need to come to terms not only with the contexts in which communication takes place, such as a Faculty Senate, and the actors involved in the specific structure, such as a university president, but also the wider sociopolitical structures in which the communicative processes are embedded.

From this perspective, it is unwise to undertake analyses that focus exclusively on an organization's structure or are only outcomes related. Looking only to the formal structures of decision making or communication ignores the ways in which messages are created by the participants in the organization's culture, which in turn, impacts trust. Similarly, to argue that trust exists when individuals vote on a particular issue (as if voting raises trust and not voting decreases it) is to disregard the notion that communication transcends decisions and outcomes. Trust will not necessarily be self-evident if there is a formal means of communication such as a daily newsletter, and it will not absolutely be absent if the means of communication are highly informal. No one has ever plausibly advanced or proven the idea that any one system of decision making is better than the rest or that one style of communication is superior to others. The success of any given strategy has more to do with how the members interpret the strategy and how it is employed within a given context.

To consider the situated meaning of communication, one needs to locate trust not only in structural units but in the interstices of culture. One must identify who is and who is not involved in the organization, the venues of communication, and the formal and informal means used to communicate. Consider, for example, the multiple means of communication employed at SU. True, formal decision-making bodies existed such as the Faculty Senate, but what individuals spoke about most was the informal means of communication employed by the new president—"salons." Others pointed out that the president relied on multiple means of communication. They assumed it was a top priority for his administration to such an extent that one provost resigned, and another was brought in who not only philosophically agreed with the president but also had a similar communicative style. Informal meetings, lunches, and coffees with faculty from throughout the campus became a cultural norm.

No one style is superior or the only example of "what works." Far too often individual case studies provide a successful portrait of one or another undertaking with the assumption that all organizations should conduct their work in a similar fashion. Postsecondary organizations, however, are far too protean for such an assertion. At PHU, for example, the culture had a tradition of formalized procedures of communication and decision making that seemed to work quite well. If a new individual came in and overlooked that process, opting instead for the more informal methods at SU, problems most likely would occur. At DU as well, the need appeared for formalized procedures that were well known and understood. An informal approach to communication most likely would increase a sense of suspicion and mistrust for individuals who have grown tired of backroom deals. A research university typically has different forms of communication than a community college. A campus with a collective-bargaining agreement will differ from one where none exists. The best communicative structure cannot be determined irrespective of institution. Instead, the location of trust is via communicative strategies that differ from culture to culture.

Social networks and trust at SU

Communication exists via literate and oral means and conveys symbolic and "real" messages. A literacy event takes place when a piece of writing plays an integral role in shaping meaning and interactions among participants. Speech events are oral in nature and surround literacy events. As Heath (1982) noted, "Speech events may describe, repeat, reinforce, expand, frame or contradict written materials, and participants must learn whether the oral or written mode takes precedence in literacy events." Obviously, in any academic community, numerous literacy events occur, and speech events circumscribe organizational decisions. A student newspaper, a faculty forum, a university newspaper, a senate Web page, and the minutes and agenda for meetings are examples of literacy events. Each piece of writing pertains to some aspect of creating trust or diminishing it. Writing may be used to explain actions, to argue for or against a particular idea, or to inform debate. Written materials help constituents frame an understanding about the organization and in doing so advance notions of trust. Literacy events reflect or expand what the recipients know to be true, their lived experiences. Where literacy events are absent, or more problematically, create dissonance, trust may be undermined. At SU, the faculty appeared to have a paucity of literacy events. The senate did not communicate via a Web page or constant email message or a newsletter. The administration had a university newsletter, but individuals looked on it as "Pravda." The messages received on the Internet conveyed only routine "alerts." Although a strategic plan seemed to be in the works, the previous one was not widely disseminated or discussed.

Speech events generally take place with participants face to face and involve literacy events. Individuals may refer to a text or extrapolate from it, confer individually or as a group, and so on. They might speak formally or informally. An example of a formal speech act that involves a literacy event is the SU's Senate and the approval of the minutes. An example of a quasi-informal speech act that involves literacy events are the salons the president held where he brings with him outlines of ideas that he has. The constant lunches that the provost held are additional examples.

Speech and literacy events, then, are oral and written messages communicated to an organization's participants. The *forms* in which these messages are conveyed play a crucial role in social capital and network development insofar as they advance meaning. Messages sent about the future of the organization that go only to senior administrators may convey a sense that other individuals are irrelevant or cannot be trusted. When messages are intended only for external audiences as a way to generate donations, they most likely do little to advance trust within the organization. Trust does not simply occur; it has to be nurtured, and one crucial way to do so is in the literacy and speech events that an organization's actors employ.

Similarly, *norms of obligation* and *reciprocity* in part develop and mature through the communicative venues that are utilized. At SU, the communicative norms that the president and provost created were designed to develop a culture of trust so that they might embark on ambitious goals. They recognized that in order to advance trust, they needed to utilize the communicative venues at their disposal. Recall that the provost had tried to utilize the senate as a vehicle for decision making and to increase their scope from what he perceived as mundane day-to-day issues and toward larger strategic matters. However, the informal uses of communication appeared to play a more significant role in network development than those traditionally formal mechanisms. As opposed, for example, to the culture of PHU, where formal communicative structures had a significance that transcended the mere conveying of information, informal means of communication reigned at SU. Individuals noted that the senate did not have a constant communicative vehicle for disseminating its ideas and that the use of a listserv or electronic messages to the entire faculty were more to remind individuals about road closings or inclement weather rather than to serve as a forum for discussion.

Unlike DU, where there were few, if any, norms of obligation that transcended organizational boundaries, SU appeared to be more a university in transition. The president did not so much inherit a spoiled culture as one that did not appear to have many ingrained norms of obligation. Communication may be seen from two perspectives here. On the one hand, there were few norms of communication that existed at SU. On the other hand, because there were so few norms of communication, literacy and speech events had not played much of a role in advancing organizational norms. That is, on some campuses, individuals come to expect particular communicative norms, be they formal or informal, literacy events or speech events. On some campuses, for example, a president holds a retreat at the start of the year that everyone is expected to attend. At other campuses, a draft of a strategic plan is conveyed by way of the Internet and at informal hearings and workshops. The vehicles for communication come to be expected such that, if the beginning-of-year retreat is cancelled or the strategic plan does not involve the participation of numerous groups, then individuals feel that a norm has been transgressed. These communicative norms feed into norms of obligation, which in turn enable trust to arise.

At SU, however, insofar as communicative norms were absent and the previous administration had spent more time on external matters, there were few norms of obligation that existed to create a climate for trust. The atmosphere of rancor that permeated DU was absent, but the sense of camaraderie that pervaded PHU was also nonexistent. As noted earlier, communication, of course, has a purpose. Messages are conveyed and interpreted. Although some messages actually may have a unitary meaning that is easily interpreted by a campus community—"parking lot X will be closed for the summer"—the kind of messages that create or depress social capital are open to interpretation and imbued with symbolic meanings. When a president schedules informal get-togethers throughout a campus with multiple constituencies, she or he is trying to convey a message of interest; such was the widely interpreted meaning of the salons by SU's president. At DU, however, such an interpretation might have been entirely different and only reinforced a climate of suspicion and mistrust. These meanings help create and are created by the grammar of trust.

The grammar of trust at SU

How might trust have increased through the communicative strategies employed at SU? Individuals came to learn about plans for the university by way of constant, rather than episodic, messages such that communication was a *repeated interaction*. Obviously, communication exists in myriad forms and manners such as literacy and speech events, but as a strategy, the constituents developed a way to communicate that enabled formal and informal channels to exist and to enhance the likelihood for trust to develop. Communication had become a *dynamic process* across groups who engaged one another in trying to consider what the future of the organization might be. Rather than a top-down approach where the future was charted by senior leaders, or an approach that eschewed any sense of a cohesive strategy, the framework here was more organic and ongoing. Individuals came to understand that they had a voice in the process.

Communication exists in part as a filter for trust. Trust develops as a repeated interaction; the manner in which trust is enacted is by way of communication. I do not believe that trust and communication are equivalent so that "good communi-cation" ensures trust—as if a cookbook might be developed about the ingredients for successful communication. However, just as trust functions via multiple forms of grammar, so too must we analyze this grammar through a communicative lens.

The process also was purposeful. Senior administrators worked assiduously in trying to develop a cohesive plan about where they wanted to go and how individ-uals might participate in creating that plan. Although individuals made use of for-mal and informal structures, clearly the intent was to develop processes where votes were not mandatory on every issue. I noted at PHU that the structures served as lubricants for trust, but that was not the case at SU. Structures in some respects were irrelevant; perhaps if the president or provost had ignored or tried to overthrow academic structures, problems would have arisen. Instead, rather than ignore them, they created additional informal means of communication that served to increase the possibility for trust. Individuals felt they had a voice in the process and future of the institution.

Communication might also be thought of as an *end*. To be sure, salons and informal conversations are a process that helps build trust, but not every encounter or interaction is one that has a specific gauge for trust's increase. When a culture has a communicative process that is successful, then every interaction need not be invested with symbolic significance. When Nixon made his historic trip to China, for example, what made the event meaningful was that an American president had not done so before. A phone call or interaction between friends will not of neces-sity have as its purpose such a dynamic process, and it may simply be an end to itself. Such a communicative interaction, however, helps build trust. As I previously noted, trust generally does not arise unanticipated or by accident. Relationships develop over time as individuals gradually come to know one another. Out of this knowledge come the conditions for trust to develop. Grand gestures, such as a pres-ident's trip to China or a college president's inaugural speech, are easily understood as rich with symbolic significance. What is often overlooked is that the more microscopic aspects of daily life also carry symbolic consequences.

Trust as an *exchange* in some respects functioned in a manner akin to the events at PHU. Faculty and administration communicated with one another in a bidirectional manner. Although the administration in many respects "owned the air-waves" in terms of the formal organs of communication, faculty played a role in the central communicative structures of the organization. The administration acknowl-edged that the faculty were critical to moving the organization forward, and the fac-ulty allowed the administration to have wide leeway with regard to setting the strategic direction of the university. Although some individuals surmised that they had been appointed to a committee because they were willing to speak out, I never heard anyone speak in a manner akin to what took place at DU, where individuals were afraid to speak with me or appeared hesitant to speak at the university level.

As a research university, if a problem existed in communication, it had as much to do with the faculty's affiliation with their disciplines as with their campus. That is, the communicative challenge for the administration was to encourage the faculty to invest as much into the university as they did with their academic discipline. More often than not, research faculty feel the pull of their discipline or profession more than their campus. For individuals to feel invested in the organization necessitates that the faculty trust the administration and vice versa; for trust to occur, open pathways of communication need to exist.

A grammar of *faith* was largely absent. I want to avoid dichotomies whereby individuals or organizations either have faith or do not, either engage in risk or do not, and so on. Organizational life is much more complex than an either/or decision process, and the grammar underscores this complexity. For trust to exist in an organization, not all forms of grammar need to be present. The challenge is more to understand how the participants utilize the grammar than to determine where the organization fits on a simple-minded scorecard. Unlike DU, for example, where faith had been destroyed, at SU individuals were more agnostic than faith-less.

Communication did not so much involve an expression of faith as it did a way to think about the future. The participants in SU's culture seemed intent on building a climate where *risk taking* took place. Trust here was more in evidence such that individuals felt free to disagree with one another and the administration without fear of retribution. One might say that individuals had faith in the system because of the repetitive communicative strategies. This allowed for risk taking, but it appeared from the interviews that rather than emphasize a devotion to SU, the institution's participants were more concerned with the development of risk. Individuals created a communicative structure that fostered informal disagreement. Thus, the larger goal for SU was to create a communicative vehicle that enabled trust as an *ability*. At DU, the individuals had learned to have little faith in what board members said. They came to believe that people could not be trusted. The converse was not necessarily the case at SU—individuals neither factored in or out whether someone could be trusted by their oral and written statements.

Obviously, to analyze communication in this manner situates it as a *cultural construction*. In doing so, I acknowledge that these terms are simultaneously simple and complex, singular and interrelated. When one speaks about the importance of "communication," most individuals have a pedestrian understanding of what one means by the term just as one intuitively has some understanding of the concept of "trust." However, communication is by no means clear or self-evident. My intention is to convey how different cultures will produce different interpretations of similar communicative strategies, or that similar interpretations will have unintended consequences in one locale and not another. Communication has the potential to help produce the conditions for trust, which in turn enables better communication. Rarely can a literacy or speech event exist in a vacuum such that it does not help increase or decrease social capital and network formation.

The culture of trust at SU

As with PHU and DU, the individuals at SU have *shared experiences* and *learned experiences* that are more similar than different. As a research university, the faculty have come to SU shaped by their discipline and profession. They have been socialized about what to expect from faculty life; their daily interactions are not that different from what one might find on another campus. The tempo of the campus is similar to that of most other major colleges and universities, and the structures in which they conduct their work are more similar than different from the vast panoply of postsecondary institutions. A faculty handbook exists that delineates faculty roles and responsibilities. The Board of Trustees is vested with the ultimate authority for the institution. An Academic Senate exists that on paper does not appear that different from other universities. The president has an administrative team and the provost is looked on as second-in-command and the academic leader of the institution.

What differs is the *conditionality* in which individuals lives get enacted. Yet again, however, the challenge at SU has more to do with the imprint that the university's culture makes on the individuals, rather than the events that have taken place over time. SU's culture does not have as strong a pull on the faculty as it has at the other two institutions. At PHU, there is a specific way of doing things. To transgress boundaries will provoke a reaction. At DU, these boundaries were violated long ago. SU, even though it has a long tradition as a regional institution, does not appear to have as strong a defining role in the lives of its constituents as do the other institutions. The conditions that have been built up over time have enabled individuals to live their lives and to participate in a minor way in university life but not to have the institution's culture shape their lives. The senate's role is undetermined. Individuals participate in the academic life of the university but are more concerned with affairs pertaining to their intellectual backgrounds. Centralization is loose and there is no central organizing ideology.

I caution against a view that SU's culture, or any culture, is weak. Cultures exist. The ability for individuals to align themselves in one way and not another may be thought of as a cultural framework. Maneuverability is a cultural attribute just as is an organizational straitjacket that frames how an individual is to act. SU provided the opposite of a straitjacket; it allowed individuals to go about their business and not have their identities overly defined by the culture. The dialectic of "weak" versus "strong" is meaningless when it comes to the idea of culture.

Indeed, I have shown how DU's culture is quite strong, but that vibrancy has done more harm than good. SU's culture is an example of a canvas that provides new leaders with many possibilities. True, there are cultural norms that are assumed. A shared expectation of the academy, for example, is that the president and provost will hold a Ph.D. or terminal professional degree and come from postsecondary education. SU's faculty undoubtedly would have found it strange, if not repugnant, if leaders had been chosen who had no prior experience in the academy and held nothing higher an associate's degree. But such shared experiences have more to do with occupational socialization than with the culture of SU. The conditions of the culture at SU were defined by providing individuals with wide latitude to structure how they did their work and what was expected; this wide latitude fell within the expected norms shared by the academy in the United States.

Thus, the challenge for SU is in many respects to build shared experiences that wed people to the organization. The manner in which they have gone about building these shared experiences is through communicative efforts aimed at instilling in people a vision of the future that they might share. These communicative efforts are put forward by way of oral and literate activities in a consistent, systematic manner by multiple parties. Rather than a top-down approach, where plans are designed in isolation, SU has worked toward implementing a dialogue across the campus to invigorate a sense not only of getting the best ideas possible about what the future might be, but also to enable individuals to have a sense that they are part of creating that future. And too, the communicative strategy is being employed on many levels by multiple parties rather than singular messages emanating from the president or provost. Such activities have been made possible not because the culture is weak, but rather that the culture has left unregulated individuals' identities except through professional norms. The challenge now is to develop trust through shared experiences that provide a structure for identities and the culture of the institution.

The cultural conditions of academic work at SU

I premised this work on the assertion that networks help create social capital, which in turn generate the conditions for trust, and that trust is crucial in voluntary organizations where change is necessary. Obviously, individuals have the potential to participate in multiple networks—familial, communal, and the like—in addition to those that occur on a campus. Those networks, as I previously observed, may also be utilized on campus. However, for trust to occur so that an organization is capable of moving forward in a determined way that has the support of the constituents, some basis for academic networks needs to be in existence. SU's networks are neither in structural relationships that have been built up over time nor are they in a deeply embedded culture that determines "how we do things around here." A new president, for example, might have called upon any number of strategies to move the organization forward.

However, the thesis of this chapter is that whatever the strategy, a necessary focus to build trust should be on communicative events. People come to understand the organization through the multiple symbolic meanings they interpret by way of literacy and speech acts and who is involved in making and participating in them. The future for SU is surely not in the hands of a lone individual who communicates in one way and not another, but communication nonetheless plays a critical role in determining the success or failure of building trust in any initiative.

CHAPTER EIGHT

The Limits of Trust

The previous chapters painted a portrait of the importance of trust. At Salon University and Prairie Home University, trust was apparent. The organization's participants appeared to be working toward achieving excellence. At Dysfunctional University, the reader might rightfully conclude that, if trust were more in evidence, fewer problems would exist. The institution might have a chance at improvement. Although such conclusions from the case studies would be correct, I am troubled when complex terms such as trust are reduced to a dichotomy that suggest "x" assures success; to be without it assures failure.

Far too often in business and organizational literature, authors adopt a fad such as total quality management—as if it is the cure-all for whatever ails the industry (Birnbaum, 2000). Recently, for example, analysts talked about the import of culture and utilized Japanese corporations to define what they meant by the term (Ouchi, 1983). The assumption was that if American companies would simply mimic Japanese corporations, then organizational performance would improve. As I suggested earlier, to reduce such a complex term as "culture" to a series of acts to be carried out is not only intellectually mistaken but also will not accomplish what is desired. The point was proven when American businesses did not improve despite managers adopting what they thought were the cultural mores of Japanese firms. Indeed, the Japanese economy has been in slump in recent years, even though these companies still exhibit the same cultural behaviors.

I worry, then, that a similar fate will befall the burgeoning organizational literature on trust. Handbooks and manuals will emerge that suggest that, if employees trust their employers, then all sorts of good results will occur. Stories such as Dysfunctional University and Prairie Home University will point out the import of trust; attributes such as communication will be used to demonstrate what managers should do by examples such as Salon University. Unfortunately, when individuals try to follow these revelations, some will find that they did not achieve what they had intended. Trust will fall by the wayside, dismissed as just another fad.

Trust, like other complex terms, is not an umbrella under which all organizational action, success, and failure fall. Rather than think of trust as a static concept that improves current organizational performance, one should think of organizations from a temporal perspective and consider how trust operates within this temporality. On some occasions, trust is paramount. On all occasions, it is foundational. But the simple appearance of trust guarantees nothing more than that people trust one another at a given point in time. In what follows, I offer a case study of a campus where I interviewed 26 individuals. Trust exists at Congenial University, but it is insufficient for the university to achieve excellence over a longer time period.

Congenial University

Founded at the turn of the 20th century, Congenial University (CU) is a private liberal arts and sciences university that offers more than 40 undergraduate programs and grants master's degrees in selected areas. CU enrolls more than 4,000 students and has a 12:1 student/faculty ratio. The university is sprawled across an exceptionally beautiful campus populated with lush lawns and tall leafy trees. Over the past ten years, CU has invested close to $100,000,000 in the physical facility. "When people arrive on campus, we want them to be impressed and get the message that we're a serious university," the president remarked.

The campus has a small-college flavor from a previous era. The student body is more diverse than similar institutions. Among the 3,015 undergraduates, more than 13% identify as Latino, 7% African American, and 13% report race unknown. Almost 60% of the undergraduates report they are White, and 6% are Asian American. There are roughly 133 faculty, 93% of whom are White or Asian American, and 7% are either African American or Hispanic.

The university has a college of arts and sciences, a school of education, and a school of business. The schools of business and education originated less than a decade ago, a result of reorganization. Almost two-thirds of the approximately 133 faculty are in the college of arts and sciences. The new deans of business and education are charged with securing accreditation and developing those schools. As one might imagine, the new schools have encountered resistance in their pursuits because many university constituents hold fast to the historical emphasis on liberal education.

Traditionally, the nature of faculty work at CU involves teaching (up to six courses a year), service, and, to an increasing degree, research. Teaching is viewed as the cornerstone of faculty work. Service is viewed as a critical cultural component and is necessary to secure tenure. "Service is a must for getting tenure here. There is a strong expectation that you should be involved, and people know who you are," one faculty member explained. "We don't want new professors to be preoccupied with service," added a second person, "but we always make sure they're on some committees so they get known, get to know the place." "I'd tell a new hire 'don't shirk your service,'" added another. "We talk about service mattering," summarized a fourth person. "You need to get involved beyond your department."

Over the past decade, faculty work has increasingly involved research as the institution attempts to grow and compete with peer institutions for prestige and constituent advantage. This new direction is expressed most visibly in the recently revised faculty handbook. "In the last few years, there has been an apparent emphasis placed on conducting research. This will change the nature of faculty work and modify what faculty spend their time doing," stated a faculty member of 32 years. "Research is now more important," added another, "but it's still a distant third in terms of priorities."

Service to the university seems to be embedded in the culture, in part because of the small-town flavor of the surrounding area. However, the town has grown and is now less of a "small town." There is also an increase in faculty who live outside of the local community. "Fewer people live here," bemoaned one individual. "People used to be on campus all the time. It was expected, but now people live further away and don't come as much." An additional person explained, "Two-career marriages make living here difficult. So people commute here to work, and it's changed the place some."

For some, the move away from the local community has resulted in a weakening of the academic community. "People are less willing to get involved because when they come here, their day is packed," stated one person. A second added, "It's understandable. It's happening everywhere. But we just have less time." "Email has replaced face-to-face," opined a third person. "They're all interrelated. People live an hour away, and they use email to get their work done. But it's impacted our sense of service, what governance means. It's not terrible. Times change."

At the time of the site visit, the president of 16 years and the vice president of 10 years provided a sense of institutional stability. Additionally, the university employed many long-time faculty committed to teaching and liberal education, sustaining and reinforcing a culture that holds together the community. Over the past decade, CU experienced minimal growth in the population of students or faculty.

The university was built upon a foundation of community, teaching, service, and sturdy leadership. This foundation appears to be changing. One way to comprehend the change is through the manner that the campus makes decisions.

The campus governance structure is comprised of a 36-member board that has the traditional responsibilities of overseeing the financial, investment, and personnel matters of the university. The president has garnered a great deal of support from the board, providing him broad leeway in decision making. The president also holds weekly cabinet meetings that include the vice presidents and deans.

Faculty participate in governance mainly through their Academic Assembly. Approximately 60% of the faculty attend each assembly. The assembly was recently restructured to accommodate the new schools and reduce the number of committees; it meets once a month. Additionally, each school has an assembly that governs matters pertinent to the college and presents issues of concern to the larger assembly. There has been a gradual shift toward more involvement at the school-level rather than at the university level. Although the assembly is seen as the most important governance structure on campus, when coupled with the creation of the schools (business and education) and the decrease of individuals living in the community, all-campus governance is defined by primary involvement, and attendance in the assembly seems less strong today than a decade ago.

I have labeled the institution "Congenial University" based on the way members of this community expressed satisfaction with the governance of the campus that in turn creates a sense of contentment with campus life in general. "People sense that the administration is trying to do the right thing," explained one person. A second added, "We're listened to, and I suppose we all recognize that we give more advice than consent, but that's okay. We're moving in the right direction." The faculty express high levels of satisfaction with their work conditions and the management of the campus. Disgruntled members are in very short supply. "Things are good here," one faculty member remarked. Another exclaimed: "This is an extraordinarily civil campus. People get along and there is a sense that everyone wants what's best for the university." "Angry outbursts or yelling are extremely rare," said another, "It's not that we wouldn't tolerate disagreement. We do! It's that most of us feel that things are pretty good." The ethos of CU is marked by civility and courtesy reminiscent of mid-America in the 1950s.

The culture of governance at CU is based on trust and deference to the administration. The trustees are viewed primarily as ambassadors who help raise money. The senior administration—the president in particular—represents the locus of authority on the campus. The faculty voice is represented mainly through the University Assembly, but essentially it exists as an advisory body. Decision-making authority is freely granted to the president and there are few occasions where differing opinions are represented formally.

When asked if they had a good governance structure, the participants generally agreed based on deferential relations. Individuals' comments painted the picture of effective decision making but did not clearly delineate what good governance meant—other than that people agreed with one another: "Yes, governance works here. Everyone gets along," said one person. A second added, "Governance is always dicey on any campus, but the faculty respect the president and the vice president, so it's pretty good, yes." A third noted, "It hasn't always been good, but for a very long time we've cooperated with one another. This president's administration has focused on good relations with the faculty." And a fourth person summarized, "Governance succeeds when faculty and administration work together. That's what we've got." Thus, the members defined governance not by outcomes, such as an increase in quality. Instead, good governance meant the faculty and administration enjoyed cordial relations with one another and that the processes of governance and decision making were understood.

Every summer after commencement the president takes the vice presidents and deans away on a two-day retreat to evaluate the past year and plan for the upcoming year. "During this time, I ask each of them to really think about where we are and how we can improve," said the president. By July, each of the deans and vice presidents are asked to submit written ideas about the direction of campus. "During that process, I ask them to talk about their ideas informally to different people across the campus," the president further explained. In August, the group meets again to present ideas and compile a plan that will guide the campus. "Afterwards any faculty member or board member can call me and comment on the plan," said the president. The plan is published in October and serves as the administrative agenda for the year.

One person commented on the process by noting:

> There is a veneer of decision making on the part of the faculty. We're told that a certain number of positions exist, and we can then decide with the provost what we should do. But that's a predetermined decision. Who's to say that we can only hire three new faculty this year? Other decisions lead into that one, but we're not involved in those. It's like the table is set and we get to choose where we want to sit. But who decided to set the table with that many chairs?

Other individuals also believed that faculty participation "was not as significant" as they'd like and that "the president has broad authority." But overall, individuals appeared content. The portrait was neither of an autocrat who governed through intimidation nor a faculty that was disengaged. Rather, individuals were satisfied with the direction of the institution because they largely trusted the president and his staff, even though some might have desired a bit more influence. "He has developed a reservoir of support through the years," said one person. "It's not hero worship," said another. "It's just that we understand the system and it appears to work. What's the problem?"

The creation of two new schools and the revisions to the faculty handbook were the most frequently mentioned recent changes. Both initiatives came from the administration. When asked about the faculty's role in creating or rejecting major initiatives, one professor responded: "Minutes ago in the assembly meeting, we were just verbally contemplating the issue of how much power we actually have. The problem I saw was that few assembly members could answer the question."

"The plan to create the schools of education and business was fashioned before the faculty were asked about it," one professor stated. The process of decision making at CU involved what one assembly member called "selective consultation" by the president. The decision to create the new schools was announced by the administration. Many faculty members recalled that announcement as the first time they had heard of the restructuring. When asked about the faculty's response to the decision to create two new schools, an education professor explained that "there was not much reaction to the decision. The faculty just went about doing the work of getting it done without having much to say." A former dean recalled: "The faculty in many of the programs that would be moved into one of the schools were not even consulted during the process of decision making." When asked about the decision to create the schools of business and education, once again many faculty expressed satisfaction and concern but did not mention disappointment with the process of decision making. A business professor remarked:

> The president has a good track record with the faculty, and most people trust him to do the right thing. Some people had questions about creating new schools, but those voices were so faint that the administration didn't hear them. I would say that people are just accustomed to the president making decisions. Most faculty don't really seem to mind and the few willing to challenge him recognize that they are the minority.

The Academic Assembly was viewed as an information-sharing venue more than a governing body. A long-time English professor expressed little confidence in the assembly's ability to influence decisions: "The assembly is useful for information, but it has no power." An assistant to the vice president stated that "the assembly is sort of a show-and-tell that is manipulated by the administration. I even remember a faculty search that was manipulated by the administration as an example of just how compliant they [faculty] can be." Of interest is not simply the individual's comment but the manner in which it was said. When individuals comment that something is a "show-and-tell," it is often said to demonstrate distrust and dissatisfaction. However, this speaker, as many other interviewees, expressed little unhappiness or distrust. Faculty and administration were aware of the processes of governance and appeared content.

Revising the faculty handbook into "the handbook for faculty" was another example of an action in which the administration led the changes. A member of the assembly recalled:

> Originally the faculty were charged with revising the handbook. There were some things that really needed to be changed, but, like most places, the faculty fumbled around with [the handbook], never being able to get it done. The provost then headed up the process, which was fairly contentious at times. What was interesting to me is that, as the process went along, you could see the administration positioning itself to take decision making authority out of the hands of the faculty. Ironically, the handbook for faculty, as it's now called, is the document that puts into effect these changes.

Others agreed that revising the handbook was a process that involved the faculty and administration in an adversarial relationship. "Everyone has a story. Some will blame the vice president and others, one or another professor. What's important, though, is that we resolved them. We worked through the process. The vice president deserves credit." "It's an example," claimed another, "of one of those things that could have gone either way. It could have ended badly, but I think the history of how we work with one another saved us." They also agreed that the process was "at times litigious" because of changes to tenure requirements, which placed a slightly greater emphasis on research and created an amended salary structure. Still, faculty accepted the fact that the administration, and to some extent the board, exerted decision-making authority—without facilitation of faculty opinion.

In spite of widespread satisfaction with governance, many faculty were of the opinion that they did not have "real" power. "The faculty, at best, serves an advisory capacity and most people seem to be okay with that," one English professor stated. When asked about his relationship with the faculty, the president explained that "there's almost too much trust. I can set pretty strong agendas. People give me the liberty and will to do so." He then stated that "it's nice to be liked, but it's more important to be respected and trusted."

A recent newcomer to the campus summarized the pervasive culture of deference by saying:

> There is a structure that allows for dialogue, but the president is so well liked that the faculty defer their will and rights to him. It's an enormous display of trust. I've been here for two years and have been amazed at how central the decision making is and even more amazed at how satisfied the faculty are with this kind of structure.

The challenges and changing environment facing CU will likely create a significantly different decision-making context in the near future. Almost 40% of the CU faculty, for example, will be eligible for retirement within six years. At the same time, the schools of education and business are expected to undertake significant recruitment. The assistant to the provost explained:

> We are really concerned about what our faculty will look like in the near future. With the changes to the university, there is a concern that new faculty will care less about teaching and more about research and won't be concerned the least bit about service.

There are also concerns about socializing new faculty to the ways of CU, according to a professor of philosophy and member of the campus for 15 years:

> I fear that the faculty will turn over at such a rate that we won't be able to acculturate them or subject them to the type of social pressure to serve the way we once could. When I first got here, there was an unspoken rule that to be a member of the community, you had to be involved with the work of the campus. That's how you gained your acceptance. As we look to expand, I don't think that we'll be able to leverage that kind of pressure.

In addition to faculty turnover, concerns about a changing student population exist. Not only is CU expected to increase its traditional student population, it also intends to increase enrollment among professional students, which means holding classes at night and possibly online. "We were one kind of campus," said one individual, "and now we're becoming another." Another summarized: "You can't stay stuck in the past. But I hope as we get new students, new faculty, a new president and administration, there's still some of what makes us 'us' left."

I asked participants about the effects such changes might have on CU over the next five years. Most expressed a mixture of optimism and fear. It is a well-known fact that the president is nearing retirement. Additionally, the changes that will result from the new schools create a sense of uncertainty across the campus. The dean of one school commented:

> I would bet on this place. If the president sticks around through the capital campaign, you'll see that we've incorporated the new schools. We will grow our enrollments, move up in the rankings, and we'll have a more diverse student population in the professional schools.

Concerning governance, a professor of 33 years and chair of a School Assembly predicted:

> I think you'll see that we've changed. The governance activity will be separate and I think that the faculty work load will change, which in turn affects the number of days people come to campus. This essentially means that we'll be a different campus.

The chair of the University Assembly stated:

> There will be a new president and administration. Governance for the most part will be secondary because people will be so busy with their work. What all of this means is that the university will be much more segmented and the culture of service at CU is at risk of being broken down into service for self and service for the school.

Another dean explained:

> With the new schools, there is going to be a need for more autonomy. For example, right now, in order to make any purchase over $500, forms must pass through the administration for processing and approval. Well, you can't even buy a computer with $500, and it makes building a school difficult with those kinds of constraints in place. So my guess

is that we are going to have to disburse much of the responsibility that once existed in the central administration down to the school level to enable us to do our work effectively.

Although some could point to changes, few were able to tie the future to an explicit sense of quality or excellence. Rather, most individuals talked about the environment from a rationalist perspective and suggested ways that the organization might react to the change. Faculty will retire and new faculty need to be hired. Schools need to grow and there will be autonomy. A long-term president will step down. Although many of these issues are social "facts" in the sense that they will occur, what one did not hear at CU is how individuals associated change with any explicit sense of organizational excellence.

When asked, for example, where the institution will be in five years, one person said: "We'll be bigger, that's for sure. I can't predict much more." Another stated, "I hope we still have a fairly inclusive structure, not hierarchical." A third person commented on structures: "We need to figure out how to get the committee work under control; the faculty review process is unwieldy." Another faculty member said, "We'll be pretty much the same. We're pretty satisfied with what we're doing now." A final person predicted, "We'll be about what we are today. I sure hope we are."

What might one make of trust at such an institution? On many levels, the institution appears strong. Campus facilities are attractive and abundant. Basic indicators such as enrollment, endowment, completion rates, and student satisfaction are good when compared to peer institutions. The faculty trust the administration and the administration asks for input from the faculty on many issues. The structures of governance appear to be what exist on manifold campuses—departments, schools, and a campus-wide governing body—and they entertain typical issues such as revisions to the faculty handbook, curricular reform, and issues pertaining to student life. The vitriol and suspicion that mark many campuses are absent. Thus, one might conclude that Congenial University is a campus with trust, and of consequence, is an effective organization. People trust one another, and the result is a culture that enables the institution to move forward. In what follows, however, I offer a caution.

Discussion

Congenial University is a campus where individuals trust one another on some levels. The administration and the faculty have exceedingly cordial relations. If distrust is often associated with a spoiled culture, then is trust emblematic of an effective one? Congenial University, in many ways, is a model campus for communication and trust between campus constituents. One professor proclaimed: "I guess we are more efficiently run as a result of the president's ability to make decisions and our trust that he'll do the right thing." Common sense suggests that fundamental trust and civility among members of any organization are useful for progress. I wish to suggest that trust "in the present" is not sufficient to enable quality to occur and grow over time.

Locating trust at CU

Trust appeared to exist in the structure and culture of the organization. However, in large part, trust seemed to be invested in the long-term senior administrators, especially the president. Individuals trusted one another; however, institutional structures such as the Faculty Assembly appeared more as appendages than central deliberative bodies (such as existed at PHU). The culture of the organization enabled individuals to rely on one another's judgments rather than on a process defined by votes or legislation.

A culture of trust and deference may enable individuals to "get along," in the words of one individual at CU. This, however, does not ensure long-term quality. Trust needs to be more than the absence of conflict and the ceding of authority and voice to one group. A simple veneer of trust does not signal the conditions for quality.

Frequently when individuals disagree with one another what may result is a better decision than if everyone simply viewed a topic from the same perspective. Disagreement, of course, does not signal distrust, and it may even suggest widespread trust. Organizations are dynamic entities; they need to be viewed in a manner that enables trust to evolve, rather than simply to be incorporated into the manner in which activities are done. Governance needs to be linked to an increase in institutional quality rather than simply a series of harmonious structures. At CU, those very structures that might enable debate are underutilized. In the words of one faculty member:

> Although the assembly exists, it doesn't have power to do anything. The president and the administration really run the place. What's amazing is [the president] has, for the most part, made decisions that the faculty can live with. Although we may not like something, there is not much discussion about it and no real prescribed steps to do anything about it. I guess that's the down side of entrusting a campus to the president and his administration. For this very reason, a lot of people will be nervous about the selection of his successor.

An additional concern is whether the current structures are able to accommodate conflict and disagreement. The lone example from CU when the faculty and president could not agree over an issue is illustrative. A faculty member explained:

> For a long time, there has been discussion about moving our interim session. The decision went to the assembly, but the faculty could not make any decision about what to

do with it. Finally, the president decided for them. The interim session is important to many faculty here for a number of reasons. Well, the faculty were dissatisfied with it being moved to the summer and many have decided not to participate. Since the move, we have had trouble with that session because many faculty refuse to teach.

A rare faculty disagreement with the decision of the president provided the campus with a glimpse of the current strengths of their culture and the potential dangers of deference. To be sure, the president was able to implement an idea without a faculty vote because they trusted him. However, over the past decade, CU has experienced few decisions that create disparate positions. Inclusive decision making structures that are based on trust in individuals and trust in an established process are able to legitimize contentious decision making.

Social networks and trust at CU

Again, a seeming paradox occurs insofar as *forms* of social capital exist in contrast to the absence of them at DU. Governance functions, albeit not in a manner similar to what takes place at PHU. Individuals know how to communicate with one another, how decisions are made, and how decisions are relayed and implemented.

Norms of obligation and *reciprocity* are also in evidence, although expectations are changing. At one point, for example, the assumption was that individuals should live in the community and be readily available to students and colleagues. Service appeared to have more importance a generation ago than it does today. Individuals believed that involvement in the life of the university was important, but over time, the strength of the academic profession seems to have become more important. Research is now a key factor in promotion and tenure; residence in the local community is no longer so important. Thus, although norms previously existed and to a considerable degree they still persist, the times have changed. Now, the norms seem to be to defer decision making to the administration rather than to have the faculty play a central role in the strategic plan of the institution.

I surely am not arguing that an organization's culture should be one that is distrustful or that norms of obligation and reciprocity are irrelevant. However, the opposite is also incorrect. Simply because everyone defers to a long-time leader does not ensure organizational quality. CU is well situated for the future, if trust is viewed as a dynamic concept. They have the conditions for quality to arise insofar as the culture is based on trust. Rather than focus on changes based on rational choice that are sure to occur—the retirement of the president, and the like—the organization's participants will be well served if they concentrate on cultural values and discussions about how values might enable the promulgation of quality.

Consonant with the issue of decision making culture is faculty responsibility. Two instances of important decision making at CU were assigned to the faculty during the time under investigation. The revising of the faculty handbook and changing the interim session were issues originally sent to the assembly for faculty to decide. In both cases, the CU faculty admitted to being unable to forward a resolution. "The faculty fumbled around with the [handbook]," said one member of the assembly. Another commenting on the interim session stated that "the faculty could not make any decision . . . finally the president decided for them." In the interest of promoting cultural values that ensure institutional quality, faculty are obligated to assume responsibility for making informed and timely decisions. The inability to do so silences faculty voice in decision making and compromises institutional quality, even if individuals trust the leader to make a fair decision.

The grammar of trust at CU

I maintain that one may locate trust at CU and that the networks exist that enable the development of trust. However, in some respects, various forms of the grammar of trust were underutilized. This enabled the appearance of trust to exist that did not create the conditions for quality over the long term. For example, as a *repeated interaction,* one might assume that trust existed—for example, individuals attended meetings—but these interactions conveyed little sense of a *dynamic process.* To be sure, at an institution such as DU, trust could not exist because there were no repeated interactions that engendered trust. But at CU, one sensed that the structures and culture were not in dynamic motion. An analogy might be of an overweight person who wishes to get in shape and peddles on a stationary bicycle for 45 minutes a day, while leisurely reading a magazine without breaking into a sweat. Any health expert will acknowledge that a sustained workout is necessary for good health. But if that workout is simply a rote process, then little real change will take place. I do not think that CU is in ill health, but the lack of dynamism is one cultural problem that needs to be overcome. If structures such as faculty assemblies exist and faculty attend meetings, then the possibility for trust is apparent. If the meetings are meaningless and the faculty never make any decisions, then one wonders about the conditions for quality in a culture that assumes meaningful interactions across groups.

Similarly, the simple existence of a structure is an insufficient indicator of quality even when those structures are necessary for trust to take place. Trust as an *end* enabled individuals to lack suspicion and afforded the administration broad leeway in decision making, but the *faith* individuals exhibited also seems to have inhabited the kind of communicative vehicles I discussed in Chapter 7. Again, an analogy is useful: most theologians will argue that the kind of faith one ought to develop is not simply an unthinking allegiance to a deity. Faith involves having worked through particular mysteries, acknowledging that there may not be logical certainty. But because of previous interactions, the individual believes in the deity. Faith that induces trust, especially in an intellectual organization, needs to provoke questions that ultimately lead to support rather than blind allegiance.

Trust at CU appeared to involve little *risk taking*. A positive interpretation is that one does not need to take a "risk" if trust is implicit. As I previously noted, when I get in my car and drive to school without a police escort or a gun, one might mistakenly say that I trust my journey will be safe. Clearly, not all actions involve a risk, which is why contexts matter. When I drank a glass of water this morning, I did not assume a risk. If I lived in a village with poor sanitation, then such an action would take on a decidedly different risk.

Life at CU appeared to involve little risk taking. Individuals had become comfortable with one another, which is important. The question I raise here is whether such an environment produced the conditions for quality and excellence. Trust needs to be renewed insofar as its relationship to social capital works from the assumption that capital is spent and earned. Social capital does not simply accrue. The investor spends social capital; for it to be maintained, the individual (or organization) needs to continue to earn and accumulate capital just as with economic capital. At CU, it appears as if they work implicitly from a static notion of capital.

The president utilized trust as an *ability*. His informal manner and longevity in the position earned a good deal of respect from the faculty. In effect, trust was a grammar that enabled individuals to short circuit formalized processes so that they frequently relied on what the president had decided. I do not believe that the president made a series of flawed decisions that endangered the institution. However, as a *cultural construction*, trust needs to function in manifold forms. At CU, the actors utilized a *rational choice framework*. The appearance is one where individuals make logical choices and the result is one based on trust. My concern, then, is that even though trust was apparent, the culture of trust was not sufficient for creating excellence over time, especially when the culture is in a period of change.

The culture of trust at CU

CU is an institution in transition. The *shared experiences* and *learned experiences* at CU have been built over time in a manner that created common understandings of the culture. True, as with the other institutions, the members have been socialized by their professions and disciplines, but unlike PHU or SU, for example, the actors at CU would point out the centrality of the organization's culture over the last generation. The president has been in office twice as long as the presidents of the other case studies portrayed here, and he has been president much longer than the norm in academe. The citizens of CU used to live in the community and meet casually off-campus. The expectation was that faculty would be in their offices daily. Thus, individuals participated in and experienced similar events and ceremonies with one another.

The structure and manner of hierarchical decision making have become a norm; individuals appear content. The president has assumed a degree of authority that would be unheard of at DU—the Board of Trustees at DU has a greater say in the life of the organization than the president at CU, but the crux of the matter at DU turns on the faculty's resistance to the arbitrary and capricious decisions of the Board and the manner in which they are made. The culture of trust is nonexistent at DU, whereas it has become embedded at CU. CU's president has never made a decision to rival what has angered the faculty at DU, but the structure of CU's decision making also would be resisted at DU. The point, of course, is not that one system is right and another wrong, but that the *conditionality* of trust frequently helps determine how trust is perceived and enacted. At CU, the stability of the culture has created the conditions for trust up to now, but one wonders what will take place in the future.

That stability is about to change. The president is set to retire. The provost will depart. Over half of the faculty will most likely turn over within five years. Living in the community is problematic for two-career families. A greater interest in the disciplines and professions has led to a change in the tenure code; a more outward-looking faculty will continue to follow the trend of recent hires. None of these "facts" should be construed as indictments or as an indication of the downfall of the academic community. But curiously, a culture that created the conditions for trust is now also one that will undergo significant change in a relatively short time period. If the institution's participants are concerned about academic quality and improvement, has the culture created a climate for trust that not only lets change occur but also creates a dynamic that involves people in those manifold decisions that lead to academic improvement?

Unlike SU where the imprint of the organization's culture was relatively light on the faculty, the opposite has been the case at CU. At PHU, structures and processes buttress the culture so that when individuals enter and exit, the organizational structures such as the Faculty Senate remain vibrant. At SU, the culture does not appear to have structural stability. The question then turns on how change occurs in a dynamic culture that will simultaneously encounter far-reaching changes and the need to improve performance. How will neophytes learn about the culture and what will they learn? Have the conditions been created to not simply create trust today but also maintain it tomorrow?

The cultural conditions of academic work at CU

The vibrancy of the various networks of the faculty appears to be changing; the intellectual networks are increasing, and the institutional networks seem to be on the wane. Although at PHU, faculty had a significant affiliation to external networks, a commitment remained with the institution as well. I saw little evidence that such a commitment will remain for CU's faculty. The familial and communal networks external to CU that fed into the organization's culture are certain to fade. The structures at CU are not unlike what exists at SU such that the networks are not deeply embedded into the culture. Unlike SU, however, a reliance on communication has yet to take hold. Although the culture is relatively vibrant, the concern is that academic work is undergoing significant change at a time when the organization itself is also set to undergo change.

I previously noted that networks are fragile. Insofar as humans create networks, these same routes for social capital formation are contingent on individual nurturance and maintenance. Although one test of institutional vitality is based on indicators of current performance, the intent of this chapter has been to focus the idea of trust on the future. An institution's well-being for the future is in part determined by the conditions set in the past. The present conditions that create trust at CU may not be a sufficient variable to increase organizational quality in the future. Trust is a process rather than an end.

The case of CU highlights the dilemma of deference and trust. The president at CU is of the opinion that the faculty trust him too much. This, in some ways, signifies not so much an abandonment of faculty responsibility but the danger of a culture where trust is seen as an end in and of itself. Neither the president nor the administration is characterized as autocratic. Instead, a culture has been created where "getting along" has been at a premium. My concern is surely not that trust is useless, but rather that, in a time of change, organizations need to develop cultures that have the expectation of improving quality. In order to improve quality, individuals need to create and sustain ways to engage one another effectively about the institution's goals and how to achieve them. In this light, the essential grammar of trust is one where it is a dynamic process that is conditioned and evolved by all of the organization's actors.

Campuses with cultural systems that I define as deferential might examine the expectations of the faculty. Although the CU faculty were service oriented, their service involved carrying out decisions of the administration. Faculty more meaningfully involved in decision making might likely assert themselves as responsive partners in campus governance rather than as workers. Such a conception affords a distinctly different view of trust.

Organizational life should aim to improve organizational quality rather than placate constituencies. The case of Congenial University serves as one example of the potential dangers of a culture based on agreement. The importance of trust, the issue of faculty responsibility, and the coordination of cultural processes with an organization's structures represent areas that provide significant insight to the understanding of the complexities of organizational change and quality.

This case also serves as an example of the need to create cultures able to withstand transitions. Many of the CU constituents were concerned about what will happen when the current president retires, which indicates that their confidence is based on the current collection of personnel. A vibrant culture is related to the people who populate the culture but is one that should also transcend individuals. As it stands, CU faculty are without effective formal mechanisms that support their involvement in the life of the organization. Additionally, the institutional transition will likely incite disagreement, increased autonomy, and a more ambiguous mission—all factors for contentious decision making, especially when trust has not been seen as a synonym for agreement.

PART THREE

Trust and
the Public Good

CHAPTER NINE

Public Trust
and the Recreation
of Academic Community

After a marathon 12-hour meeting, the chair of the Board of Regents at the University of Hawaii announced, "Sadly, we have come to the realization that the President no longer has our trust, and there is no longer a unity of purpose between the Board and the President" (Creamer, 2004, p. A1). The board unanimously agreed to fire Evan Dobelle, the 12th president of the University, after slightly less than three years in office. The public manner in which the firing was conducted and the cancellation of the benefits package the president was to receive—reportedly close to three million dollars—made national news.

Dobelle was hired with great fanfare and hope for the beleaguered Hawaii system of higher education. After a decade of crushing budget cuts, the system suffered from low faculty and staff morale and the public perception of a system adrift. The Regents hired Dobelle at a salary in the top tier of all university presidents in the nation. He proceeded with an energy that initially excited some and eventually turned off others. Although one serious political blunder on Dobelle's part was to endorse publicly the Democratic candidate for governor (the Republican won), no single event led to his downfall. Some saw him as a braggart, and others complained that he hired too many of his friends from the mainland and gave them huge salaries. Still others protested that he misappropriated money.

It appeared, however, that rather than criminal misdeeds, he made perceptual errors. Tickets to rock concerts and upgrades to first class on airplanes may not be illegal. But to some individuals, Dobelle had taken on the role of an academic

Marie Antoinette. While the legislature tried to figure out how to provide meager raises to the faculty during stringent fiscal times, the president was flying his friends first class around the world. One individual summarized, "The only obvious thing is that there is a lack of trust. . . . If the people that you work for don't trust you, then you are in an impossible situation" (Gima, 2004, p. A1). The result was a system in chaos. The greatest amount of publicity the University received in the last decade was over a public firing of a president because he had lost the trust of the Regents and, by inference, the elected representatives of the state and its citizens.

I want to avoid a reductionist logic which argues that a president has to be trusted or he or she will run into public problems such as Dobelle's. No single act or idea defines an individual's success or failure. But I have argued here repeatedly that trust is foundational within an organization. Without trust, as the individual noted above, "you are in an impossible situation." I now turn to the environments in which postsecondary institutions exist and consider how trust functions in these contexts. Public trust of a nonprofit institution and its leaders is again foundational. How that trust is defined changes over time. For academic institutions, a new relationship needs to be forged that will not only resituate postsecondary education within the public imagination but also reconfigure academic life within the organization.

Although what I suggest has obvious and significant implications for public higher education, virtually all institutions in the United States are impacted by the public's perception and support of postsecondary education. Tier I universities receive substantial public monies for research. Federal and state student financial aid forms a major portion of academic budgets. Public trust affects students' decisions to apply and/or enroll in certain institutions. Public trust is also relevant to private donors. Even for-profit institutions receive significant direct support from the government through grants and loans for their students as well as indirect support by way of the ability of those institutions to make use of public facilities such as libraries for their students. How the public learns to trust academe turns on the meaning of "public good." I argue that such a term is inevitably contested and ever-changing. The challenge ahead is to reconfigure what is meant by public good, which will resituate academe in the civic imagination.

The public trust and the public good

Public trust

Some institutions, such as the Universities of California and Michigan, are defined as a "public trust" under their respective state constitutions (Douglass, 2000, p. 97). Even if institutions were not established as trusts, a preponderance of public and private institutions have Boards of "Trustees," who hold the "trust" of and for the institution. Presumably, the trustees ensure that the institution does not betray its trust to those who support it. For a public institution, that trust is vested in the citizenry by way of the state government. For private institutions, there is an array of potential constituencies that warrant support. Specific groups such as religious denominations for faith-based institutions, or a particular segment of the population for colleges and universities that cater to a particular clientele, are examples of constituencies that expect their institution not to betray their trust. Although public and private institutions obviously must adhere to typical fiduciary reporting requirements, what perhaps stands out most potently is the significant degree of autonomy that has been granted to postsecondary institutions and has been ceded to the trustees and faculty.

Trustees generally were not perceived as serving two competing groups—the external constituencies that provided the institution fiscal and moral support and the internal organization composed of faculty, administration, and students. The assumption was that the activities of the organization were in sync with the expectations of society. The overheated debates that take place today when trustees say they have assumed their position to ensure that the public does not get cheated by the college have always been with us, but they were less pervasive a century ago. Instead, individuals became trustees to guide the organization in a manner in keeping with what the public expected; the assumption was that the best way to ensure trust was for the state and related citizenry to keep an arm's length from the internal operations of the institution.

Even before the idea of academic freedom took hold in the early 20th century, postsecondary institutions were seen as a breed apart from other institutions. States generally provided lump sum monies to public institutions and let the trustees determine how those monies were to be spent. In California, for example, a legislature's attempt to pass a statutory law related to the management of academic programs or operations by state universities was viewed as nonbinding (Douglass, 2000, p. 97). The trustees had the direct authority to make such decisions; they vested the decision with the administration. The legislature might proffer suggestions, but ultimately, they were little more than recommendations.

Similarly, the faculty's determination of academic quality and the creation or elimination of curricula was not to be influenced by external agents. The assumption was that the internal operations of academic organizations were best left to the organization's actors. Thus, for a significant portion of the 20th century, the trustees and faculty of colleges and universities had a remarkable degree of autonomy to chart their own direction without intrusion from external agents—even those who provided the fiscal support to run the institution. Consider, however, what frequently takes place today. Legislatures seek to change curricula, set hiring standards, or dictate how monies are to be spent. Individuals frequently campaign to secure a position on a board of trustees in order to influence activities on campus whether they are athletics or academic programs.

To be sure, some public institutions had greater leeway than others. A state's legislature or governor could always speak up on behalf of a specific idea and try to influence the direction of the institution. A concern for vocational training and the professions has frequently been greater than for the humanities or social sciences. Donors played a significant role even in the early part of the century and undoubtedly influenced a particular institutional direction. Newspapers and commentators from time to time tried to shed light on a particular topic or issue of an institution. Nevertheless, the general historical portrait one receives of postsecondary institutions is that of trustees, faculty, and administrators who were able to chart a course less defined by politics and external constraints than what exists today (Couturier & Scurry, 2005). Why would individuals devise a system without what appears today as very much oversight? Perhaps more importantly, why has the opposite occurred in the early years of the 21st century to such an extent that, even while fiscal support continues to decline, regulations and oversight continue to increase?

To say little more than that the public trusted academics a century ago, and does not today, is far too simplistic. Instead, I turn to a discussion of colleges and universities as public goods and investigate how the perception of a public good has changed over time. These changes have impacted, and are impacted by, the relationship of trust developed between postsecondary institutions and their various public constituencies.

Public good

The idea of a public good is a deceptively simple term that individuals employ with increasing frequency but has different meanings and interpretations. Traditionally, a public good has been used by economists to signify something that costs no more to provide for many individuals than it does for one; everyone will be able to enjoy the good once it has been produced (Hansman, 1987). Brian Pusser added that public goods "are commonly identified by two characteristics, nonrivalry and nonexcludability. Public goods are presumed to be under-produced in markets, as those two fundamental characteristics prevent individual producers from generating sufficient profit" (2002, p. 48). The clearest example of a public good is national defense. When the country spends money to defend the country, as an individual, I am protected as well as everyone else in the country. Similarly, when a state decides to provide pure drinking water to its citizens, everyone enjoys the water, not just an isolated few.

Of course, a theory of a public good always meets social reality. If national defense is the clearest example of a public good, the assumption is that the cost of a good should be similar for all. But even that example is flawed. Although the cost of protecting individuals against nuclear attack may be the same for the citizens in the continental United States, surely the costs rise when the citizens of Guam need to be protected as well. Although, as an American, I will be defended against nuclear attack (because defense is a public good), I am probably less vulnerable to such an attack if I live in Guam rather than New York City. The costs of providing pure drinking water may be equivalent in much of a state, but there are always rural areas where reaching individuals will be more difficult and costly. They may either have to forego the public good—in which case it is not an ideal type of a public good—or the cost will be differentially based on location—in which case it is not a pure public good either.

Nevertheless, the underlying economic principles for what has been meant by a public good are relatively clear, especially so when the idea of private goods are considered. A frequent example pertains to security in a city. The police are a public good. They exist to protect everyone—not just a privileged few. If I do not feel secure, however, I may decide to buy a security alarm, hire a security company to watch my house, or live in a gated community with a private security system and our own security guards. Whatever I pay for private security is a private good. The "good" is confined to my house or gated community; if we were to extend that good to others, then the costs will rise with each additional person or family. Simply because I enjoy the service does not mean anyone else does.

The perception that a public good is insufficient for individuals' purposes and that consequently they turn to private goods has two policy-related ramifications. First, the perception and/or the reality that a public good is ineffective has the effect of decreasing support for the public good. Second, there has been an increased demand to make private goods more public. Any public good receives fiscal support from the state and that support derives in one way or another from tax revenues—general individual taxes, taxes on business, or taxes specifically earmarked for that good. The assumption is that the community supports the public good and is willing to pay a portion of their income for that good. A municipal bond that will increase taxes to upgrade highways, school buildings, or subways is an example of votes that the citizenry make about whether to support a public good. Increasingly, however, individuals argue that they are unwilling to pay for goods that they perceive to be ineffective. Conversely, if those public goods do not meet the needs of the citizens, forcing them to buy additional services, they might seek some form of direct tax relief or indirect tax support through a credit on their tax form.

Nowhere has the debate of public goods been more vociferous than in the domain of public schooling. In line with the idea of public education, the United

States has assumed that a right to an education extends to everyone—whether they are male or female, rural or urban, black or white, rich or poor. In part, the Supreme Court's decision in *Brown v. Board of Education* pertained to the denial of a public good to a particular race of people. The Supreme Court ruled that "separate but equal" negated the concept of a public good.

Special education has also been a continuing area of controversy and underscores the imperfect definition of a public good that I referred to earlier. Students who require special education have been assured a right to a public good—public schooling—but clearly the cost of that education differs. Special education students require additional services. Again, in part, the Americans with Disabilities Act (1990) codified that equal access to a public good should be extended to all citizens, not just the abled.

Throughout much of the 20th century, a continuous debate revolved around Catholics who desired to send their children to a parochial school. Why, they asked, should they support public education while paying for their child to attend another school that provided a religious education? Insofar as the Catholic child was not taking up a place or using resources in the public school, should not those monies that the public system saves be used to support the Catholic school? The argument was that the educational public good pertained to individuals, not to institutions. It was the individual citizen's decision about how to enact that public good. In effect, Catholics were paying twice for their child's schooling; they sought to change the rules. The response, of course, was that parents chose to send their child to a private school. They were welcome to send them to a public school supported by public monies. A strict separation of church and state required that no public funds be given to religious schools.

The debate over individual resources and parochial schools did not initially revolve around the inadequacy or ineffectiveness of the public schools but instead focused on additional services that a particular segment of society desired. However, in the last 20 years, the argument has shifted. Parents have become increasingly dissatisfied—whether justified or not—with the education provided in public schools. The result has been a great deal of experimentation, including charter schools. These experiments revolve around the idea of what has come to be known as "school choice." Although school choice is an interesting idea, if it were decoupled from public funding, the demand would not have brought into question the idea of a public good. Individuals might have multiple providers, for example, which receive public support; these providers will reach the same ends but use different paths to achieve them. One public high school might focus on the arts, and another might focus on the sciences, but the students all take agreed upon curricula approved by the state and receive a state-sanctioned high school diploma.

The argument over school choice has been as much about the need for a public good as for school choice. Why pay for a public good, ask critics, if it is ineffective? Why not simply let individuals pay out of their pocket for a service that does not need to be a public good? These same critics argue that an individual cannot create an army or protect him or herself against nuclear attack. The necessity of public funding for such an activity seems clear. But individuals can educate their children without the support of the state, the critics point out. In the 19th century, the rise of public education was as much to ensure some form of a common culture for the country as to educate individuals for jobs. The Governor of New York, DeWitt Clinton, said as much in 1822: "The first duty of a state is to render its citizens virtuous by intellectual instruction and moral discipline, by enlightening their minds, purifying their hearts, and teaching them their rights and obligations" (Lincoln, 1909, p. 1100). Such a necessity has changed, suggest some. In consequence, the need for education to be seen as a public good should be eliminated.

Although an argument may be made that a common culture is no longer of the utmost priority, or at least as great a priority as a century ago, economic productivity is essential for the health and well-being of the country. Further, not all individuals can afford an adequate education. Some level of schooling must be accorded all children irrespective of wealth, which returns the argument to the need for education to be seen as a public good.

As I shall elaborate in the subsequent section on postsecondary education, increasingly the argument shifts between two questions: Should education be seen as a public or private responsibility? Should support be provided to institutions or individuals? Such questions extend to most areas where public goods exist and underscore the contested nature of the idea of public good. Some, for example, will argue that all adults have the right to use freeways if they have a driver's license; the "free" way is a public good and all individuals should be ensured of safe travel on adequate roads. But if freeways are chronically unsafe and dangerous, then a question will arise about whether individuals would be better off by not paying for an ineffective means of transportation and be left to their own devices—perhaps support should not go toward the freeway system in the United States but some other means of individually supported transportation. The response, of course, will be akin to the argument I just made about public education. Not everyone can afford private jets. For the economic health of the country, some level of public transportation must exist. If it is ineffective, then it must be improved.

Thus, while I am in sympathy with David Labaree's (1997) critique of the American debate over educational goals, he misses the point when he reduces that struggle to a tension over "democratic politics (public rights) and capitalist markets (private rights), between majority control and individual liberty, between political equality and social inequality" (p. 41). The question for many of those who criticize public education has as much to do with the effectiveness of the public good and plausible alternatives as it does with the ends that are desired. Some believe that education ought not to be a public good, for example, and that schools are ineffective. Others acknowledge that education is a public good but recognize that there may be alternatives to public providers. Even if the country were ineffective in defending itself against nuclear attack, few would argue that national defense is not a public good. I cannot build my own missile defense system. Instead, the public good must be improved in order to be effective. However, plausible alternatives exist with other public goods (such as transportation).

As individuals have grown dissatisfied with public education, they have advanced three critiques that suggest that education need not be a public good as it has been defined over the last century. First, insofar as the execution of the public good is inadequate, the citizenry have a right to look elsewhere. Second, a public good need not be defined and carried out in the same way for all individuals. Third, given that the contexts for the public good have changed, so too should the assumption that education needs to remain both "public" and a "good."

From this perspective, a public good is not an expansive list that needs to incorporate all matters of society. Instead, a public good is a finite list of activities that should extend to all citizens. What Labaree overlooks is that how a public good is defined changes over time. Clearly, a century ago, the public good of national defense did not take into account nuclear attack. Only 20 years ago, terrorism would not have registered in a manner that it now does. Thus, although citizenship education might have been a prerequisite at the turn of the 20th century, and could have counted as a public good, many today will argue that no such need exists—hence, one reason for the demise of schooling as a public good.

What remains unresolved is how society should deal with those who cannot afford a private good that was once a public good. Some will argue that such a concern has less to do with the definition of public good and more to do with the position of the state vis-à-vis particular rights. Homeless shelters exist for those who cannot afford a home of their own. Public monies being spent for homeless shelters have never implied that all individuals have the right to a home based on the principle of a public good. Clearly, such an assertion defies my initial definition. Further, most students of public goods do not suggest such an expansive notion of the concept.

How a society defines a public good changes over time. Fire stations, for example, were once private; individuals contracted with different companies. If a family contracted with one company and their neighbor's house started to burn, the company would protect the family's house but not their neighbor's. Over time, the public decided that fire stations should be part of the public good and all citizens should be protected. Those involved in the process of interpretation have also changed. I noted earlier that public institutions such as the University of California are a public trust, epitomizing a state's definition of a public good. Over the last century, however, the means by which the state of California supported that public good has shifted as dramatically as the movement from public schools to school choice. What has not changed in California is the perception that the Board of Regents is the buffer between the state and the institution.

Such a role for a board is increasingly uncommon. Indeed, three days after the Regents fired President Dobelle of Hawaii, the governor stated that she believed the Regents should make the acting president permanent. Such an assertion by a governor would have been astonishing at one time. It inserts the university into a political process and makes it appear that the presidency is akin to a cabinet position. From this perspective, the Regents do little more than evaluate candidates for the governor. In the 21st century, however, the external world of public higher education has shifted. When Governor Bill Richardson assumed office in New Mexico, for example, he said he expected the resignation of all appointees to public positions so that he might put in place individuals who agreed with his philosophy. To assume that a state's board of regents is akin to the members of a public utilities commission is to place the postsecondary system in a dramatically different light from the past.

Other states have suggested even more dramatic action. The governor of South Carolina opined that perhaps all of the state's postsecondary institutions might wish to go private and do as they wish; the result would be that South Carolina no longer needed to support them. Virginia's major institutions are moving toward private status. Colorado has considered implementing a voucher system whereby individual institutions could set tuition and fees (Couturier & Scurry, 2005). Students would receive the bulk of public funding rather than the institution. One may well debate the fiscal wisdom of such actions, but I leave that argument to others. What intrigues me in these actions are the interrelated assumptions at work regarding trust. The first assumption is that the public, by way of the legislature, no longer trusts postsecondary education in a manner they once did. In consequence, the second assumption is that if the institutions do not have the trust of the public, then they do not need to be a public good. The third assumption is that the marketplace can replace what has been done. In what follows, I quarrel with, but do not overtly reject, those assumptions and then suggest an alternative configuration which reiterates the need for trust.

Higher education as a public good

Traditional conceptions and critiques of higher education as a public good

A public good provides public benefits; otherwise, there would be no reason for an investment of public funds in the undertaking. Just as national defense provides citizens with the benefit of safety from attack, public higher education also must provide benefits to the society. Unlike national defense, however, higher education as a public good demonstrates its benefits through the individuals who use the system. As a citizen, I do not "use" national defense. It is impossible to gauge the effectiveness of national defense through an individual's use or nonuse. Students, however, are consumers of the public good of higher education. By their education, they will benefit society in an economic or social manner. Such an assumption assumes that the individual consumer of the public good benefits not merely the student who utilizes the public good but everyone.

Although no two public goods are alike, it is important to point out the distinction I am making here. National defense, clean drinking water, and public transportation benefit everyone. The benefit of necessity must come through a specific organization. The way we judge the effectiveness of the public good is that everyone is safe from attack, no one gets ill from drinking contaminated water, and individuals are able to get where they want to go. The good occurs by the ability of an organizational entity to deliver its services to everyone. No other entity is able to provide that service. Thus, public monies go to national defense and public utilities rather than to private militias or private companies.

Higher education is different. Benefits in general do not occur through the institution but instead through the individual. Individuals presumably accrue economic and social benefits—which, in turn, benefit society. For example, with regard to economic benefits, educated individuals earn more money. This is an individual benefit, but by these earnings, they will contribute more to the tax base—a social benefit. Educated individuals are more likely to be employed and less likely to be reliant on social welfare services, thereby lessening the need for public services. Educated individuals are more likely to meet manpower needs which will enable the country to remain competitive, and so on.

Social benefits relate to the noneconomic consequences of individuals attending postsecondary institutions and earning a degree. Educated individuals, for example, are more likely to vote, more likely to participate in the public sphere, and more likely to engage in civic activities. A social benefit that accrues to the organization rather than the individual is the investment in long-term research that contributes to basic knowledge (as opposed to knowledge for the marketplace).

Presumably, the marketplace will not invest in basic research because there will not be an immediate payoff, whereas public institutions see as part of their responsibility the ability to conduct such research regardless of economic gain.

Further, clean drinking water benefits all individuals in an equal manner while a postsecondary degree has differential benefits. The individual who earned a two-year degree rather than a four-year degree is likely to have a lower salary; the student who majored in creative writing rather than engineering will generate different earnings. Thus, the public good of higher education is much more reliant on individual benefits than most other public goods and potentially less reliant on the provider of those goods.

National defense and other such public goods generally have one primary means of delivery—through an institution or organization. The commitment to higher education as a public good, however, has involved two primary means of delivery: individual and organizational. For over a century, the commitment has been a combination of individual supports, incentives through grants and loans, and support for public institutions. The GI Bill, Pell Grants, and the potpourri of state grant and loan programs are examples of support to individuals. The land-grant college movement, the expansion of community colleges in the 20th century, and the dramatic increase in federal funding for science and technology during and after World War II demonstrate support for institutions. Although boards of regents and trustees have primarily focused on the welfare of their specific institutions, state and federal legislators and higher education coordinating commissions have focused more of their efforts on individual benefits. This combination of individual and institutional support is unique in the delivery mechanisms for a public good. Conceivably, if the country were under attack, the government might provide individuals with arms to defend themselves, but the bulk of funding for public goods comes through public means. The public good of higher education, however, has seen reduced funding on the organizational and individual level, and those who work in public higher education have pointed out with increasing anxiety their concern for declining public support of the institution.

The market has been dismissed as antithetical to the advancement of a public good. As Adrianna Kezar has written, "Wholesale adaptation to market pressures compromises the longer-term public and democratic interests that have always characterized higher education" (2004, p. 430). A market-based ideology does not meet the criteria I used above to define a public good. Nor do individuals believe that the market would extend benefits to everyone. In a market, goods and services go to those who can afford them, which by definition means that some individuals will not be able to participate. "A key distinction between nonprofit and for-profit production of higher education," according to Pusser and Doane, "is that for-profit providers are fundamentally oriented to the production of a private benefit: enhanced labor-market outcomes for individuals. While nonprofits are also committed to producing that benefit, their missions have long incorporated the production of public benefits as well" (2001, p. 21).

The assertion that public higher education is a public good that creates unique public social and economic benefits of this kind raises several critical issues. First, in a universe as diverse as the postsecondary system in the United States, clearly not all institutions provide equivalent public benefits; the individual who receives a certificate in computer technology at a community college receives a quite different public and private benefit than the person who gains a bachelor's degree in philosophy from a major university. Second, many institutions offer benefits more closely associated with the market such as a job, insofar as the goal of the education has little to do with social goals and instead is entirely focused on labor market outcomes for individuals. Although one may claim that employment is a public good because the individual is more likely to vote, more likely to earn an income that generates tax revenue, and so on, the same may be said if the individual had received the training from a for-profit institution.

Third, no evidence exists that public institutions are actually successful at increasing civic participation or creating social cohesion, or that they do so at greater rates than their for-profit counterparts. Presumably, it is the education itself and not the public nature of the funding or organization that generates such benefits, in which case the distinction of institutions becomes problematic. Fourth, private institutions are a combination of public and private investments that appear to be overlooked in such a definition. Even without the rise of for-profit institutions, the public good of postsecondary education always has been more dependent on the benefits that individuals accrue rather than the organizations that deliver them. From this perspective, if higher education were to remain a public good, then the focus should be on increasing individual access to postsecondary education rather than on maintaining a unitary provider.

A reasonable response would be that public higher education accounts for 80% (Department of Education, 2002) of all students; without such a system, goods afforded to all would only be provided to a few. However, what is being brought into question is not simply whether higher education should be a private good but the delivery mechanisms for such goods. Are public institutions better able to provide those goods than other providers? Some critics will say that higher education may be a public good but argue that the provider does not necessarily need to be a public institution. Why not increase benefits to individuals and let them accrue the public economic and social benefits in any way that they see fit?

I raise the distinction of delivery mechanisms in a book on trust because in large part X no longer trusts Y to do Z. The view of encapsulated trust that I defined has broken down where X is the public, Y is the public postsecondary provider, and Z is educational services. I noted earlier that although one ought not to personify institutions, in many cases employees do; those within the organization think of individuals when they decide whether to trust the organization. Subordinates learn to trust the organization or not because of their experiences with their managers. However, external constituencies frequently think of trust in relation to the organization and not individuals. Indeed, in an age when the public face of postsecondary institutions are the college presidents and these individuals frequently last less than six years, legislatures, policy analysts, and the broad public come to think of the institution before the individual when they arrive at their decisions trust. Such a point is crucial with regard to the assumption that higher education is a public good. Ullmann-Margalit explains:

> Talk of trusting an institution ought to be construed in terms of our degree of confidence that the institution will continue to pursue its set goals and to achieve them regardless of who staffs the institution. There is a *principle of substitutability* at work here: whenever the idea of substitutability comes up, the question to ask is what remains constant under the substitution. When we express trust in an institution we express our belief that, even if the present officeholders in that institution were to be replaced with others, the performance of the institution would remain constant. In other words, so-called trust in an institution is tantamount to a belief in the *impersonality* of its performance, in addition to the belief that its goals are compatible with our interest. (2004, p. 77)

The public has doubts about whether to trust public higher education because the goals of the public may no longer be compatible with what those who work in postsecondary institutions wish to do. I am not arguing that those individuals involved in higher education are in any way trying to confuse the public or that those who work in postsecondary institutions are even doing work that is an abrupt departure from what they did a generation ago. One reason that distrust emerges, however, is because the organization has drifted from the goals that it intended to pursue, or the organization's participants have sought to achieve those goals in an ineffective or wasteful manner.

The contexts in which higher education currently exists has shifted, which has resulted in modified goals. Higher education has been slow to respond. Lethargic responses have resulted in a lack of trust in the organization's capability to respond, which in turn has partially been the cause for a lack of investment in public higher education. Just as the creation of networks that develop social capital within an organization builds trust which creates benefits to the individuals and the organization, so too, does organizational capital function. The extent and quality of a university's participation in the local community, for example, builds an organization's social capital in the community, which in turn, develops trust. Organizational networks develop social capital in the larger community.

However, such has not been the case with many nonprofit postsecondary institutions. Instead, institutions and the publics in which they are embedded have created a dynamic that yields few opportunities for network building, which in turn develops low social capital, and subsequently, little trust. The ensuing activities have benefited neither the public nor private institutions. Legislatures and policy analysts have called for increased monitoring and accountability, and public institutions have complied with varying degrees of willingness. Such (re)actions ultimately render organizations rigid and dysfunctional. A metaphoric catch-22 ensues where the public grows increasingly distrustful of the organization that provides the public good; this in turn generates additional rules and regulations that receive minimal compliance while those in the organization try to capture funds from alternative sources to replace what has been lost. If public higher education is to remain a public good, then what might that suggest with regard to the maintenance and renewal of trust?

To raise such a question ought not to engender an unthinking response that either the state should disavow any relationship to education as a public good or that the way the state once defined a public good is sacrosanct, cannot be changed, and must be reinstated. Rather, as Powell and Clemens argue, the notion of the public good has always been "unsettled and contested and is part of the unsettled and contested nature of politics itself" (1998, p. 433).

Thus, in what follows, I sketch an idea of the public good in the 21st century and consider how it impacts trust and postsecondary institutions. The one supposition I offer is that, commonsensically, a public good refers to communal interests. Although self-interest remains central to a democratic polity, so too does the notion that individuals have common bonds that enable them to support philosophical and economic public goods such as national defense, the environment, and postsecondary education.

Rethinking higher education as a public good

Michael Walzer has helpfully summarized four rival ideologies that competed with one another in the 20th century for defining civil society in the United States (1998). Although his summations, as all intellectual summaries must be, are ideal types, they are useful in reconfiguring what the public good might be in the 21st century. Each view advances a singular notion of the good society.

One view is decidedly *communitarian* and holds that collective engagement and working toward a common destiny is what should hold the polity together. Such a view has expansive implications for public higher education as a public good. The second and third views are economic in nature. One view might be thought of as *democratic socialism* where the focus of the polity is to ensure economic equality; the collective ensures that everyone can be productive and equal. Again, higher education as a public good is interpreted in a broad manner.

The other ideology is market driven and focuses on *capitalism;* it aims to free the individual to generate as much capital as he or she can and to hold onto the benefits derived from one's labor. In contrast to the first two positions, this view assumes that living well has little to do with engagement with the polity and more to do with personal choice. A market-driven view of public goods in general and higher education in particular will be quite narrow. Certainly there is a need for national defense, but the individual should be left to his or her own devices to earn an education. The final view is intensely *nationalistic,* where living well means learning and passing on the national heritage. Public goods will be defined in relation to the advancement of the state; to the extent that higher education can develop a convincing argument that it is in the state's welfare, it will be supported.

Clearly, each views overlaps with another insofar as one could be nationalistic and communitarian. A nationalistic ideology could emphasize personal autonomy and be in sync with capitalism. Democratic socialism could be an extension of the communitarian ideology. However, each ideology on its own is insufficient to our current society. Although I find much support in the communitarian idea of public engagement, such a view is a nostalgic call for an America that perhaps never existed—and certainly does not today. Walzer points out that, "The rule of the demos is in significant ways illusory; the participation of ordinary men and women in the activities of the state is largely vicarious" (1998, p. 126). Democratic socialism suggests a utopia where once productivity is free from state-created constraints, then social division and conflict will go away, and with them, the state. Such a perspective, although again tempting, has little basis in historical reality and assumes a mythic goodness of the human spirit. In effect, individuals would live in a nonpolitical state where conflict is absent.

Rampant capitalism, of course, also calls for a singularity of purpose and outcome but of an entirely different kind. Although many currently call for the state to "get out of the way" (and to wither away as well), the reality is that for capitalism to flourish, the state needs to play a central role. Entrepreneurs are the heroes of this system and a multitude of choices is evidence of the good life. Such a view ignores that not everyone will be successful in a strictly entrepreneurial world; gross inequalities are sure to exist. A system slavishly devoted to personal autonomy is one that accepts large numbers of people living on the margins of society and belies any notion of democracy.

Nationalism creates the tension of cultural politics that in many respects exists today. As with the other perspectives, although some form of concern for one's history and country is essential in a democracy, a rigid view falls into fascism and internalized paranoia. While self-sacrifice for the good of one's country is a trait to be admired, those societies that have ultimately disintegrated frequently developed a blind loyalty to the "fatherland" where they resisted engagement with other nations or have tried to subdue them.

Thus, as with Walzer, I find each view insufficient, and even more so, in the rapidly changing conditions of the 21st century. In an environment marked by emerging technologies that redefine communication, national agreements, and personal relationships, among other things, a rigid adherence to one's nationality does not bode well for the success of the country in a world dependent on interrelationships. A melancholy call for a return to an environment of active engagement seems to ignore the pace of contemporary life where information, communication, and decisions occur instantaneously over the Internet. The assumption that the state is unnecessary other than as a marketing firm, or that conflict will ultimately retreat into the interstices of history, overlooks the environments that currently exist where new relationships between the individual and the state need to be forged. But what might such relationships be, and what do they suggest for rethinking the public good in general and trust in higher education in particular?

The idea of the public good is a centerpiece to what Michael Walzer has termed a *civil society* that incorporates all of the ideologies I outlined. Rather than a singularity of purpose, a democratic state that accepts present realities incorporates all four ideologies into its way of being. The state remains central to such a society and compels members to think about a common good beyond an individualistic conception of the ideal life. Most will agree that the state also needs to control the most voracious activities of rampant capitalism, such as multinational corporations. In such a society, the civility that exists must be learned so that democracy may be enacted, transmitted, and continued. Involvement, however, does not mean that all activity centers on advancing the polity; associations flourish in much the way that social capital forms in the discussion I provided in Chapter 1. Walzer notes:

> Theorists of civil society have a more realistic view of communities and economies. They are more accommodating to conflict—to political opposition and economic competition. Associational freedom serves for them to legitimate a set of market relations, though not necessarily the capitalist set. The market, when it is entangled in the network of associations, when the forms of ownership are pluralized, is without doubt the economic formation most consistent with the civil society argument. (p. 133)

Such a pluralist perspective rejects a romanticism of the past or an uncontested static sense of identity handed down from generation to generation. Citizens of a civil society seek a contemporary balance between the Rousseauian ideal of self-determination and engagement and the demand for individual autonomy. The civil society calls for engagement, but it is an engagement on multiple levels where individuals enter and exit at will. Rather than assume that the end result is a singularity of ideas and action, as each of the previous ideologies put forth, the idea of a civil society is that the search for such singularity is fruitless. Contestation and conflict are inevitable, and in many ways are to be treasured, a centerpiece of the democratic project. Of consequence, what the citizens make of the public good is essential for understanding how they interpret their society and democracy.

Higher education remains as a public good, then, but in a more competitive atmosphere. As opposed to assuming that higher education is by definition a public good, or that it definitely is not, postsecondary education must make the case about why it is a public good. Rather than assume that the state will fund whatever those in the institution desire, the argument should be made for what institutions will do that others cannot. In such an environment, the grammar of trust as faith is less likely to be persuasive; the polity will not have blind faith and trust institutions to do whatever they desire. However, some form of trust is mandatory for a public good to be enacted.

Simply by claiming that a term such as the public good is contested does not, of course, assure that the definition that gets decided upon will be sufficient. Contests are won and lost. If the public good is up for grabs, then it is just as open to demagogic exploitation as for democratic engagement and just as likely (if not more) to be determined by the interests of dominant groups to the detriment of those on the margins. The public good in the early 19th century, for example, excluded racial and ethnic minorities and women from participation. At the same time, it was in part out of these discussions and debates that those who were once excluded were eventually accorded the legal right to participation. "If enough people take this view a society will not be able to produce efficiently a large number of goods that require subtle and complex forms of human cooperation," notes Mansbridge. "Such forms of cooperation . . . depend not only on self-interest but also on many individuals acting in the public good on primarily internal rewards" (1998, p. 5). In short, simply because the contest is complex and loss is possible does not excuse the citizens of a democracy from entering into the debate.

By arguing for a renewed concern for the public good, I am actively incorporating the multiplicity of strategies suggested for a civil society. The debate over the public good needs to ask whose good is being considered, and in consequence, whose is left out. The term is also a debate about what is public and what is good. Such a debate ultimately asks citizens to leave behind a radical version of autonomy where communal interests are absent, but it also asks that the questions of whose good, whose public, be defined clearly, logically, and narrowly. The public good is not a term to be invoked casually whenever a need is desired but not necessary, for it asks of the community to give up some sense of self for the whole.

A contest over the public good also cannot be determined by way of a ledger sheet that adds up pluses and subtracts minuses. There is a continuous reshaping of public identity that must take place such that rather than a static logic irrespective of temporal or cultural contests, the discourse instead situates itself as a social and cultural project. "The public good needs to be seen as a dynamic, as a project in which varied actors participate, speaking through different cultural understandings, never altogether agreeing on just what the public is, yet producing it continuously if incompletely through their very discourse," Calhoun argues (1998, p. 24).

Of consequence, the discussion focuses on difference rather than homogeneity. Such engagement demands not merely a giving up of one's individuality but also recognizing that in the polity difference is essential and overriding. Again, to ask of individuals that they give up something, it must be made clear to them what they are getting in return—that they are not giving away their independence. From this perspective, the dialogue over the public good is less a discussion of sameness along simplistic nationalistic terms and more the creation of communication across complex lines of difference.

Calhoun notes that the nurturance of such a public sphere requires "not simply to identify commonalities with each other but to rebuild civic institutions" (p. 34). Those civic institutions which I am most concerned with here are, of course, colleges and universities. Calhoun goes on to write about the loss of faith and cynicism that pervades the public sphere about public institutions, while at the same time pointing out that these institutions are the ones that "make much of the story of the uniqueness and greatness of American democracy real and not just a chauvinistic claim" (p. 34). One might make a similar claim about postsecondary education. A lack of trust pervades academe's relationship with its multiple publics. What I appreciate about Calhoun's claim is that he does not simply bemoan the cynicism that pervades public life but also calls for institutional reform. What might such reform mean for postsecondary institutions and what role does trust play in the renewal?

Conclusion

In 1978, Mortimer and McConnell wrote, "The legitimacy of university and college governance based on mutual trust and cooperation among constituencies is more important, we believe, than the form or structure for participation in university affairs" (p. 284). I concur. I have argued that the restoration and maintenance of trust are multifaceted and complex. To suggest that those in colleges and universities have lost the public trust solely because of an action or series of actions would be as foolish as to suggest that postsecondary education is merely a pawn in the machinery of globalization and there is nothing that can be done. Indeed, I take seriously Calhoun's claim that public institutions need to do more than simply worry about how to restore their standing as public goods; part of their obligation is to stimulate dialogue about what the polity means by a public good. Higher education is less a public good today than yesterday, as much because of the public's redefinition of what they mean by "public" and "good" as for any internal actions of the organization. In part, then, to remain a public good, public institutions along with the state need to have shared commitments for future courses of action. Undoubtedly, this is easier said than done, but some states and public systems have made efforts in this regard. These efforts have built networks that have the potential for social capital formation, which in turn generates trust.

One of the challenges for any organization in general (and postsecondary institutions in particular) is that the institutions must reflect the needs of society. Those needs change. For some public goods, needs expand. Whether real or perceived is not to be debated here, but the public demand for more expansive protection against terrorism has led to a concomitant increase in the public's willingness to pay for that protection. The same cannot be said for higher education. Or rather, the demand for access to higher education has remained stable, if not increased, but questions have arisen whether public institutions need to be the providers for that education. If the state of California, for example, had no public institutions and decided today that a postsecondary education was essential for all high school graduates, they most likely would not create a system that currently exists where undergraduate education subsidizes graduate education, and a great deal of facile research is done that benefits no one. If trust is to be pervasive throughout postsecondary systems and institutions, then greater willingness needs to exist about the purpose and role of those systems and institutions.

Public goods are values that the polity agrees are important in a civil society. The institutions and organizations that enact those goods need to develop commitments about what they will do within and external to the organization. How to go about enacting those needs is what this book has been about. I suggested in Chapter 1 that the creation of trust comes by way of the expansion of social capital. Walzer points out that for trust to be enabled within the academic community, ways must be found to expand avenues for social capital above the import of associational affiliations for a civil society. Further, I outlined the various forms of the grammar of trust and considered in case studies how they are employed in various contexts. When we see trust as a interpretive cultural construction, we are better able to consider ways that it might be shared, learned, and maintained even in a highly dynamic environment such as now exists.

The case studies highlighted the hard work of building and maintaining trust. Although PHU demonstrated the ability of an institution to maintain networks that strengthened trust, DU pointed out a spoiled culture where networks were nonexistent and trust was absent at all levels. Both institutions are public. One need not be a scholar of higher education or organizational theory to decide which institution is better able to engage their publics about the meaning of how the institution might best meet the commitments of the public good. When four of the last five presidents at the University of Hawaii have either been dismissed or resigned because of a lack of trusting relationships, how able is the institution to engage the public about institutional purpose and commitment?

For such engagement to occur, the constituents must be able to partake in ongoing, systematic, formal, and informal communication. A college or university needs not simply to get its message across, as if the institution has to do little more than employ a public-relations firm to succeed. Rather, as Calhoun implies, those who work in colleges and universities ought not to think of the institution simply as the repository of knowledge but instead as the generator for knowledge production. Yes, professors of classics will investigate ancient texts, and archeologists will undoubtedly unearth truths not yet known, but I am suggesting something more here for the role of higher education. A university in the best sense must be a conduit for communication; it needs to help the polity decide the directions it takes. Such a claim is vastly different from the metaphor of postsecondary institutions as monasteries where faculty and students withdraw from society to understand it. Instead, I suggest that for a civil society, what higher education now needs to be is more communicative, more engaged, and by doing so, more likely to be develop trust. I have not intended to put forward trust as a cure-all for everything that ails academe, and Chapter 8 highlights an institution where individuals trust one another but have a long way to go to secure excellence.

Nevertheless, trust is a foundation on which to build relationships in academe that not only provide for a more secure organizational environment but also enable greater support for the manifold problems that now confront civil society. The United States is beset by market forces that suggest a radical redefinition of the polity's obligations and commitments to one another. Nostalgia for a past that may never have existed seems foolhardy. Instead, those of us in higher education have work to do at creating trust within and outside the organization, with one another and our multiple publics, in order to build a more democratic society.

A Note on Method
and Design

This is a text that occurred in part by happenstance. In 2001, I received a grant from the Atlantic Philanthropies to undertake a longitudinal study of governance in higher education. The project involved a multitude of tasks, and one of them was a series of case studies designed to understand the challenges for governance in colleges and universities. I conducted those case studies between 2001 and 2003 with a postdoctoral scholar at the Center for Higher Education Policy Analysis, James T. Minor. I had not anticipated how often the word "trust" would come up in our interviews on the multiple campuses we visited. Our protocol and design initially had not focused on trust but rather on the processes of governance on diverse campuses and the problems that the different constituencies faced.

By way of grounded theory, I came upon the burgeoning literature on trust, and we subsequently asked additional questions of individuals that probed further into what they meant by trust and how it differed from campus to campus. That is, my purpose was not to prove or disprove any particular notions about trust. However, as the interviews occurred, individuals continually brought up a concern for trust. I did not choose campuses on whether individuals trusted one another or not but choose instead, on the basis of what the campus had to say about governance.

Although the parameters of the case studies excluded community colleges or for-profit institutions, initially choosing a handful of institutions remained a daunting task. As with all case studies, I did not seek to choose a dozen institutions that would be representative of the 2,000 four-year colleges and universities in the

United States. We did, however, select institutions that were in diverse geographic locations, were a mixture of public and private, large and small, and were representative of Carnegie classifications. I wanted a broad overview of governance in American higher education rather than an intensive sample of one type of institution, such as small liberal-arts colleges. I knew ahead of time that DU had a tempestuous relationship between the board and the faculty, and that PHU had a quite explicit approach to governance, but in neither case did I suspect that trust was as important as it turned out to be. I chose SU and CU based on the generic parameters mentioned above and had no preconceived notions about what we might find with regard to governance or trust.

I guaranteed the interviewees at the institutions anonymity, which is why the initial information in the case studies uses approximate numbers rather than specifics, and why I mask the identities of the individuals with whom I have spoken. As I mentioned in the case study about DU, such anonymity was particularly critical for that institution. The vast majority of interviews were tape-recorded and the quotes were taken from subsequent transcriptions. But in some cases, the quotes derive from hand-written notes taken in an interview. Again, especially at DU, many individuals did not want to be taped.

The chapters, obviously, draw on interviews conducted on campus and by telephone. I also followed up with several individuals via email or met them off-site at a conference or another setting. Insofar as the focus of the case studies was on governance, I did not interview very many students or clerical workers. Although I appreciate that they also play a critical role in the life of an institution, I preferred to concentrate on a select group of constituents across a sample of institutions rather than to have an intensive focus on one campus. The sample of interviewees reflected a broad spectrum of administrators and faculty; I interviewed faculty leaders as well as faculty who seemed relatively disengaged from the day-to-day governance of an institution. I sought senior and junior faculty, new and old faculty, men and women, majority and minority faculty, and faculty from a diverse array of disciplines and professional fields.

I also observed meetings and interactions on different campuses. I read the minutes and documents related to campus life and governance such as faculty senate meetings, strategic plans, accreditation reports, campus newspapers, email correspondence, and the like. The use of observations and written documents was useful as secondary data, but the primary focus of the case studies was the interview.

Over the years, I have followed a quite standard procedure in collecting and analyzing data. Immediately after an interview, I write up my own notes about an interview, filling in a cover sheet for everyone with whom I spoke. After a site visit, I write a five-page synopsis of what I heard. As the cases develop, I write a similar overview of converging and diverging themes. When I have finished the initial round of data collection, I then have five forms of notes to analyze. Although such a process is time-consuming, I find that different notes taken at different times in different forms help me to analyze themes rather than to rely on only the transcript. The constant synthesis and analysis that begin in my work at the outset of my data collection help me create and discard categories and themes as I proceed, rather than waiting until a final moment when I would have to make sense of one singular mound of data. In follow-up interviews with individuals, I engaged in member checks where I tried to refine my results in light of their subsequent interpretations. Some individuals also read drafts of the case studies in order to provide an opinion of my interpretation of the campus. I revised the case studies based on their comments.

I was also aided in the analysis of the data and the themes by my colleagues and research assistants in the Center, especially James Minor. James helped collect some of the data for the case studies at SU and CU; he has made use of that and other data for his own work on governance. Vicente Lechuga, Karri Holley, and Jarrett Gupton provided useful comments on the text and responded to the numerous requests I had for one or another piece of data with lightning speed. I also held a seminar in the Center where we read Putnam's *Bowling Alone* and discussed the idea of social and cultural capital, and how it related to the notions of trust that I have developed here. These conversations were extremely helpful for me in formulating my initial approach to the relationship between social capital and trust.

Much later in the process, I presented a draft of some of my work to colleagues at a seminar I hold in Santa Fe, New Mexico every summer. Their comments, especially those of Ken Mortimer and Ann Austin, helped me tie the theoretical notions of trust developed in Part One to the pressing problems that individuals face on their campuses that I eventually developed in Part Two. Ken, in particular, pushed me toward distinguishing between trust in individuals versus trust in the laws, structures, and culture of the organization. One distinction I have tried to maintain is the idea of trust in an individual due to a charismatic personality and a possibly fleeting context, as opposed to trust that permeates an institution regardless of who populates a particular role.

Still other readers criticized what they saw as an overemphasis on the internal focus of the book. How, they asked, could I write of trust within an organization, focus on culture, and exclude a discussion about the protean environment in which academe currently exists? Part Three is an attempt to respond to these comments and also unite the idea of trust with that of the public good. I anticipate that these twin themes will only grow in importance over the coming decades as academe works out its changing relationship to the public.

Although I understand the comments by other readers, I have in large part avoided their suggestion to interrogate notions related to trust, namely distrust. One can attempt only so much in a book, and as I mentioned in Part One, there is currently a paucity of literature about trust in postsecondary education. This book is not a primer for "how to" develop trust, nor is it the final word on all matters pertaining to trust. Undoubtedly, some people are untrustworthy and how to deal with them in an organization and still build and maintain trust is important. Some individuals or groups also may not find it is in their interest to trust. Distrust is not simply the absence of trust. It is a concept that demands more investigation and elaboration than I would have been able to do justice to here. Clearly a great deal more work awaits those who are intrigued by the idea of trust in postsecondary organizations. I hope, if not trust, that the reader will find some of what I have presented here useful scaffolding for undertaking additional investigations.

References

Adler, P. S., & Kwon, S. (2002). Social capital: Prospects for a new concept. *The Academy of Management Review, 27*(1), 17–41.

Agres, T. (2003, August 25). The cost of commercializing scientific research. *Scientist, 17*(16), 58–59.

AHA Council Decisions (2001, June). *Perspectives, 39*(6) [electronic version]. American Historical Association. http://www.historians.org/perspectives/issues/2001/0109/0109aha2.cfm

American Anthropological Association (2002). *Final report of the American Anthropological Association El Dorado task force.* Washington, DC: American Anthropological Association. Available at http://www.aaanet.org/edtf/index.htm.

Becher, T. (1987). The disciplinary shaping of the profession. In B.R. Clark (Ed.), *The academic profession: National, disciplinary, and institutional settings* (pp. 271–301). Berkeley: University of California Press.

Bigley, G., & Pearce, J.L. (1998). Straining for shared meaning in organization science: Problems of trust and distrust. *The Academy of Management Review, 23*(3), 405–421.

Birnbaum, R. (2000). *Management fads in higher education: Where they come from, what they do, why they fail.* San Francisco: Jossey-Bass.

Blau, P. M. (1964). *Exchange and power in social life.* New York: Wiley.

Bourdieu, P. (1986). The forms of capital. In J.G. Richardson (Ed.), *Handbook of theory and research for the sociology of education* (pp. 241–258). New York: Greenwood Press.

Brennan, G. (1998). Democratic trust: A rational-choice theory view. In V. Braithwaite & M. Levi (Eds.), *Trust and governance* (pp. 197–217). New York: Russell Sage Foundation.

Calhoun, C. (1998). The public good as a social and cultural project. In W.W. Powell and E.S. Clemens (Eds.), *Private action and the public good* (pp. 20–35). New Haven: Yale University Press.

Carroll, L. (1994). *Through the looking glass.* London: Penguin Books. (Original work published 1872)

Chaffee, E., & Tierney, W.G. (1988). *Collegiate culture and leadership strategies.* New York: Macmillan.

Clark, B. (1987). *The academic life.* Princeton, NJ: The Carnegie Foundation for the Advancement of Teaching.

Coleman, J. (1990). *Foundations of social theory.* Cambridge, MA: Harvard University Press.

Couturier, L., & Scurry, J. (2005). *Correcting course: How we can restore the ideals of public higher education in a market-driven era.* Providence, RI: The Futures Project at Brown University.

Creamer, B. (2004, June 16). Regents fire Dobelle [electronic version]. *Honolulu Advertiser.* Retrieved November 22, 2004 from http://www.honoluluadvertiser.com/

Creed, W.E.D., & Miles, R.E. (1996). Trust in organizations: A conceptual framework linking organizational forms, managerial philosophies, and the opportunity costs of controls. In R.M. Kramer & T.R. Tyler (Eds.), *Trust in organizations: Frontiers of theory and research* (pp. 16–38). Thousand Oaks, CA: Sage Publications.

de Souza Briggs, X. (1997). Social capital and the cities: Advice to change agents. *National Civic Review, 86,* 111–117.

Dee, J. (2004). *The accountability/autonomy dialectic in higher education governance.* Paper presented at the Research Seminar on Governance, Santa Fe, NM.

Department of Education (2002). *Digest of education statistics.* Washington, DC: US Department of Education, National Center for Education Statistics.

Dika, S. L., & Singh, K. (2002). Applications of social capital theory in educational literature: A critical synthesis. *Review of Educational Research, 72*(1), 31–60.

Douglass, J.A. (2000). *The California idea and American higher education, 1850 to the 1960 Master Plan.* Stanford: Stanford University Press.

Dreher, R. (2002, February 11). Sins of the fathers: Pedophile priests and the challenge to the Catholic church. *National Review, 54*(2), 27–31.

Dunn, J. (1988). Trust and political agency. In D. Gambetta (Ed.), *Trust: Making and breaking cooperative relations* (pp. 73–93). New York: Basil Blackwell.

Durkheim, E. (1966). *Suicide: A study in sociology* (J.A. Spaulding & G. Simpson, Trans.). New York: Free Press. (Original work published 1867)

Elangovan, A.R., & Shapiro, D.L. (1998). Betrayal of trust in organizations. *The Academy of Management Review, 23*(3), 547–566.

Fordham, S. (1996). Blacked out: Dilemmas of race, identity, and success at capital high.Chicago: University of Chicago Press.

Fordham, S. (1998). Racelessness as a factor in Black students' success: Pragmatic strategy or Pyrrhic victory? *Harvard Review of Education, 58*(1), 29–84.

Fordham, S., & Ogbu, J. (1986). Black students' school success: Coping with the burden of Acting White. *Urban Review, 18,* 176–206.

Gambetta, D. (1988). Can we trust trust? In D. Gambetta (Ed.), *Trust: Making and breaking cooperative relations* (pp. 213–238). New York: Basil Blackwell.

Gilbert, J., & Tang, T. (1998). An examination of organizational trust antecedents. *Public Personnel Management, 27*(3), 321–336.

Gima, C. (2004, June 16). Dobelle fired [electronic version]. *Honolulu Star-Bulletin.* Retrieved November 22, 2004 from http://starbulletin.com/2004/06/16/news/story1.html

Hansman, H. (1987). Economic theories of nonprofit organization. In W.W. Powell (Ed.), *The non-profit handbook* (pp. 27–42). New Haven: Yale University Press.

Hardin, R. (1993). The street-level epistemology of trust. *Politics and Society, 21*(4), 505–529.

Hardin, R. (2002). *Trust and trustworthiness.* New York: Russell Sage Foundation.

Hardin, R. (2004). Distrust: Manifestations and management. In R. Hardin (Ed.), *Distrust* (pp. 3–33). New York: Russell Sage Foundation.

Heath, S. (1982). Protean shapes in literacy events: Ever shifting oral and literate traditions. In D. Tannen (Ed.), *Spoken and written language: Exploring orality and literacy* (pp.91–117). Norwood, NJ: Ablex.

Hymes, D. (1974). *The foundations of sociolinguistics: An ethnographic approach.* Philadelphia: The University of Pennsylvania Press.

Kevles, D. (1996). The assault on David Baltimore. *The New Yorker, 27,* May, 94–109.

Kezar, A. (2004). Obtaining integrity? Reviewing and examining the charter between higher education and society. *Review of Higher Education, 27*(4), 429–459.

Kramer, R.M., Brewer, M.B., & Hanna, B.A. (1996). Collective trust and collective action: The decision to trust as a social decision. In R.M. Kramer & T.R. Tyler (Eds.), *Trust in organizations: Frontiers of theory and research* (pp. 357–389). Thousand Oaks, CA: Sage Publications Inc.

Kramer, R.M., & Cook, K.S. (2004). Trust and distrust in organizations: Dilemmas and approaches. In R.M. Kramer & K.S. Cook (Eds.), *Trust and distrust in organizations: Dilemmas and approaches* (pp. 1–18). New York: Russell Sage Foundation.

Kramer, R.M., & Tyler, T.R. (Eds.). (1996). *Trust in organizations: Frontiers of theory and research.* Thousand Oaks, CA: Sage Publications.

Labaree, D. (1997). Public good, private goods: The American struggle over educational goals. *American Educational Research Journal, 34*(1), 39–81.

Lane, C. (1998). Introduction: Theories and issues in the study of trust. In C. Lane & R. Bachmann (Eds.), *Trust within and between organizations* (pp. 1–30). Oxford: Oxford University Press.

Lewicki, R.J., McAllister, D.J., & Bies, R.J. (1998). Trust and distrust: New relationships and realities. *The Academy of Management Review, 23*(3), 438–458.

Lincoln, C.Z. (Ed.) (1909). *Messages from the governors, Volume II.* Albany: J.B. Lyon Company.

Luhmann, N. (1979). *Trust and power.* New York: Wiley.

Luhmann, N. (1988). Familiarity, confidence, trust: Problems and alternatives. In D.G. Gambetta (Ed.), *Trust: Making and breaking cooperative relations* (pp. 94–107). New York: Basil Blackwell.

Mansbridge, J. (1998). On the contested nature of the public good. In W.W. Powell and E.S. Clemens (Eds.), *Private action and the public good* (pp. 3–19). New Haven: Yale University Press.

Mauss, M. (1967). *The gift: Forms and functions of exchange in archaic societies* (I. Cunnison, Trans.). New York: Norton. (Original work published in 1924)

Mayer, R., Davis, J., & Schoorman, F. (1995). An integrative model of organizational trust. *The Academy of Management Review, 20*(3), 709–734.

McNeal, R.B. (1999). Parental involvement as social capital: Differential effectiveness on science achievement, truancy, and dropping out. *Social Forces, 78*(1), 117–145.

Mehm, J.G. (2002). Sexual abuse research and the (shaken) Catholic faith. *Connecticut Psychologist, 56*(2), 3.

Meyerson, D., Weick, K.E., & Kramer, R.M. (1996). Swift trust and temporary groups. In R.M. Kramer & T.R. Tyler (Eds.), *Trust in organizations: Frontiers of theory and research* (pp. 166–195). Thousand Oaks, CA: Sage Publications.

Morse, J.R. (1999). No families, no freedom: Human flourishing in a free society. *Social Philosophy and Policy, 16,* 290–314.

Mortimer, K., & McConnell, T.R. (1978). *Sharing authority effectively.* San Francisco: Jossey-Bass.

National Center for State Courts. (1999). *How the public views state courts: A 1999 national survey.* Williamsburg, VA: Author.

Ogbu, J.U. (1991). Immigrant and involuntary minorities in comparative perspective. In M.A. Gibson & J.U. Ogbu (Eds.), *Minority status and schooling: A comparative study of immigrant and involuntary minorities* (pp. 3–33). New York: Garland.

Ortega Y Gassett, J. (1944). *Mission of the university.* New York: Norton.

Ouchi, W. (1983). *Theory Z: The Japanese challenge to America.* New York: Avon Books.

Portes, A. (1998). Social capital: Its origins and applications in modern sociology. *Annual Review of Sociology, 24,* 1–24.

Powell, W.W., & Clemens, E.S. (Eds.) (1998). *Private action and the public good.* New Haven: Yale University Press.

Pusser, B. (2002). Higher education, the emerging market, and the public good. In P.A. Graham and N. Stacey (Eds.), *The knowledge economy and post-secondary education* (pp. 105–126). Washington, DC: National Academy Press.

Pusser, B. & Doane, D.J. (2001, September-October). Public purpose and private enterprise: The contemporary organization of postsecondary education. *Change, 33,* 18–22.

Putman, R.D. (1995a). Bowling alone: America's declining social capital. *The Journal of Democracy, 6*(1), 65–78.

Putman, R.D. (1995b). Tuning in, tuning out: The strange disappearance of social capital in America. *PS: Political Science & Politics, 28*(4), 664–683.

Putnam, R.D. (2000). *Bowling alone: The collapse and revival of American community.* New York: Simon and Schuster.

Rhoades, G. (1998). *Managed professionals: Unionized faculty and restructuring academic labor.* Albany: State University of New York Press.

Rousseau, D.M., Sitkin, S.B., Burt, R.S., & Camerer, C. (1998). Not so different after all: A cross-discipline view of trust. *The Academy of Management Review, 23*(3), 393–404.

Seligman, A.B. (1997). *The problem of trust.* Princeton, NJ: Princeton University Press.

Sennett, R. (1998). *The corrosion of character: The personal consequences of work in the new capitalism.* London: W.W. Norton & Company.

Sheppard, B.H., & Sherman, D.M. (1998). The grammars of trust: A model and general implications. *The Academy of Management Review, 23*(3), 422–437.

Smircich, L., & Stubbart, G. (1985). Strategic management in an enacted world. *Academy of Management Review, 10*(4), 724–736.

Stanton-Salazar, R. D. (1997). A social capital framework for understanding the socialization of racial minority children and youths. *Harvard Educational Review, 67*(1), 1–40.

Stepick, A. (1992). The refugees nobody wants: Haitians in Miami. In G.J Grenier & A. Stepick (Eds.), *Miami now* (pp. 57–82). Gainesville: University of Florida Press.

Stokes, D. E. (1997). *Pasteur's quadrant: Basic science and tecnological innocation.* Washington, DC: The Brookings Institution.

Suarez-Orozco, M.M. (1987). Towards a psychological understanding of Hispanic adaptation to American schooling. In H.T. Trueba (Ed.), *Success or failure? Learning and the languages of minority students* (pp. 156–168). New York: Newbury House.

Tierney, W.G. (1988). Organizational culture in higher education: Defining the essentials. *Journal of Higher Education, 59*(1), 2–21.

Tierney, W.G. (1989). *Curricular landscapes, democratic vistas: Transformative leadership in higher education.* New York: Praeger.

Tierney, W.G., & Bensimon, E.M. (1996). *Promotion and tenure: Community and socialization in academe.* Albany, NY: State University of New York Press.

Tierney, W.G. & Minor, J. T. (Eds.) (2003). *Challenges for governance: A national report.* Los Angeles, CA: Center for Higher Education Policy Analysis.

Ullman-Margalit, E. (2004). Trust, distrust, and in between. In R. Hardin (Ed.), *Distrust* (pp. 60–82). New York: Russell Sage Foundation.

Walzer, M. (1998). The idea of civil society: A path to social reconstruction. In E.J. Dionne (Ed.), *Community works: The revival of civil society in America* (pp. 123–144). Washington, DC: The Brookings Institution Press.

Whitener, E., Brodt, S., Korsgaard, M., & Werner, J. (1988). Managers as initiators of trust: An exchange relationship framework for understanding managerial trustworthy behavior. *The Academy of Management Review, 23*(3), 513–530.

Williams, B. (1988). Formal structures and social reality. In D.G. Gambetta (Ed.), *Trust: Making and breaking cooperative relations.* New York: Basil Blackwell.

Zaheer, A., McEvily, B., & Perrone, V. (1998). Does trust matter? Exploring the effects of interorganizational and interpersonal trust on performance. *Organization Science, 9*(2), 141–159.

Index

138-44, 145-46, 155-56, 156-63,
163-64, 164-65
characteristics of, 75-79
communication and, 144, 145-46
conditional, 64
cooperative behavior and, 42
cultural, 63-71
cultural contexts and, 68, 132
deference and, 169
definition of, 71
encapsulated, 66
environment and, 62
faculty and, 19-20
faith and, 111, 112, 166
grammar of, 41-43, 131-32, 148-53, 189
higher education and, 5, 7, 42
interorganizational, 73
levels of, 71-74
limits of, 6, 155-56
occurrences of, 75
organizations and, 44, 59-61, 63, 66
phases of, 74-75
public, 44
social capital and, 20, 107
social networks and, 107-10, 129-31,
146-48, 165-68
structure and, 61-62
values and, 62-63
trustworthiness. *See* trust
Tyler, T. R., 42

-U-

Ullman-Margalit, E., 45, 185
University of California, 174, 181
University of Hawaii, 173, 181, 192
University of Michigan, 174
use-informed research, 10

-V-

Van Luchene, S., vii

-W-

Walzer, M., 187, 188
Weick, K. E., 51
Werner, J., 49, 77
Whitener, E., 49, 77
Williams, B., 71

-Z-

Zaheer, A., 73

Studies in the Postmodern Theory of Education

General Editors
Joe L. Kincheloe & Shirley R. Steinberg

Counterpoints publishes the most compelling and imaginative books being written in education today. Grounded on the theoretical advances in criticalism, feminism, and postmodernism in the last two decades of the twentieth century, Counterpoints engages the meaning of these innovations in various forms of educational expression. Committed to the proposition that theoretical literature should be accessible to a variety of audiences, the series insists that its authors avoid esoteric and jargonistic languages that transform educational scholarship into an elite discourse for the initiated. Scholarly work matters only to the degree it affects consciousness and practice at multiple sites. Counterpoints' editorial policy is based on these principles and the ability of scholars to break new ground, to open new conversations, to go where educators have never gone before.

For additional information about this series or for the submission of manuscripts, please contact:

Joe L. Kincheloe & Shirley R. Steinberg
c/o Peter Lang Publishing, Inc.
29 Broadway, 18th floor
New York, New York 10006

To order other books in this series, please contact our Customer Service Department:

(800) 770-LANG (within the U.S.)
(212) 647-7706 (outside the U.S.)
(212) 647-7707 FAX

Or browse online by series:
www.peterlang.com